Edward Foley (Ed.)

Religion, Diversity and Conflict

D0897127

International Practical Theology

edited by

Prof. Dr. Chris Hermans (Nijmegen),
Prof. Dr. Maureen Junker-Kenny (Dublin),
Prof. Dr. Richard Osmer (Princeton),
Prof. Dr. Friedrich Schweitzer (Tübingen),
Prof. Dr. Hans-Georg Ziebertz (Würzburg)

in cooperation with the
International Academy of Practical Theology (IAPT),

represented by

Bonnie Miller-McLemore (President)
and Jean-Guy Nadeau (Vice President)

Volume 15

LIT

Religion, Diversity and Conflict

edited by

Edward Foley

LIT

Gedruckt auf alterungsbeständigem Werkdruckpapier entsprechend
ANSI Z3948 DIN ISO 9706

Bibliographic information published by the Deutsche Nationalbibliothek
The Deutsche Nationalbibliothek lists this publication in the Deutsche
Nationalbibliografie; detailed bibliographic data are available in the Internet at
http://dnb.d-nb.de.

ISBN 978-3-643-90086-9

A catalogue record for this book is available from the British Library

©LIT VERLAG GmbH & Co. KG Wien,
Zweigniederlassung Zürich 2011
Klosbachstr. 107
CH-8032 Zürich
Tel. +41 (0) 44-251 75 05
Fax +41 (0) 44-251 75 06
e-Mail: zuerich@lit-verlag.ch
http://www.lit-verlag.ch

LIT VERLAG Dr. W. Hopf
Berlin 2011
Fresnostr. 2
D-48159 Münster
Tel. +49 (0) 2 51-620 320
Fax +49 (0) 2 51-922 60 99
e-Mail: lit@lit-verlag.de
http://www.lit-verlag.de

Distribution:
In Germany: LIT Verlag Fresnostr. 2, D-48159 Münster
Tel. +49 (0) 2 51-620 32 22, Fax +49 (0) 2 51-922 60 99, e-mail: vertrieb@lit-verlag.de

In Austria: Medienlogistik Pichler-ÖBZ, e-mail: mlo@medien-logistik.at

In the UK: Global Book Marketing, e-mail: mo@centralbooks.com

In North America by:

Transaction Publishers
New Brunswick (U.S.A.) and London (U.K.)

Transaction Publishers
Rutgers University
35 Berrue Circle
Piscataway, NJ 08854

Phone: +1 (732) 445 - 2280
Fax: + 1 (732) 445 - 3138
for orders (U. S. only):
toll free (888) 999 - 6778
e-mail: orders@transactionpub.com

Preface

From 30 July to 3 August 2009 the International Academy of Practical Theology (IAPT) held its ninth biannual meeting in Chicago, Illinois (USA) hosted at Catholic Theological Union. The meeting was presided over by Prof. Ruard Ganzevoort, President of the IAPT (2007-2009) and Professor of Practical Theology at the Vrije Universiteit in Amsterdam. The theme of the meeting was Religion, Diversity and Conflict. That theme was elaborated in this way:

> *Religion, Diversity and Conflict.* In 1893 the city of Chicago was host to World's Parliament of Religions, celebrated as a key moment in modern interreligious dialogue. In 1993 the Parliament held its centennial observation in Chicago, where significant attention was given to discussions of global ethics. Like many urban centers of the world, 21st century Chicago is a city of enormous cultural, political, social and religious diversity. Such diversity can be a source of dynamism and grace, as well as conflict and strife. The 2009 Congress of the International Academy of Practical Theology will consider various aspects of both inter- and intra-religious diversity in the context of this polyphonic cityscape and other situations around the world. In particular, participants are invited to explore how the resources and varied approaches of practical theology can address the inter- and intra-religious conflicts which arise in the midst of such diversity, as well as propose paths for dialogue, mutual respect and ethical practices in the face of such conflict. The conference will explore ways in which the disciplines of practical theology can contribute both to the emerging world dialogue between conflicting religious traditions, as well as addressing parallel issues at the national and local levels.

Major presenters at the meeting included Prof. Patrice C Brodeur of the University of Montreal, Joyce S. Dubensky of the Tanenbaum Center for Interreligious Dialogue (New York), Prof. Robert Schreiter of Catholic Theological Union, Prof. David Tracy of the University of Chicago, Prof. Esther Reed of the University of Exeter, and Prof. Ganzevoort. Besides these keynote presentations, forty-five seminar papers were presented by various members and guests of the IAPT. This volume is a distillation of many of the papers and presentations from the 2009 meeting, reshaped for publication.

The division of articles here is admittedly arbitrary and all of them could, in fact, have been collected under a single division heading. There are contributions that employ empirical methods that are not gathered under that heading, and others about "peace building" or "leading ideas" that are similarly not included there. In many respects, all of the contributions are about "expanding the boundaries of practical theology." The partitions that follow, therefore, are less rubrical than heuristic: ways of considering these distinctive yet not separate contributions that weave a powerful vision of religion in all of its diversity and in view of its many conflicts through practical theological lenses.

I am very grateful for the wise assistance of Friedrich Schweitzer and Hans-Georg Ziebertz throughout this editing process, editors for the International Practical Theology Series for Lit Verlag. I am also grateful for the steadfast support and engagement of Bonnie Miller-McLemore, the current IAPT President, and IAPT Executive Board Member Neil Pembroke. Finally, the Academy is deeply grateful to Lit Verlag for their continued support of our work.

We also want to give special thanks to Sylvia Scheller form the Insitute of Practical Theology inWürzburg (Germany) who prepared the manuscript for publication. We are very grateful to benefit from her professional support.

This volume is lovingly dedicated to Prof. Don Browning (+ 3 June 2010), the founding President of the IAPT and a singularly articulate and respected voice in the field of practical theology. The Alexander Campbell Professor of Religions Ethics and the Social Sciences Emeritus at the University of Chicago at the time of his death, Prof. Browning was instrumental in shaping the 2009 meeting of the IAPT. His vibrant spirit and unflagging presence at that gathering remain a vivid memory. May he rest in peace.

Edward Foley
First Sunday of Advent, 2010

In Memory of Don S. Browning
mentor, colleague and friend

Table of Contents

Leading Ideas

A Look at Religion, Diversity and Conflict through a Practical Lens

Joyce S. Dubensky

Abstract: *This article profiles the Tanenbaum Center for Interreligious Understanding (Tanenbaum), a secular, nonsectarian non-profit dedicated to overcoming religious violence and intolerance in a range of settings. The piece examines the motivation for Tanenbaum's work and the organization's concrete responses to sensitive religious tensions. As such, it showcases Tanenbaum's approach to putting interfaith respect into practice and thereby creating models of practical theology as a lived reality.*

Introduction

When an invitation to speak to the International Academy of Practical Theology (IAPT) arrived, I thought it an error. I am a nonprofit executive and not a theologian. But it was not a mistake, and it provided the opportunity to make a presentation to IAPT about the Tanenbaum Center for Interreligious Understanding and how it pragmatically responds to the interrelated issues of religion, conflict and diversity.

Three Foundational Opening Premises

I begin these reflections where Tanenbaum starts its work. Though a secular, non-sectarian organization, our thinking is based on the obvious premise that religion is a powerful societal force. Today, 72.1% of people in the world self-identify as religious, and 88% say they believe in god (World Values Survey Association 2006; Pew Forum on Religion & Public Life 2006). Being religious is not only one of the most common of personal identities, it can also be among the most salient components of a person's identity or culture.

A second premise that underlies our work is that being "different" is the norm. Because it is normal, it is critically important that we learn to live with differences in everyday life. Even in homogeneous religious communities, there are still males and females, young and old, healthy and ill, the more and less powerful, the more orthodox and those who may practice or believe somewhat differently.

For decades, the effort to understand difference has been at the center of social and academic discussions. These conversations often addressed personal issues of identity, power and respect. Starting with slave history and race, they expanded to include a range of identity factors including gender, sexual orientation, ability status, age and ethnicity. Only recently has this 20th century conversation broadly begun to include religion in a meaningful way.

At Tanenbaum, we tackle the challenges posed by numerous religious and non-religious belief systems. A look at the US shows just how complicated this task is. In the US there are over 4500 different religious traditions depending on how you count and your sources (Barrett et al. 2001). While some suggest that there are only 200 religious traditions in the US, this calculation undoubtedly considers all denominations of Christianity (including Roman Catholicism, all Orthodox and all Protestant denominations) as one. This diversity of beliefs is compounded by conflicting expert interpretations of text and layers of individual interpretations and traditions. Thus, the actual practice of religion is far more complicated and diverse than the numbers.

Tanenbaum's final foundational premise encapsulates two opposing propositions. We accept that religion is a cause of conflict—at least sometimes. Religion and religious differences are a cause of tension, bias and outright discrimination in everyday life, as well as a stimulus to armed conflict and unspeakable violence. Concurrently, we recognize that religion is also a resource for resolving conflicts and overcoming the very intolerance and hatred that is perpetuated in its name.

The balance of this essay will be divided into two sections: the first will address religious differences in everyday life, focusing on the ways that religion and religious diversity create conflict and how practical behavioral changes can reduce or prevent these daily occurrences. The second will focus on ways in which religion and religious diversity are resources for overcoming violent conflicts, whether fueled by religion or not.

The Convergence of Religion, Diversity and Everyday Conflicts

Religious conflicts erupt in a range of everyday settings, often manifesting as microaggressions that deeply injure the individuals affected. Understanding how this occurs is the first step in identifying proactive responses for reducing or even preventing them. The three arenas in which such conflicts occur more than we generally acknowledge are schools, work and the health care system.

At School

There is insufficient data on the direct impact of religious diversity on school children. Yet there is ample information to suggest that religious diversity is an issue in US schools and that it impacts students and their classrooms.

Over the past 40 years, the foreign born population in the US has more than tripled. Historically, that population was predominantly from Europe and the new residents brought with them familiar religious practices (United States Census Bureau 1970). Today that is no longer the case. Most foreign born residents come from Africa, Latin and South America, and Asia, bringing non-Christian traditions and syncretic beliefs that differ markedly from the nation's predominantly Christian heritage.

While much of our "diversity data" references country of origin and ethnic differences, such characterizations blur with religion. For example, someone from Africa not only brings a less familiar ethnic background to the US, but also likely brings indigenous practices and perhaps less-familiar religious beliefs as well. Consider New York State, which ranks fourth in diversity in the US regarding countries of origin, ethnic backgrounds and religion (Sable and Garofano 2007). In public schools there is a 61% likelihood that any two students in New York City will have different ethnic backgrounds (*The New York Times* 2009). The fact that they have contact, however, does not mean that they get along.

Data shows that bullying and silent ostracism of children who are "different" permeates schools: those differences include religion, ethnicity and country of origin. In a national study of U.S. adolescents, the *Journal of Adolescent Health* reported that 29.9% of students experienced frequent bullying in the two months prior to the survey. Of that group, 13% were bullies, 10.6% were victims and 6.3% were *both* (Wang et al. 2009). Besides physical harm, bullying impacts a child's social development and contributes to adjustment problems, including poor mental health and "more extreme violent behavior." (Juvonen et al. 2003)

When children grow up bullying or as victims of bias-based harassment, stereotypes and prejudice calcify. In November 2009, the Federal Bureau of Investigation reported that New York State ranked first among all 50 states in instances of religion-related hate crimes. While a majority of the hate crimes in most states are racially motivated, 45.6% of such bias-based crimes in New York are motivated by religious hatred (United States Federal Bureau of Investigation 2009). These acts of violence outnumber those based on race, sexual orientation and ethnicity.

Anecdotal data from educators and media reports support the conclusion that religion and diversity stimulate conflict and bullying among students. One teacher reports that some students mocked others because their food was "dirty" (not religiously pure). Another tells how her Bangladeshi student sat isolated, ashamed of his country of origin and his religion. Another admits not knowing what to do when a child cannot participate in a birthday celebration because she is fasting for Ramadan, or is a Jehovah's Witness.

To reduce everyday conflicts that emerge around religious and other differences, Tanenbaum offers its *Religion and Diversity Education* program. The program's goal is to change how educators teach so that students learn to conduct themselves with respect. We focus on educators because they are a point of leverage from which to reach thousands, even tens of thousands of students. Our outcomes are respectful *behaviors*. While we would be thrilled to change hearts and minds, we believe the first step is to change actions and behaviors. Hearts and minds may follow; if they do not, we still will have made progress.

The name of the program is significant. While there are many diversity education programs, most mention religion (at best), but fail to include lessons about religion or religious differences. Tanenbaum's program is a diversity program with a difference. In addition to providing multicultural and diversity training, we prepare educators to teach students *about* the impact of religion and the existence of religious differences, and to act respectfully.

Tanenbaum's program starts with a pedagogy, i.e., *The Seven Principles for Inclusive Education.* Rarely part of general educator pedagogical training, *The Seven Principles* can be used by any educator and infused into their academic lessons, whether in an after-school program, an elementary school or high school math class. *The Seven Principles* are:

1. Teaching All Students (using several approaches to teaching the same material because different students learn differently);

2. Exploring Multiple Identities (encouraging compassion through learning about each person's multiple identities including group identities like race and religion, and individual identities like birth order, being an introvert or an extrovert);

3. Preventing Prejudice (learning to identify and proactively debunk stereo-types);

4. Promoting Social Justice (focusing the class on social justice and fairness);

5. Choosing Appropriate Materials (critically reviewing curricula and materials and choosing accurate, diverse images);

6. Teaching and Learning about Cultures and Religions (including learning from peers);

7. Adapting and Integrating Lessons Appropriately (not simply following curricula that omit opportunities to educate about stereotypes or social justice; rather, adapting them to implement the *Seven Principles*).

Tanenbaum provides training for educators in our pedagogy through intensive, week-long workshops and also offers academic curricula for elementary and high school students that imbed the pedagogy.

When used regularly, students learn skills of global citizenship including how to relate to the "other" and how to conduct themselves respectfully amid differences. At Tanenbaum, we define those skills and behaviors as: acceptance of differences as normal; viewing difference as something interesting that promotes curiosity rather than fear; skillfully asking questions about differences; being an attentive listener;

identifying a stereotype and having the skills to debunk it (e.g., bringing in contrary data) and recognizing that there are many different religions, religious beliefs and practices.

Tanenbaum's goal is to empower educators and students at all levels with these skills. Admittedly, it is a lofty goal, but as we work with ever more educators and schools, we establish a foundation for today's students to navigate a global society more successfully. Students tell us we're right. Khalil, a 4th grader from our *World Olympics* program, says, "I'm going to go to [all] the countries we talked about when I'm older."

At Work

More and more companies today are global. Managers and employees alike often work with colleagues from around the world, while the composition of local offices reflect many of the same immigration trends that are shaping our schools across the US and Europe. Data show that this mix is often combustible.

In a benchmark national survey of US employees conducted by Tanenbaum in 1999, two-thirds of respondents reported that they could identify some indicator of religious bias or discrimination in their workplace. Interestingly, human resources professionals did not recognize this phenomenon, perhaps because the vast majority of the employees who actually experienced such treatment (75%) never reported it. Nonetheless, it is clear that religious bias and discrimination have a significant impact. Of those who experienced discrimination, almost half reported that their productivity had been negatively affected and 45% thought about quitting their jobs (Tanenbaum Center for Interreligious Understanding 1999).

While no parallel survey of employees has since been conducted, the challenges around religion at work have only escalated. The number of legal complaints has increased. The religious discrimination complaints made to the US Equal Employment Opportunity Commission have risen 87% over the past 10 years (United States Equal Employment Opportunity Commission 2009). Likewise, the press has reported significant settlements for religious bias in workplaces. In July 2009, AT&T was ordered to pay $1,307,597 to two male customer service technicians who were suspended and fired for attending a Jehovah's Witnesses Convention (United States Equal Employment Opportunity Commission 2009). Furthermore, tensions around Islam have escalated in the US and Europe, as media portrayals after September 11 and general ignorance have contributed to increased stereotyping about Muslims and confusion about the distinctions between Muslims, Sikhs and Arabs.

Key issues repeatedly trigger religious diversity conflicts in workplaces including prayer, attire, diet and scheduling.

Prayer: If a company has an office in Saudi Arabia, most employees will be Muslim and time for daily prayer will be built into the schedule. In contrast, the same company's office in the US is likely to have a minority of Muslim employees. Their desire for daily prayer times and longer congregational prayer on Fridays may not be accommodated by the office schedule, and requests for such times may be unanticipated by managers. Managers may not be prepared to respond, while colleagues may resent time other employees "take off," especially when deadlines loom.

Attire: What should a company do when a Hindu employee wants to come to work barefoot for a month in preparation for her religious pilgrimage, but the company's policy requires proper attire (including shoes) at the office?

Diet: What about the business luncheon with two options, beef or fish, but no options for the Buddhist business guest who is a strict vegan?

Scheduling: What happens when the Board meeting at which the Chief Operating Officer is to make his annual report is scheduled on the eve of Yom Kippur and the Chief Operating Officer is an observant Jew?

Tanenbaum works with companies to develop practical policies to address these issues. By institutionalizing religion-respectful policies and practices respectful of local office procedures, micro-aggressions, tensions and conflicts can be reduced.

For example, a company could implement a prayer-break policy that seeks to accommodate sincere believers, provided they make up any time taken for prayer and meet deadlines. The company can implement this corporate policy by broadly communicating that it is designed to respect *all* employees' beliefs and practices, as long as work gets done and the company is not overly burdened. Training managers on how to implement the policy would be important, as well as holding them accountable through evaluations, raises and promotions that measure and reflect their success.

The barefoot Hindu woman may present a more complicated issue, but an attempt to accommodate may minimize any resulting tensions. What if bare feet are not allowed because it is unsanitary and can spread disease? Here, the response would be that the employee must wear shoes. Alternatively, it might be possible to allow the employee to work off-site, depending on her responsibilities, or allow her to take her vacation or unpaid time to meet her religious obligations (provided, again, that it does not unduly burden the company).

Regarding diet and scheduling, the solution is changing corporate practices to anticipate such issues. For gatherings where food is served, meeting planners should be trained to expect that different participants will have different food requirements. Accordingly, meeting invitations should ask all potential participants to identify their food preferences and needs. This is not only a practical act of respect for people whose religious practices are not known, it also acknowledges other, non-religious dietary needs.

Similarly, when scheduling meetings, the company can require all schedulers to consult calendars that indicate major religious holidays and plan accordingly. While occasional issues may still arise with respect to less recognized holidays that may be important to a particular employee, instituting this general practice acknowledges that religious beliefs are important for many company employees.

Enhancing policies and formalizing certain practices can preempt many tense situations but not all. The interpersonal religion-based conflicts at work, whether between managers and employees or among employees, vary in degree and may require different responses. When the issue is not clearly addressed by policies, the approach should balance competing interests, ensure that the workplace functions optimally and strive to create an environment characterized by mutual respect for differences.

In Health Care

Most physicians report that religion is not relevant in medical care and that health care is about science—not religion. As rising religious diversity intersects with the health care system, however, challenges and conflicts emerge. Worldwide migrations are changing the religious make-up in many countries. In the US there is increasing ethnic, country of origin, and religious diversity among providers *and* their patients.

In one study, less than 10% of providers asked their patients about religion, even though over 80% of those patients sometimes want them to ask (McCord et al. 2004). In addition, 41% of patients report having made a health care decision based on a religious belief (McCord et al. 2004). This phenomenon has a real-life impact, ranging from disparity in the ability to access care to treatments to provider responses that address the wrong problem.

Consider the Muslim community in Maine—largely comprised of Somali refugees—where women did not access routine health care. The local hospital was concerned and informally investigated. They learned that the women were following their understanding of the Islamic mandate to live modestly. The gowns they were given to wear at the health care clinic were skimpy and violated their community's practices. This resulted in the women opting not to seek care, effectively losing access to the preventative treatments that reduce medical emergencies and costs. The local hospital implemented a practical response: patient gowns were redesigned to provide more coverage and the women from the local Muslim community started coming to receive the care they needed.

Issues also arise around diet, medicines and medical regimens. For example, in religions that forbid the eating of pork (e.g., Islam and Judaism), observant patients may not want to ingest food or medicines made from pig. An alternative diet can help, but only if all of the individual patient's religious practices around food are known. Knowing the dictates of the person's religious texts is often not enough, as they may not reflect the individual's personal beliefs and practices. Likewise, alternative medicines can be sought once it is understood that an objection is not to taking medicine per se, but to taking medicine derived from porcine sources.

Such patients may also refuse procedures such as valve replacements in which the valve comes from a pig. If the surgeon does not recognize the underlying reason, the patient may end up not having a necessary surgery. Understanding a patient's beliefs and rationale in such instances is critical, especially because a mechanical valve may be available or a religious leader might influence the patient's perspective, saving the patient's life.

Tanenbaum believes that the practical solution to these challenges starts with changing how the medical field views religion, and then providing skills training so that providers across the spectrum appropriately communicate about religion. To do this, the system needs to be infused with religio-cultural competence through several practical strategies. First, the training in medical and nursing schools as well as residency programs needs to incorporate religious diversity training into the curricula so that new providers understand the role religion plays in compliance, decision making and outcomes.

Simultaneously, accreditation and legislative mandates for training providers in religio-cultural competence is essential. This is starting to happen in the US. The Joint Commission now requires cultural competency in hospitals for them to be accredited (The Joint Commission 2006) and various states like New Jersey (New Jersey Administrative Code 2008), New Mexico (Senate Bill 2007), Washington (Senate Bill 6194 - 2006) and California (California Health and Safety Code 2008) now require ongoing training in cultural competence. Such mandates will ensure continuing education in this arena. Similar laws are needed across the country so that all providers will be required to learn how to address these issues.

Finally, resources like Tanenbaum's *The Medical Manual for Religio-Cultural Competence* are a must for practitioners so they can learn how various traditions practice and have accessible communication guidelines for talking about religion with patients. Such discussions should never involve proselytizing but, rather, should provide practitioners with information on patients' personal practices and beliefs (including atheism) and the extent to which they may follow religious dictates that affect health care decisions.

Conflict and Deadly Violence: The Convergence of Religion, Diversity and Armed Conflicts

Religious differences are at least a contributing factor in many of the armed conflicts within and across borders globally. The many perpetrators who cite religious justifications are well known. Our focus is on their counterparts: the lesser recognized, yet forceful individuals whose religious beliefs move them to peaceful action in some of the most violent and unstable regions of the world. At US Ambassador Richard Holbrooke's urging, Tanenbaum began what is now known as its *Peacemakers in Action* initiative—a multi-layered program centered on identifying these religiously motivated individuals and documenting how they are key players in successful conflict resolution. Our long term goal is to change how diplomacy and peacebuilding are conducted to ensure that these vital actors are included appropriately.

Our premise is that relatively unknown men and women—not famous heroes like Mandela and Gandhi—are struggling to reduce and stop violent conflicts, whether or not they are perpetrated in the name of religion. To identify the best in the field, we articulated criteria: Tanenbaum *Peacemakers* are individuals motivated by any religion (not necessarily clergy), relatively unknown, working in an area of armed conflict, locally based, who have put their lives or freedom at risk. To identify them, Tanenbaum conducts an open, worldwide nomination process. To select them, we work with an Advisory Council comprised of globally recognized scholars and practitioners in religion and conflict resolution.

To understand how these criteria translate, one need only consider Franciscan Friar Ivo Markovic, the first Tanenbaum *Peacemaker*. Friar Ivo is a self described "Practical Theologian." A Catholic, he is a Bosnian-Croat scholar, teacher and musician who lived in Sarajevo's Franciscan Seminary during the recent war. He remembers when that war began. He urged other religious actors not to support or bless the fighting but, instead, to encourage the people to demonstrate for democracy.

Devoted to stopping the hatred, Friar Ivo was working far from home when he received word that the Bosniaks (mostly Muslim) had destroyed his home and village, killing his father and other members of his family. Initially filled with rage, he fell into despair. Then, recalling how his father was his ally against violence, he recommitted himself to fighting the insanity.

Driven by his religious beliefs and conviction that justice required him to see the humanity in the other, Friar Ivo took action. On one occasion, as two armies faced each other across a field, he marched from his seminary to a nearby Muslim village in search of the local Imam. As he passed between the armies, rifles were aimed at him and he was ordered to stop. In response, Friar Ivo challenged, "Would you shoot me, you idiot?" He then continued on his mission. Later, he found the Imam and together they returned to the commanders and persuaded them to put down their guns. No one died that day.

Friar Ivo is representative of Tanenbaum's *Peacemakers* and displays the characteristics we find in most of them. Religion is a driver for these individuals: in multicultural terms, it is one of their most salient identities. When they gathered at one of the Tanenbaum working retreats, they defined themselves as *Peacemaker-Practitioners*. They are local agents for conflict resolution, transformation and peace: either coming from the conflict region itself or having been there over the long term so that they are now part of the community. They are trusted and have credibility to act because they are seen as fair and authentic, though not always neutral.

While these women and men have very different personalities, they share core qualities. They are highly intelligent and have an exceptional degree of emotional intelligence and empathy. For them, injustice is intolerable and it spurs them to action. *Peacemakers* feel compelled to respond to violence to honor and preserve the humanity in each person.

By early 2010, Tanenbaum identified 26 *Peacemakers in Action* from over 18 countries, including those named *Peacemakers* through a special initiative to raise the profile of religious women in the Middle East and North Africa. Naming them, however, is just the beginning of this program, which has two trajectories: first, to work directly with *Peacemakers* to provide skills training, develop a practitioners' network and support their work in a range of ways; second, to document the *Peacemakers'* methodologies and personal stories, with the objective of encouraging and, ultimately, institutionalizing the recognition of these conflict resolution specialists and Track II diplomats as key resources in resolving armed conflicts and mainstreaming their vocation.

Our first trajectory is accomplished in several ways. In addition to providing a small monetary award to newly named *Peacemakers*, Tanenbaum organizes periodic working retreats which facilitate training in concrete skills among themselves and with outside experts, e.g., working with the UN, fundraising for a small NGO, and negotiating a hostage situation. On rare occasions Tanenbaum joins a *Peacemaker* to work on a specific project. At their request, we are now working to identify how this group of very busy, local *Peacemaker-Practitioners* can operate as a global network with a larger footprint in the struggle against violence and injustice.

In addition to short profiles for media outreach, Tanenbaum creates in-depth case studies to document *Peacemaker's* stories, the influence of religion on their lives and work, and the techniques they use to overcome conflict or establish foundations for peace. In 2007, Tanenbaum published an analysis of the *Peacemakers'* most frequently used and replicable techniques along with 16 case studies (Little 2007).

Some techniques used by *Peacemakers* are identical to those practiced by secular conflict resolution practitioners. Others derive from the *Peacemakers'* unique motivation, and offer powerful religion-based vehicles for peace, e.g., using the power of the pulpit to mobilize for social justice; creating religious debates that establish the shared values of seemingly antagonistic traditions; and mobilizing mediation or prevention through an interfaith model in areas where religious actors are among the most trusted leaders.

One specific example is the technique masterfully employed by Rev. Bill Lowrey, who drew on local rituals and customs in the Sudan. Living among the Nuer and the Dinka during a time of tribal unrest, Bill understood the communal decision-making processes of both tribes and created a neutral, newly built village in which to negotiate peace. Through storytelling, listening without interruption and the use of a shared ritual for starting afresh—slaughtering and then stepping over a bull—he helped the tribes end their fighting and establish a time of peace.

Peacemakers in Action (Little 2007) moves the second trajectory of our program forward. To fully mainstream the vocation of religious *Peacemaker-Practitioners*, seminaries and divinity schools are necessary partners. We know that many employ our publication as a resource for preparing the next generation of religious leaders. There are even more ways we can collaborate to accomplish our goal. For example, Tanenbaum conducted a small-scale survey of 12 institutions of higher learning, mainly seminaries and divinity schools in the US, to assess the teaching and training now being offered. It is clear that the vocation of religious peacemaking is being taught and even formalized in some of these institutions, although approaches differ and the extent of offerings varies from a course or two to a Ph.D. concentration in religion, conflict and peacemaking.

It is also clear that as the field receives greater recognition, it attracts the interest of the next generation. Classes are overflowing and the demand among faculty is great. Going forward, it will be critical to build on this emerging movement and establish a field of study that prepares religious leaders to address conflict, whether within congregations (where peacemaking is a skill-set) or in zones of armed conflict (where peacemaking is actually the vocation of powerful activists). A corollary to further encourage religious peacemaking is changing perspectives within the diplomatic community, so that religious actors are viewed as potential partners for overcoming armed violence. There is evidence that this shift is occurring. Senior diplomats including the US's Madeleine Albright have noted the importance of addressing the power of religion in statecraft, and many of the most prominent conflict resolution programs in universities are now including this subject. The Council on Foreign Relations recently created a new initiative and website on religion and foreign policy through which they share information and bring leaders of religious communities and organizations together with diplomats and policy experts.

As these trends converge, the vocation of religious peacemaking will be main-streamed. *Peacemaker-Practitioners* will become visible as on-the-ground, Track II Diplomats, who can partner with their Track I counterparts to establish, then secure cultures of peace.

Final Thoughts

The three societal forces that are the subject of this essay—religion, diversity and conflict —are powerful individually, and often converge in daily life and in violent, armed conflicts. When they do, tensions and emotions run high. To reduce these tensions, practical responses can be implemented that change how people act and what victims experience. The motivation can be simply to reduce religious tensions or to bring peace in the name of religion's highest values. Either way, it results in a practical approach for living the Golden Rule.

References:

Barrett, George, George Thomas Kurian and Todd M. Johnson. 2001. *World Christian Encyclopedia*. New York: Oxford University Press.

California Health and Safety Code. 2008. Section 152.

The Joint Commission. 2006. 2006 Hospital Requirements Related to the Provision of Culturally and Linguistically Appropriate Health Care. Http://www.jointcommission.org/NR/rdonlyres/A2B030A3-7BE3-4981-A064-309865BBA672/0/HL_STANDARDS.PDF (accessed 1 September 2010).

Juvonen, Jaana, Sandra Graham and Mark A. Schuster. 2003. Bullying Among Young Adolescents: The Strong, the Weak, and the Troubled. *Pediatrics* 11, no. 6:1231-237.

Little, David. 2007. *Peacemakers in Action: Profiles of Religion in Conflict Resolution*. New York: Cambridge University Press.

McCord, Gary, et al. 2004. Discussing Spirituality with Patients: A Rational and Ethical Approach. *Annals of Family Medicine* 2, no. 4:356-61.

New Jersey Administrative Code. 2008. 13:35-6.25.

New Mexico Bill. 2007. Chapter No. 2007-114.

The New York Times. 2009. Diversity in the Classroom. http://projects.nytimes.com/immigration/enrollment (accessed 1 September 2010).

Pew Forum on Religion & Public Life. 2006. U.S. Religious Landscape Survey. Http://religions.pewforum.org/pdf/table-belief-in-god-or-universal-spirit-by-religious-tradition.pdf (accessed 1 September 2010).

United States Census Bureau. 1970. 1970 Census of Population. Http://www2.census.gov/prod2/decennial/documents/1970a_us1-01.pdf (accessed 1 September 2010).

United States Equal Employment Opportunity Commission. 2009. AT&T Pays $1.3 Million to Satisfy Judgment in Religious Discrimination Lawsuit. Http://www.eeoc.gov/eeoc/newsroom/release/7-31-09.cfm (accessed 1 September 2010).

United States Equal Employment Opportunity Commission. 2009. Religion-Based Charges FY 1997 - FY 2009. Http://www.eeoc.gov/eeoc/statistics/enforcement/religion.cfm (accessed 1 September 2010).

United States Federal Bureau of Investigation. 2009. "Hate Crime Incidents per Bias Motivation and Quarter by State and Agency." Http://www.fbi.gov/ucr/hc2007/table_13ny.htm (accessed 1 September 2010).

Sable, Jennifer and Anthony Garofano. 2007. Public Elementary and Secondary School Student Enrollment, High School Completions, and Staff from the Common Core of Data: School Year 2005-06. United States Department of Education Institute of Education Services. Http://nces.ed.gov/pubSearch/pubsinfo.asp? pubid=2007352 (accessed 1 September 2010).

Tanenbaum Center for Interreligious Understanding. 1999. *Religious Bias in the Workplace.*

Wang, Jing, Ronald J. Iannotti and Tonja R. Nansel. 2009. School Bullying Among Adolescents in the United States: Physical, Verbal, Relational, and Cyber. *Journal of Adolescent Health* 45, no. 4:368-75.

Washington Senate Bill 6194. 2006.

World Values Survey Association. 2006. World Values Survey. Http://www. worldvaluessurvey.org/ (accessed 1 September 2010).

Conflict, Peacebuilding, and Practical Theology

Robert Schreiter

Abstract: *This chapter is a practical theological reflection on Joyce Dubensky's previous essay on the Tanenbaum Center's "Peacemakers in Action" project. Recent work in peacebuilding and the renewed interest in practical theology have been growing side by side over the past thirty years. Both use an inductive methodology to examine experience, critique assumptions and produce new knowledge in their respective fields. The parallel methodologies bespeak a fruitful cooperation between the two that allows peacebuilding to grasp more clearly religious motivations and dimensions in peacebuilding, and practical theology to respond to an important and growing field of human endeavor.*

Three points of intersection are examined. First, practices of peacebuilding are about building alternative social formations—something practical theology has long done in its mediation of seen and unseen worlds. Second, ritual is important to both fields: ritual strengthens alternative social transformations and helps transport participants out of intransigent situations; practical theology comes to understand better how religious ritual engages important forms of human action. Third, when peacebuilding focuses on the generation coming of age in a conflict situation, it is building for the future; practical theology can revisit its understandings of rites of passage with an eye to social change. This chapter concludes with the reflections on the roles of the practical theologian as peacebuilder

Introduction

In the previous chapter Joyce Dubensky presented the Tanenbaum Center's efforts at tracking, encouraging, and supporting the work of peacemakers around the world. The stories that the Center has gathered are impressive and moving. They contribute to our understanding of the religious dimensions of peacebuilding in very important ways, especially peacemaking efforts at the grassroots and mid-range levels of society.

The purpose of this chapter is to explore the work of religious peacemakers as practical theology. "Religious peacemakers" can be understood here in two different ways. It may first mean peacemakers who are religiously motivated in their efforts to transform conflict. That religious motivation may be either overt or implied. If a peacemaker is identified as a religious leader, the peacemaker may be seen as interpreting, in a more or less authoritative way, a religious tradition's understanding of peace. In so doing, that religious tradition is enacted in the situation. Religion, then, is part of the public discourse of the interactions on behalf of peace, even though religious difference is not the ostensive source of conflict. In other instances, religion itself may be less in direct evidence, affecting the peacemaker's motivation for pursuing peace, but played out below the surface of concrete interactions. For instance, ethnicity may seem to be the coin of exchange, but because in many instances religion and ethnicity are interwoven, religiosity or religious motivation may not be immediately obvious.

In a second scenario, religion is the stated difference that drives the conflict, even though the actual features and genealogy of the conflict may be more complex than this. The number of conflicts that turn on religion alone is quite rare. The tensions that lead to conflict usually draw on a host of factors—economics, contested resources (such as land), power, memories of suffering—with one of the features then becoming iconic for the conflict itself. The conflicts in Northern Ireland in the last third of the twentieth century would be an example of this. Religious difference was foregrounded, but a host of other causative factors lay not very far below the surface.

The Tanenbaum Center is committed to greater religious and interreligious understanding, especially in practical ways. It approaches such understanding in a secular, non-sectarian way. "Secular" here in no way means anti-religious, but rather that it works out of no single religious perspective and also works with those who have no religious persuasion. In doing this, the Center acknowledges the presence of religious value and practices within a complex web of other social motivations. Rather than ignoring or discounting religion within that web (as is so often done in models of social and international relations), the Center holds up the religious dimension without making an explicit judgment on the quality of the religious contribution, other than showing how it might affect the transformation of conflict, especially in a positive way. One could say that the Tanenbaum Center's program of peacemakers in action understands "religious peacemaking" in the first of the two senses of that term outlined above.

Here I will consider from a more explicitly religious perspective the work the Center is doing among religiously committed people in order both to make explicit the theological meaning of the practices in which peacemakers are engaged, and to draw from that lessons for a practical theology that works in the contexts of diversity, conflict and peacemaking. I will proceed in three steps. First, I will make some general remarks about the current state of practical theology as it deals with diversity, conflict and peacemaking. The experience arising out of Tanenbaum's work has a distinctive contribution to make to practical theology at this moment of practical theology's history. Second, I will consider some of the practices of peacemaking Tanenbaum's work is uncovering, and try to explore their practical theological dimensions—what those practices do in peacemaking and how those practices engage religious traditions. Finally, I discuss some of the stances or roles of the practical theologian as peacebuilder. Throughout I will be illustrating these with examples from the cases that Joyce Dubensky has presented.

A brief note about terminology before proceeding: I will be using the terms "peace-making" and "peacebuilding." "Peacemaking" is the older of the two. As understandings of how peace is brought about become more specific, the term "peacemaking" in contemporary discourse is often restricted to establishing peace after conflict has ended. "Peacebuilding" is now being used increasingly as a more comprehensive term to describe what might be called the three stages of such work: prevention in the pre-conflict situation, work to end conflict during the active (armed) conflict itself, and the work of post-conflict reconstruction (Schreiter, Appleby and Powers 2010). The efforts of the people studied in the Tanenbaum Center's "Peacemakers in Action" project certainly range across both conflict and post-conflict situations, and even look to building longer-range peace in their societies. In what follows I will be using the terms more or less interchangeably, in order to honor both the studies that the Tanenbaum Center has undertaken and the wider discourse about peace now being developed.

Practical Theology and Peacebuilding: Two Endeavors Growing Up Together
I understand "practical theology" to be theological reflection on practices, or about the theological moments in a larger praxis that includes both action and reflection. This understanding of practical theology is still relatively new in the theological field as a distinctive and conscious discipline, and still struggles to distinguish itself from applied theology and pastoral theology. Only since the 1980s has practical theology emerged as a way of doing theology, something that distinguishes it from the more established forms of academic theology, on the one hand, and the application of academic theology to pastoral and other social situations, on the other. As such, practical theology is still very much a work in progress.

What is interesting is how peacebuilding as a field of inquiry has been growing and developing virtually at the same time. One would probably date the beginning of what is now being called peacebuilding to work undertaken in the 1970s at Harvard University. It was there that a more disciplined effort at understanding what is called "conflict resolution" was pursued.

Concern for peacebuilding as a discipline and as a practice began to grow following the fall of the Berlin Wall in 1989. In the immediate period after that momentous event, there was a huge upsurge in armed conflicts around the world. What distinguished these conflicts was that they were occurring among warring parties within countries rather than between them (the more commonly understood concept of war). This spike in the activity of war continued into the first years of the turn of the twenty-first century. These conflicts had some particularities that were more complex than those found in conventional warfare. The warring parties were not always clearly distinguishable: erstwhile neighbors and sometimes members of the same family or clan now found themselves on opposite sides. When armed conflict ceased, it made re-establishing peace at the local level that more difficult because the warring parties lived side by side. A similar pattern arose in the European countries that had been in the Soviet bloc, when government informers turned out to be neighbors, friends and even close relatives.

Many of these situations could not be easily demarcated as "conflict" and "post-conflict." At most, there would seem to be a temporary cessation of armed conflict that would threaten to flare up again. Indeed, during this period, countries in which such conflicts were occurring had a fifty percent chance of having the conflict renewed within five years. For development and relief agencies, both secular and religious, this presented particular problems. On the one hand, years of development work could disappear within a very short time in such conflicts. This was the case with Catholic Relief Services in Rwanda that saw thirty years of development projects disintegrate in three months of genocide in 1994. Relief workers used to providing emergency services regarding housing, sanitation, and medicine were not trained to deal with combatants from both sides of a conflict now residing together in displaced persons' or refugee camps (as was the case also in the Rwandan conflict). From the mid-1990s, this resulted in such agencies taking the lead in developing new tools for peacebuilding. Perhaps the largest was done over a twelve-year period by Caritas Internationalis, the umbrella organization for 162 relief and development agencies in the Roman Catholic Church. This effort produced both a handbook and a training manual that have been translated into numerous languages and are being used far beyond the Caritas confederation (Caritas Internationalis 1999, 2002).

What is intriguing here is that practical theology as understood within the International Academy of Practical Theology, and these efforts to understand better the practices of peacemaking, have been growing up together: not only at the same time, but also in the same manner. It has been a rare opportunity to see, on the one hand, practices trying to become a thoughtful and critical praxis and, on the other hand, religious traditions trying to stretch themselves to comprehend theologically what these practices are trying to achieve. It is as though both the theory (or theology) and the practices are very much works in progress, rather than the one trying to catch up with the other.

When considering peacemaking practices, most of the theological reflection heretofore had been on the macro-level of peacebuilding, among the major, public actors negotiating ceasefires and peace accords at the national or international level. At this macro-level, just war theory and the advisability of use of different strategies of nonviolence were the theological concerns. In the new practical theology of peacebuilding that is emerging, attention is directed more specifically at the grassroots level, toward those who work at the mid-level of society and have credibility both with the grassroots level and have access to the top-level decision makers. Such mid-level actors are essential to the success of peacemaking efforts. The peacemakers Tanenbaum is studying are precisely these mid-level actors who are increasingly seen as the key or hinge-people indispensable for peacemaking to succeed. So this new practical theology of peacebuilding can benefit immensely from the work of projects such as Tanenbaum's "Peacemakers in Action."

Also notable about the practical theology of peacebuilding is how practices or action is being foregrounded ahead of words or ideas. Words and the values and meanings behind them remain important, especially at the level of motivation of actors in the peace process. However, as interreligious peacebuilding shows (e.g., the case of Osnat and Najeeba in the Galilee), actions can be undertaken jointly even when values may not be entirely shared. This is important especially when dealing with situations of conflict, where overcoming harmful division is central on the agenda.

This pointing toward what might be called "the interreligious dimension of peace-building" has methodological implications for practical theology as well. As many of its practitioners acknowledge, practical theology is not only about a style of the-ology in the academy or in the church, but in the wider society as well—in terms of what is sometimes known as "public theology." Peacebuilding of the kind being presented here usually must move across all sorts of boundaries, e.g., between reli-gions and between the religious and the secular. Insights into these dynamics might help practical theology negotiate its boundaries with the public sphere, especially in the case of "post-secular" societies where secularity and religion both have voices in the public forum.

Emerging Insights into a Practical Theology of Peacebuilding

What are we learning in peacebuilding, and how is this taking shape as a practical theology of peacebuilding? Let me focus on three things, evident in the examples from the Tanenbaum project.

First, *the practices of peace are about building alternative social formations.* "Alternative social formations" entail a kind of re-mapping of the conflict ("map-ping" being a strategy familiar to those who work in conflict resolution). In conflict, social relationships harden and constrain the parties in conflict from thinking or acting differently. Conflicts become intractable because the parties involved get "stuck": stuck in their perceptions, their associations and their expectations. Getting people "unstuck" often involves imaginative new proposals, coupled with persistent or iterative presentation of the alternative until it gains people's attention. A key part of Friar Ivo's peacemaking effort was constantly crossing lines that others had drawn as boundaries and barriers, and forging new relationships. By doing so, he was redrawing the map and suggesting alternative social formations that could point a way through the conflict. His negotiation of a ceasefire in the village was an example of that.

Key to creating alternative social formations is imagining something different. In peacebuilding, this capacity to imagine something different—and discovering the disciplines of cultivating such an imagination—has increasingly come to the fore as an essential component of successful work in peacebuilding (Lederach 2005). From the view of practical theology, the imagination that is the resource for this is a spiritual or moral one, drawing either upon one's belief in God and the consequences of those beliefs (in the case of Friar Ivo) or strongly-held moral principles that are clearly not now evident in the conflict situation (Azi, Osnat and Najeeba). For practical theology, the seen world is not all that there is. In Christian theologies of peacebuilding, the starting point of the healing that is needed after conflict is God. The Christian "grand narrative" of God reconciling the world in Christ becomes the source and paradigm of any healing that can be done in the world (Schreiter 1992). It is this larger framework that makes possible a situating and "re-mapping" of a conflict situation so that some resolution might be reached. The need to have such a capacity of re-mapping, based on terms other than those sustaining the conflict, is becoming more recognized in peacebuilding work, but applies in other settings as well. To echo the slogan of the World Social Forum: "Another world is possible." Not only announcing that "other world," but especially also enacting it in new social formations, quite literally *embodies* peace. For believers, the source of this other world is the divine economy—the action of God—that trumps the conflicted, visible economy. Religiously motivated actors, as well as religious leaders, constantly negotiate between this unseen world and the visible world around them. This is precisely the realm of the practical theologian, although the negotiation of those worlds is by no means restricted to such figures. Appeal to shared moral values follows the same dynamic.

Second, *ritual and play are central embodiments of those alternative social formations.* Friar Ivo organized a choir and orchestra in Bosnia. Osnat and Najeeba set up visits to houses of worship and organized sports programs in the Galilee. Shared music, pilgrimage and sports are all potential bases for alternative social formations. Alternative social formations are more than ideas. They must be embodied and rulebound. Ritual is a central embodiment of these alternative formations. The familiar, reliable, rule-bound patterns of ritual can stabilize an unstable situation. Playing music in an ensemble or singing in a chorus requires sharing a set of rules. Living and acting within those shared rules not only remind us that another way of living is possible; it can also transport us to another time and place. Ritual allows us to move from the present to another time, either in the past (through memorial and memory), or to the future (by embodying relationships we hope will develop). Play, especially sport, is a form of ritual, in that it is rule-bound even as it allows for learning about social forms of cooperation and competition, of winning and losing. It also can be a forum for expressing a range of emotions that are cathartic, sources of bonding, and diversionary from larger concerns. Religion is of course a rich source of ritual. Considered from a genealogical perspective, dance, sport and shared music often took first form in human societies within religious ritual (Wade 2009). Moreover, ritual and play can embody a poetics and a politics of emotion that engages populations often far more than appeals to rational self-interest. Because negotiation is a prime form of mediation of conflict, it is sometimes assumed that rational self-interest is the most important tool for overcoming conflict. More emphasis is now being placed on the emotions that play into conflict and its resolution. Rational self-interest, for example, may be completely overwhelmed by memories of humiliation (Moisi 2009).

As evident in the examples from the Tanenbaum project, ritual and play both were central enactments of alternative social formations. Ivo organized a choir and orchestra (making music together can bring otherwise separated parties together, e.g., Daniel Barenboim's orchestra of young Palestinians and Israelis). Osnat and Najeeba set up visits to houses of worship for young Muslims and Jews in the Galilee, and organized sports programs where they could compete and contest with the safe framework of the rules of the game. Inasmuch as ritual studies has become an important part of liturgical studies and of practical theology, it is also becoming increasingly important for peacebuilding as well (Schirch 2004).

Third, *in peacebuilding focus on the generation coming of age is often the best strategy, both as an immediate solution and longer-term investment in a different kind of future.* Work on healing the social effects of trauma is showing that often about the only thing that can be provided to those who suffered the trauma of conflict as adults is simply some measure of relief. The longer-term reshaping of society often falls to the children of those adults who have suffered trauma. They find ways to be faithful to their parents' suffering yet forge new ways into the future. Hence, attention to the young is key to post-conflict healing. Friar Ivo's orchestra and chorus, and Osnat and Najeeba's work with youth embody this emerging knowledge. Furthermore, helping people shape the lens through which they will see and judge the world—the task of education—is pivotal for preventing a continuation of a conflict, and of preventing the creation of another generation of victims. Azi's work with the madrasas in Pakistan— often the only source of education for young men there—bespeaks this principle. Education and creating alternative social formations among young people are key moves in re-mapping the conflict.

Religion has long seen this in its practices of rites of passage or initiation for people passing from childhood to adulthood. Such was a time not only for socialization into the roles of adulthood, but also a critical moment of intervention. Not surprisingly, rites of initiation (be they in ethnic groups or confirmation celebration in many Christian churches) are marked by the rituals that create the "liminal" spaces that in themselves are not only an alternative social formation, but also remind the participants that the world they see and immediately experience is not the only one.

Roles of the Practical Theologian as Peacebuilder

So how does the practical theologian contribute to peacebuilding? What roles might the practical theologian play? The foregoing reflections on alternative social formations, the role of ritual, and the focus on the young are all suggestive of ways in which what the practical theologian knows from a religious tradition may redound to the work of the peacebuilder. Here I want to focus briefly on the role of the practical theologian as a *resource* to the process.

The practical theologian has special access to the religious tradition as *motivation* for building peace. The great religious traditions all speak in one way or another about the release from suffering and the primacy of peace. A task of the practical theologian is to identify motivations from the religious tradition that can sustain the practices of peace. That involves identifying both concrete principles ("we are all brothers and sisters under God") and the practices that help access and sustain those principles (spiritual acts, worship, prayer). Just as we have learned that certain moral or spiritual practices are needed to sustain a path of nonviolence, so too must such links be made in other acts of peacemaking. Ivo's struggle with finding these in his setting in Bosnia was well presented. Azi's capacity to show how studying mathematics and science could be harmonized with study of the Qur'an was another.

Second, the practical theologian is an *educator* in peacebuilding. Tanenbaum's current study of the training programs for ministry in seminaries and divinity schools in universities has focused upon this dimension in a special way. We need not only to educate future ministers, but also build their capacity for being educators for peace themselves.

Third, the practical theologian is a *mediator*—not in the sense of mediating conflicts, but finding new connections between practices of peace and the religious tradition. This occurs both by identifying the theology implicit in current practices, but also in suggesting new practices based on the tradition: in other words, by engaging in a practical theology of peacebuilding *par excellence.*

Conclusion

We thank Joyce Dubensky for sharing with us the important work the Tanenbaum Center is doing. It has been for us an invitation to think about practical theology in the midst of division and conflict, but also about the very nature of practical theology itself. The results that continue to emerge from the Peacemakers in Action Project pose extremely fertile points of reflection on the practices that make for peace and as such invite theological reflection. Inasmuch as religion is one of the key motivators for many people caught in situations of conflict to think different, to seek alternative social formations in their own settings, I would hope that ways could be found to continue the conversation between Tanenbaum's project and the work of practical theologians.

References:

Caritas Internationalis. 1999. *Reconciliation: A Caritas Handbook*. Vatican City: Caritas Internationalis.

_____. 2002. *Peacebuilding: A Caritas Manual*. Vatican City: Caritas Internationalis.

Lederach, John Paul. 2005. *The Moral Imagination: The Art and Soul of Building Peace*. New York: Oxford University Press.

Moisi, Dominique. 2009. *The Geopolitics of Emotion: How Fear, Humiliation and Hope Are Reshaping the World*. New York: Doubleday.

Schirch, Lisa. 2004. *Ritual and Symbol in Peacebuilding*. Hartford CT: Kumarian Press.

Schreiter, Robert. 1992. *Reconciliation: Mission and Ministry in a Changing Social Order*. Maryknoll NY: Orbis Books.

Schreiter, Robert, R. Scott Appleby and Gerard Powers, eds. 2010. *Peacebuilding: Catholic Theology, Ethics, and Praxis*. Maryknoll NY: Orbis Books.

Wade, Nicholas. 2009. *The Faith Instinct: How Religion Evolved and Why It Endures*. New York: Penguin.

Scriptural Pragmatism at the Crisis of International Law

Esther D. Reed

Abstract: *This paper grew from my involvement with the Theology and International Law Project based at the Center of Theological Inquiry (CTI), Princeton—which arose, in turn, from discussions at Princeton Theological Seminary in 2006 about torture and detainee abuse. The Project was limited initially to members of the Christian faith. The time is now ripe for the colloquy to be widened to include members of religions worldwide, and especially the Abrahamic. At issue in so doing is whether and/or how collaboration between the religions is best facilitated by appeal to the universality of human rights. Rather than supposing a philosophically-constructed global ethic or a priori appeal to human rights, this paper points to how some of the possibilities inherent in Scriptural Pragmatism might be developed in the search for "a common word" to speak against torture and other human rights abuses or violations of jus cogens norms.*

Introduction

This paper grew from my involvement with the Theology and International Law Project based at the Center of Theological Inquiry (CTI), Princeton—which, in turn, arose from discussions at Princeton Theological Seminary in 2006 about torture and detainee abuse. Members of the Project included Jeremy Waldron, Mary Ellen O'Connell, Amanda Perreau-Saussine, Nick Grief and Roger Alford, all of whom brought expertise from the philosophy and practice of international law. David Hollenbach S.J., Robin Lovin, David Gushee and Christiane Tietz brought academic theological insight from Roman Catholic and diverse Protestant backgrounds. William Storrar is Director of the CTI and the person who made the Group possible. I joined as a practical theologian in June 2007, and am deeply indebted to all the members of the Project. This paper would not have been possible, at least in its current form, without our conversations; this was an exceptional group of people committed to the furtherance of critical interaction between theology and international law and from whom I learned much.[1]

Torture Memos and the Need for Renewal of International Law

Uppermost in our minds throughout our time together were the so-called "torture memos" prepared by lawyers in the administration of US President George W. Bush. These memos claimed, in effect, that the President had the legal authority to permit the use of torture during interrogation (O'Connell 2008, 1). We were concerned about how a fundamental human right was conceived as something to be balanced against security (Waldron 2003, 193), and intensely aware also that Pope

---

[1] The opinions expressed in this essay are my own and should not be attributed to others in the Working Group.

John Paul II had spoken shortly before his death of the need for a "profound renewal of the international legal order" similar to that which occurred after World War II (John Paul II 2004, §6). John Paul II's challenge was not "of the moment of emergency" but far deeper rooted, namely, that the Church continue to direct international law to the common good of the whole human family; that individuals and nation states learn afresh "the 'grammar' of the universal moral law" (John Paul II 2005, §3). As a group, we tried to keep in view both the immediate crisis of international law that were witnessing with respect to apparent violations of international law in the treatment of detainees, etc., and John Paul II's vision for the renewal of the international legal order.

I cite more of John Paul II's message for the celebration of the World Day of Peace 2004 because its words were cited by several of the working party throughout our time together:

> Peace and international law are closely linked to each another: law favours peace (§5).

> Today international law is hard pressed to provide solutions to situations of conflict arising from the changed landscape of the contemporary world (§8).

> International law must ensure that the law of the more powerful does not prevail. Its essential purpose is to replace "the material force of arms with the moral force of law (§9, citing Benedict XV 1917, 422).

> International law is a primary means for pursuing peace: "For a long time international law has been a law of war and peace. I believe that it is called more and more to become exclusively a law of peace, conceived in justice and solidarity. And in this context morality must inspire law ...." (§9).

John Paul II's vision is not for an empirically-observed or philosophically-constructed global ethic or common morality but for sustained study of the different aspects of orderly coexistence and respect for the international order. Respect for the law, he writes, is necessary in the new international order that we inhabit today for the maintenance of peace. Law favours peace. Consequently, he urges leaders of the nations, jurists, and all teachers of the young, to recognize the temptation at times of friction and dispute to resort to the law of force rather than the force of law. He pays tribute to the work of the United Nations in bringing about a renewal of the international legal order after the horrors of WWII, and also of the role of non-governmental organizations in furthering respect for human rights. His plea, as in the 1988 encyclical letter *Sollicitudo Rei Socialis* is for 'a *greater degree of international ordering*' ([emphasis original] John Paul II 1987, §7). Mindful that international law has been considered far less frequently in Christian tradition than civil law and related jurisprudence, members of the CTI Project aimed to keep faith with John Paul II's vision and the scholarly complexity of our various disciplines.

From Dialogue to Participation

As a working group, our discussions were limited to members of the Christian faith. Founders of the Project deemed it wise that the working group meet, at least in the first instance, across ecumenical and not multifaith differences. Subsequently, the hope is to widen the colloquy to include members of religions worldwide, and especially the Abrahamic. At its outset, however, the CTI working group knew of the outrage expressed by members of many faith traditions via the National Religious Campaign Against Torture (NRCAT). The NRCAT *Statement of Conscience* was signed by leaders from Reform Judaism, US National Baptist Convention, Mennonite Church, World Sikh Council, Antiochian Orthodox Christian Archdiocese of North America, the Islamic Society of North America, United States Conference of Catholic Bishops, United Synagogue of Conservative Judaism … the list goes on. "Torture," it says "violates the basic dignity of the human person that all religions, in their highest ideals, hold dear. It degrades everyone involved—policy-makers, perpetrators and victims. It contradicts our nation's most cherished ideals. Any policies that permit torture and inhumane treatment are shocking and morally intolerable" (NRCAT 2006).

A multifaith coalition against torture formed in 2006 as a campaigning coalition against US-sponsored torture, the NRCAT comprises people of different faiths working together across points of theological incompatibility because all believe themselves called to compassion, to take a stand against injustice and among the most vulnerable, to create cultures of peace, etc. It presupposes that each faith tradition will grapple with its own sacred texts when asking whether and/or why torture is abhorrent. By reasoning both separately and together over sacred and other texts, the NRCAT assumption (which I share) is that faith traditions can learn together to discern the ethical imperatives in their own traditions, not for the sake of reason *per se* (as if human reason could provide self-grounding justifications for action) but for the sake of practice, or *tikkun olam*, to use the Jewish phrase for the moral labor of mending the world.

In many respects, this challenge is not new. Members of the International Academy of Practical Theology have been engaged in multifaith dialogue for years. Yet the need for multifaith collaboration around issues of concern in international law is urgent and requires new commitments one to another around matters of shared concern—even if this leads only to affirmation of the status quo around the Geneva Conventions and 1977 Protocols, their application to the use of force against terrorist groups, customary international humanitarian law and more. This paper is about how, in small and local ways, members of the various religions or faith communities might engage with these issues. There are, no doubt, members of all major faiths who hesitate to denounce torture in every circumstance. My concern here is not to convince them otherwise but, rather, to consider how those who signed the NRCAT statement, and others of like mind, might press forward together toward the repair of international law such that the human right not to be tortured is never again reduced to a consideration that may be balanced against security.

Religions and the Universality of Human Rights

An issue that presents itself at this point is whether and how collaboration between religions is best facilitated by appeal to the universality of human rights. As members of the major world religions continue to take opportunities to work together in the pursuit of justice and peace, questions arise about the nature of appeal to the universality of human rights. Such a topic far exceeds the scope of this paper yet a few comments may be offered with respect to the concern that debate about human rights in the 21st century is sustainable in terms of its multicultural and multifaith dimensions.

Drafters of the United Nations Universal Declaration of Human Rights (UNDHR) were silent in the Declaration on matters of faith and philosophy. Today, some theorists urge those working with human rights to maintain this deliberate silence with respect to substantive beliefs and to seek no more than *de simplicitur* appeals to the universality of human rights. Theorists such as Michael Ignatieff, for instance, urge those working with human rights to maintain this deliberate silence with respect to substantive beliefs. Ignatieff urges " thin" (describing only the rights themselves) rather than "thick" (contextualizing rights in the religious, cultural, economic and other complexes of a given society) appeals to human rights because, he suggests, this tends to keep human rights instruments out of political debates about the relation of rights to traditional, religious and authoritarian sources of power (Ignatieff 2001, 76). The UNDHR is a strong testament to the universality of human rights *precisely because* it floats free of any underlying justification: "The Declaration's vaunted 'universality' is as much a testament to what the drafters kept *out* of it" writes Ignatieff "as to what they put *in*" (Ignatieff 2001, 78).

Ignatieff's challenge is not merely that religion should remain confined to the private spheres of life but that seeking religious justifications for human rights potentially undermines their currently established universality. "The universalism" of human rights (i.e., the interpretation and application of human rights in different contexts) has long been recognized as contentious whereas the "universality of human rights" (i.e., the universal quality or global acceptance of human rights evidenced by the adoption of the UNDHR around the globe) has held relatively firm (Baderin 2003, 23-6). Against this backdrop, the implied warning from Ignatieff is not only that the "inspirational rhetoric" of the world religions in talking explicitly and in public about the "why" that underlies their support for human rights lacks utility but that it puts "the universality" of human rights in question.

A problem, of course, is that *de simplicitur* appeals to the Article are vulnerable to the same philosophical weaknesses as appeals to any textual authority without explanation of the grounds and methods of interpretation. The humorist P.J. O'Rourke captures this when he asks why we are we all equal:

> We hold this truth to be self-evident, which on the face of it is so wildly untrue.... are we all equal because we all showed up? ... Are we all equal because it says so in the American Declaration of Independence and the UN Universal Declaration of Human Rights? Each of these documents contains plenty of half-truths and non-truths as well. (O'Rourke 2007, 40)

Merely to appeal to a piece of paper, or even to the fact that lots of people have agreed to the words on it, is not ultimately a reason for believing these words to be true.

Nor can it be assumed that the human rights regime is culturally neutral. As the Moslem scholar Abdullahi An-Na'im has argued, a normative system cannot be culturally neutral; all normative systems are the product somehow of contextual specificities (An-Na'im 2000, 3). Today's challenges differ from those of 1948. Extraordinary progress has been made in that, today, the defence of human rights is widely accepted as a vitally important path toward social justice and the relief of suffering. Human rights undoubtedly provide an accessible language in which innumerable victims of injustice have resisted oppression and an international legal grammar in which basic claims to life and life-supporting goods can be recognized and enforced. As the UN High Commissioner for Human Rights said recently: "December 10 marks the 60th anniversary of the Universal Declaration of Human Rights, a single short document of 30 articles that has probably had more impact on mankind than any other document in modern history" (Pillay 2008). Yet questions about the relation between the universal scope of human rights and their cultural specificity are increasingly pressing. Robert Post hits the nail on the head when he writes that a fundamental challenge for our times is the construction of "a jurisprudential theory able to reconcile the universality of human rights with the partiality of positive law" (Post 2006, 3). This observation is part of his Introduction to Seyla Benhabib's plea in *Another Cosmopolitanism* for the integration of cosmopolitan norms into democratic practice. She calls for the "democratic iterations" of cosmopolitan norms, i.e., multiple processes of iteration whereby cosmopolitan human rights norms find homes in local, democratically accountable legal structures. Using Jacques Derrida's notion of "iteration," she looks for the repeating in diverse democratic contexts of cosmopolitan norms of justice: "every repetition is a form of variation. Every iteration transforms meaning, adds to it, enriches it in ever-so-subtle ways" (Benhabib 2007, 47).

The tension between the cosmopolitan norms of human rights and the need for legal rights that are universal and unconditional is ever more complex. Benhabib is surely correct to point to the lack of consensus around the globe with respect to human rights standards, and to seek after agreement. Yet morality rarely starts "thin" and "thickens" up as people mature or situations get more complex. Rather, in Michael Walzer's words, morality "is thick from the beginning, culturally integrated, fully resonant, and it reveals itself thinly only on special occasions." Thus reasoned religion in public is precisely what is required to meet the "why" of human rights (Walzer 1994, 4). Compare Benhabib's "shake-it-down" approach—i.e., shaking the *a priori* universality of human rights into the partiality of culturally-shaped positive law—with Jeremy Waldron's invitation to consider quotidian, low-profile norms "in the mundane density of ordinary life," the ordinary as well as the extraordinary, the commercial as well as the ideological (Waldron 2006, 84 & 97). He listens for the "bottom-up" articulation of cosmopolitan norms rather than repeating a philosophically derived concept or formula until it attains an approximation to the universal standard.

Amidst these debates, many religious people increasingly hold that the universality of human rights need no longer be assumed in terms of a Western philosophical construct based on the notion of "to each the same" (Aristotle) or a category derived from the faculty of judgment (Kant). The universality of human rights is not merely a philosophical or legal given but must be sought continually, identified, constructed and instantiated at law. Many are wary of "monadic" designation of rights as ahistorical ethical ideals for all individuals versus rights as social constructs, and look for alternative ways of thinking. So, for instance, the Orthodox scholar Vigen Guroian accepts "that the deepest inspiration of the doctrine of human rights has roots in Christian convictions. God is person, and so are human beings, who are created in God's image and likeness. Every human *hypostasis* has needs and makes legitimate claims to certain advantages necessary for human flourishing" but rejects much modern rights theory (Guroian 2005, 214). The risk is always that we conceive of human rights in absolute terms as a kind of foundationalist body of theory from which all uncertainty has been removed, (Wolterstorff 1984, 28-30) or as what Stanley Hauerwas calls "imperially enforced uniformity."

In "Enlightenment's wake" (to borrow John Gray's phrase) the choice between these options, i.e., between "thick" versus "thin" construals of human rights, is often cast as either disenchantment at attempts by modern philosophers to ground human rights in universal human reason or resignation in the face of deep cultural diversity as an ineradicable feature of present-day existence which means that we shall never agree about the universality of human rights. My claim in this paper is that these are not the only options available. Different paradigms are available—albeit ones which place heavy responsibility on members of the world faiths to work together.

Scriptural Pragmatism

Two (related) recent phenomena are of interest: the Scriptural Reasoning movement and the exchanges surrounding *A Common Word*. Both are scripturally-rooted movements oriented pragmatically toward reconciliation and healing. Both have enormous potential at local and international levels to promote co-operation and collaboration between members of the major world faiths, especially the Abrahamic, to contribute to public debate about attitudes to and the development of international law.

The Scriptural Reasoning (SR) movement, as I have encountered it, grew from conversations between Peter Ochs, a Jewish scholar based at the University of Virginia, David Ford, Regius Professor of Divinity at the University of Cambridge, and others; it is now spreading to include both university practitioners and a wider audience. SR is not a theory but a practice and a way of being in relation. It is a way of Jews, Muslims and Christians meeting together and reading sacred scriptures. An SR group meets with the intention of reading-and-reasoning-in-dialogue with one another around texts selected from the Hebrew Bible, New Testament and Qur'an. Open-ended and open-textured in character, SR meetings yield something more like "manna for the day" (Ex. 16:31; Num. 11:9) than analytic or systematically structured moral reasoning. We come together in tents of meeting, says Steven Kepnes, another founding figure of the SR movement, to read and reason with our scriptures: "We then return to our religious and academic institutions with renewed energy to bring criticism and healing to our institutions" (Kepnes 2005). Here, however, in face-to-face meetings around the scriptures, is surely an engine-room, or source of motivation for, political collaboration for the sake of common good.

A Common Word began as an *Open Letter to Pope Benedict XVI* after his controversial Regensburg address of September 2006. Thirty eight Islamic authorities and scholars joined together to deliver a response to His Holiness in a spirit of open intellectual exchange. One year later, in September 2007, 138 Muslim scholars, clerics and intellectuals wrote *A Common Word between Us and You* (2007). Its central claim is that the unity of God, the necessity of love for God and for neighbour is the common ground between Islam and Christianity. Welcoming responses have flooded to the website from numerous Christian and Jewish groups. The website has links to the 2004 Amman Message by King Abdullah II bin Al-Hussein in Amman of Jordan which sought to clarify the true nature of Islam. The significance of both is summarized by Allama Abul Fateh Chisti, Global Chairman of the Universal Interfaith Peace Mission: "The Amman Message and it's *A Common Word Movement* has virtually superseded all the previous world's organizations engaged in interreligious dialogue" (Chishti 2009). It is important to emphasize that this investigation is not about compromising our differences. It is not about seeking "knowledge" or a common unifying theory that underlies our diversity. There is no requirement or even desire, for instance, that evangelical Christians (such as myself) compromise their confession of the lordship of Christ. The suggestion, rather, is that a logic of repair is found deep within the sacred scriptures of the Abrahamic faiths and that the time is ripe for accessing these resources.

Leading thinkers at these interfaces include Peter Ochs and Jewish scholar Steven Kepnes. Their claim is that deep patterns in the scriptures move time and again from conflict and suffering to healing and restoration; from woundedness and recognition of the need for healing, to either healing or discernment of what is required for correction or repair. Scriptural pragmatism is the name given by Peter Ochs to this phenomenon or observed reality (Ochs 1998, 38). Drawing from C.S. Peirce, he supposes pragmatism to mean a logic of repair or method of correction. Pragmatic thinking generally begins at the point of hurt, i.e., pragmatic thinking emerges from wounds, irritation or dissatisfaction at how things are (Ochs 1998, 77). The pragmatist allows this hurt or irritation to cast doubt upon established habits of thought or practice; if something is hurting this means that something is not right. The pragmatist then tries to see the problem and represent it, in ways that expose what is wrong.

When construed theologically, this kind of pragmatism or what Ochs calls the scriptural logic of repair may be expressed in the following diagram.

The Scriptural Logic of Repair (Fig. 1)

| 1. Createdness by God as prototype of freedom | 2. The fact of suffering; a cry signifies pain |

3. There is a redeemer. Believers who are in ear-shot of a cry are obligated to hear it and join in the work of healing

Prototypical, is the *firstness of creation*; the *secondness of the reality of sin and suffering,* and the *thirdness of the hope and reality of redemption.* Alternatively stated, woundedness or suffering is recognized as the condition of someone (or a people) who cannot fix their problem. Any person who, after hearing the sufferer's cry and engaging with them in dialogue, is obligated to try to establish a relationship of trust within which the symptoms of pain can be identified and a way envisaged of living again without this damage or despair. Discernment is then needed with respect to is required for correction or repair.

Levels of Failure
In the context of our discussion about the "torture memos," it might not be obvious immediately that the language and conceptuality of Scriptural Pragmatism applies. Yet

analogies with the levels of medical practice are surprisingly relevant (Ochs 2006, 469; Adams 2008, 454). As Ochs has recounted, medicine fails at various levels:

1. the patient's body;
2. the physician's knowledge or skill;
3. the achievements of modern medicine;
4. politics or philosophy.

At level 1, the issue is whether, given the patient's account of their symptoms, the physician can identify the problem and effect a cure. At level 2, the issue is physician competence. At level 3, the issue is the limits of modern medicine. At level 4, the issue is whether societal decisions have been taken to invest in a given area of medicine or to fund the treatment.

Analogously, the failures represented by torture victims may be considered at various levels:

1. individual victims of torture;
2. their lawyers knowledge or skill (if, indeed, they have access to lawyers);
3. the achievements of national and international law;
4. politics or philosophy.

At level 1, we encounter the person who has been tortured. At level 2, the issue is the lawyer's competence and any obstacles that they encounter in the proper conduct of their affairs. At level 3, the issue is the nature of the obstacles encountered by the lawyers. So, for instance, it was not until July 2004, when the US Supreme Court ruled that prisoners held at Guantanamo Bay could take their case of unlawful imprisonment to the US courts, that detainees had any rights under the Geneva Conventions of 1949 as Prisoners of War, or subject to human rights norms under US law, due to the detainees being held outside US territory on land leased from Cuba, and to the fact that the Taliban and al Qaeda were not a High Contracting Party to the Geneva Conventions. At level 4, the issue is international. How was it possible that a fundamental human right could be conceived in nations such as the US and the UK as something to be balanced against security? How did we get to this situation? Where were the protections supposed to be? International politics seems, temporarily at least, to have failed. Philosophy too has failed. Consider how difficult it is using either utilitarian or a "right not to be tortured" versus "right to life" argumentation to assert that torture is wrong.

This extension of Scriptural Reasoning to the reading of shared extra-Scriptural texts is, in some respects, a re-posing of familiar Christian theological questions about natural law reasoning. To the extent that natural law reasoning is ethical thinking which supposes a divinely sanctioned morally-lawful universe and has moral and political content, then multifaith practical reasoning is an exercise of this kind.

The same biblical and traditional arguments by which Christians advocate natural law reasoning apply. These include, for example: 1) natural law is universal, i.e., "in all human persons"; 2) despite the devastating effects of sin, the natural law still gives true knowledge of the moral law; 3) humans have the ability to fulfil the natural law but this ability is seriously flawed by the effects of sin; 4) the content of the natural law is the law of God for humankind and has often been identified with the Decalogue and/or with the Logos or reason present by the Spirit of God in humanity; 5) the natural law is part of the natural endowment of all people and can reasonably be expected to be deduced; and 6) it is commonly associated with the claim that civil government is part of God's continuing care and a corrective for sin. The task is to hold together the reading of sacred texts—as, in some important ways, constitutive of moral reasoning in the various faith traditions—with moral reasoning about human rights, *jus cogens* norms and customary international law.

Faith and Fallibility

"It's a big task." Like the hope that international collaboration will temper climate change, it is perhaps too much to believe that members of the major world religions on the international stage might actually find "a common word" to speak against torture and other human rights abuses or violations of *jus cogens* norms. In the meantime, local Scriptural Reasoning groups might meet around both the sacred scriptures and texts such as the UNDHR in service of the common good. This is what participants in the Network for Religion in Public Life, University of Exeter (UK), have been doing in a small way since 2007. The task is not easy but our belief is that an approached informed by the type of scriptural pragmatism outlined above is the best, indeed, the only sustainable, way forward for multifaith political reasoning and for human rights politics in the 21st century. The process is vague and fallible. Yet all human reasoning is fallible. At a time, however, when the best secularist philosophical options are failing us, the need is pressing for members of the major world faiths to move from dialogue with one another to collaborative participation in political processes.

References:

A Common Word. 2007. Http://www.acommonword.com/ (accessed 22 January 2010).

Adams, Nicholas. 2008. Reparative Reasoning. In *Modern Theology* 24, no. 3:447-457.

An-Na'im, Abdullahi, Human Rights, Religion, and the Contingency of Universalist Projects. Occasional Paper, no. 2. PARC, Maxwell School of Citizenship and Public Affairs, Syracuse University: 1-32.

Baderin, Mashood. *International Human Rights and Islamic Law*. Oxford: Oxford University Press.

Benedict XV. 1917. *Appeal to the Leaders of the Warring Nations. Acta Apostolicae Sedis* 9.

Chishti, Allama Abul Fateh G.R. 2009. A Common Word Convention. Http://www.acommonword.com/en/images/stories/universalinterfaithpeacemission.pdf (accessed 22 January 2010).

Guroian, Vigen. 2005. *Rallying the Really Human Things*. Wilmington DE: ISI Books.

Ignatieff, Michael. 2001. *Human Rights as Politics and Idolatry*. Princeton: Princeton University Press.

John Paul II. 1987. *Sollicitudo Rei Socialis*. Http://www.vatican.va/ holy_father/john_paul_ii/encyclicals/documents/hf_jp-ii_enc_30121987_sollicitudo -rei-socialis_en.html (accessed: 22 January 2010).

_____ 2004. Message of His Holiness for the Celebration of the World Day of Peace 1 January 2004. Http://www.vatican.va/holy_father/john_paul_ii/ messages/peace/documents/hf_jp-ii_mes_20031216_xxxvii-world-day-for-peace_ en.html (accessed 23 June 2007).

_____. 2005. Message of His Holiness for the Celebration of the World Day of Peace 1 January 2005. Http://www.vatican.va/holy_father/john_paul_ii/ messages/peace/documents/hf_jp-ii_mes_20041216_xxxviii-world-day-for-peace_ en.html (accessed 26 June 2007).

Kepnes, Steven. 2005. *A Handbook of Scriptural Reasoning*. Http://etext.lib. virginia.edu/journals/jsrforum/writings/KepHand.html (accessed 23 February 2009).

Li-ann, Thio. 2008. The Universal Declaration of Human Rights at 60: Reflecting on the "Magna Carta for All Mankind." *Law Gazette* December. Http://www.law-gazette.com.sg/2008-12/ (accessed 1 January 2009).

National Religious Campaign Against Torture (NRCAT). 2006. Statement of Conscience. Http://www.nrcat.org/ (accessed 18 January 2010).

Nurser, John. 2005. *For all Peoples and all Nations: The Ecumenical Church and Human Rights*. Washington DC: Georgetown University Press.

Ochs, Peter. 1998. *Peirce, Pragmatism and the Logic of Scripture*. Cambridge: Cambridge University Press.

_____. 2006. Philosophical Warrants for Scriptural Reasoning. In *Modern Theology* 22:3.

O'Connell, Mary Ellen. 2008. *The Power and Purpose of International Law*. Oxford: OUP.

O'Rourke, P.J. 2007. *On the Wealth of Nations*. New York: Atlantic Monthly Press.

Pillay, Navanethem. 2008. Statement on the Occasion of the 60th Anniversary of the UDHR. Http://www.ohchr.org/EN/UDHR/Pages/60UDHRHCStatement2008.aspx (accessed 1 January 2009).

Post, Robert. 2006. Introduction in Seyla Benhabib, et al., *Another Cosmopolitanism*. Oxford: Oxford University Press.

Waldron, Jeremy. 2003. Security and Liberty: The Image of Balance. *Journal of Political Philosophy* 11, no. 2:191-210.

Waldron, Jeremy. 2003. Cosmopolitan Norms. In Seyla Benhabib, et al., *Another Cosmopolitanism*. New York: Oxford University Press.

Walzer, Michael. 1994. *Thick and Thin: Moral Argument at Home and Abroad*. Notre Dame: University of Notre Dame Press.

Wolterstorff, Nicholas. 1984. *Reason within the Bounds of Religion*. Grand Rapids: Eerdmans.

A Correlational Model of Practical Theology Revisited
In memory of Don Browning

David Tracy

Introduction

At the request of my longtime friend, colleague and—in matters of practical theology—mentor, Don Browning, I re-read my essay on practical theology of some years ago to see where I might stand now in relationship to what I wrote then. I came away with mixed reactions. On the one hand, I affirm now as then the basic correlational model for practical theology, namely,

> Theology is the discipline that articulates mutually critical correlations between the meaning and truth of an interpretation of the contemporary situation. This general notion of theology, moreover, can be further distinguished into three subdisciplines: fundamental theology, systematic theology, and practical theology. The logical spectrum for these subdisciplines is the spectrum from the relatively abstract (fundamental theology) to the concrete (practical theology). Each subdiscipline develops public criteria for its claims to meaning and truth. Those criteria also range from the necessary and abstract (transcendental or metaphysical) criteria of fundamental theology through the hermeneutical criteria of truth as disclosure and concealment in systematic theologies to the concrete praxis criteria of truth as personal, social, political, historical and natural transformation and ethical reflection in practical theology. All three subdisciplines are needed to assure the presence of the public character of theology's claims to meaning and truth (1983, pp. 62-63).

I found my earlier argument sound but, at the same time, too narrow. As emphasized then, practical theology must correlate the Christian tradition and ethics (including the ethical-political and social scientific). If anything, further instructed by liberation, political and feminist theologies and other theologies focused on justice especially for the oppressed, I hold even more strongly that this ethical-political correlation partner for practical theology is necessary. The horrors of the twentieth century as well as the massive global suffering still overwhelming us in this century make the focus upon the ethical-political still central.

The emphasis on the ethical-political in contemporary practical theology continues the prophetic center of Judaism, Christianity and Islam. At the same time, however, I now wish I had also emphasized in that early article a further need for correlational practical theology: a theological correlation with the aesthetic, the contemplative-metaphysical and the several spiritual traditions of Christianity.

The principal tasks—complementary to the correlation of practical theology corre-lated with ethics, politics and the social sciences—are the correlation of practical theology to art and to explicitly spiritual traditions: both prophetic traditions (akin to ethics and politics) and wisdom and mystical traditions (akin to aesthetics and meta-physics). Indeed, for the ancients as well as for such modern metaphysicians as Alfred North Whitehead, aesthetics and ethics (i.e., the beautiful and the good) are intrinsically related. Ethics, in this ancient and modern reading, is more a teleologi-cal ethics of appreciation rather than—as in Kant and most moderns—an ethics of obligation.

Whichever way (appreciation or obligation) a particular practical theologian construes ethics, the theologian should also add the correlation with art (thus, aesthetics) to the ethical-political emphasis first encompassed by practical theology as a method of mutual critical correlation. The addition of art, moreover, makes the further addition of wisdom and even mystical traditions of spirituality a natural move to complement the prophetic spiritualities of any practical theological correlation with ethics and politics: therefore emphasizing justice—especially for the downtrodden, marginal and oppressed throughout the world and within every society.

All ethically and politically focused practical theologies (e.g., liberation, feminist, post-colonial, gay and political theologies) will emphasize justice, as did many of the major justice-demanding prophets including Jesus (especially the Lukan Jesus). All aesthetic, metaphysical, wisdom and mystical theologies will ordinarily emphasize love, more exactly contemplative loving wisdom-in-action as in most Eastern Orthodox theologies. Western Christians—Protestant and Catholic—still have much to learn about the roles of contemplation and of aesthetics in theology, e.g. the theology of icons and the theology of liturgy as the Christian practice. Gustavo Gutiérrez is correct: all serious theology should be practical (praxis-deter-mined) as both ethical-political (prophetic) and aesthetic meditative, even mystical. All theology—especially all practical theologies designed for liberation in all forms (personal, social, economic, political, ecclesial)—should be mystical-prophetic or, in terms of correlation partners, ethical-aesthetic. To summarize, in my 1983 article on practical theology I wrote of the need to correlate practical theology with ethics. Here I wish to add the aesthetic. An aesthetic-ethical correlation should, in turn, aid the further development of mystical-prophetic practical theologies.

Art, Aesthetics and Practical Theology
Consider such exemplary modern poets as William Butler Yeats and T. S. Eliot. Yeats wanted to be a William Blake, i.e., a modern, deeply spiritual poet driven to express in his poetry an original and singular spiritual vision that could help to heal modern alienation. Yeats respected and learned from Blake's great poetic Christian vision but could not finally share it. Blake's Christianity— even in its strangeness and Gnosticism, which Yeats appreciated far more than many of Blake's fellow

Christians did—was not a live spiritual option for Yeats whose relationship to Christianity was always a distant and troubled, but not antagonistic one. Yeats learned French symbolism (especially from Mallarmé) in Paris. He still remained unsatisfied. He returned to the Ireland he loved and with his great mentor, Lady Gregory, learned the ancient Irish myths and symbols still alive among the rural peoples of Ireland. In the great poetry of his first phase, Yeats articulated a modern version of the ancient Celtic mythic world (as had Rimbaud with his pride in being a non-Parisian barbarian Celtic "pagan" of northern rural France). Yeats produced great diverse poetry in every era of his life—a rare accomplishment for any poet. Eventually, after the early fine poetry articulating the Celtic traditions, Yeats became spiritually and poetically uneasy anew. He next turned to spiritualism, especially that of the redoubtable Madame Helena Petrovna Blavatsky. He joined the theosophical society for eleven years. Thus, the second great stage of Yeats' search for a Blake-like vision occurred in his second great period: poems on the cycles of life, cosmic religion and hermetic symbols. We can hear Yeats finding himself anew, "turning and turning in the widening gyre," where the falcon cannot hear the falconer. We sense his spiritual power: "what rough beast, its hour come round at last, slouches toward Bethlehem to be born?"

Unlike so many other poets (Wordsworth, Whitman), Yeats' final poetry is just as strong, though very different from his earlier Celtic and middle hermetic periods. His final vision was a highly personal summation of his life-long spiritual and poetic journey: amazing poems on Byzantium, on "Crazy Jane among the Bishops," and his "The Tower" poems. At last Yeats finally could rest content and die. Yeats knew that he never reached a Blakean single overwhelming vision, but he discovered that—for his troubled age—perhaps it was more helpful not to be a Blake of a singular, oft-repeated vision but to be the ever-searching Yeats. His final vision was a stunning poetic vision of the spiritual Real as worked out over many years and detours. Most of us are probably more Yeatsian searchers than Blakean or Rimbaudian visionaries. We all rethink, revise and reformulate. Theologians in modernity also attempt (over a lifetime) ever new forms for articulating what we have learned of the multiform Christian vision and the diverse ways of living both genuinely Christian and authentically–modern. Like Augustine before us, we are never fully healed but convalescents trying ever new methods, practices and theories to forge ever revised practical theology.

There are, of course, many other examples of modern poets restlessly searching as there are modern philosophers and theologians continuously searching for a fuller vision of the Christian vision irretrievably united to a way of life. Most modern poets, like most thinkers and most of us, are not given a single life-lasting vision of the Real. Rather we spend a lifetime searching, trying experiment after experiment, always restless, never satisfied but longing for some aesthetic and spiritual vision of the God as manifested through Jesus Christ in the Spirit as the ultimately Real.

Intellectual historians find that they must, for clarity's sake, speak of the early and late Schelling, early and late Heidegger, the early and late Karl Barth or Karl Rahner, the early and late T. S. Eliot or Yeats. Perhaps these restless Yeatsian spiritual types will prove ultimately more helpful to our longings than even the great Blakes and the Rimbauds. One cannot but admire the great visionaries of a single vision; one need not envy them, however, as both Yeats and Eliot discovered. For eminently practical reasons, it is better for all theologians—especially practical theologians—to keep experimenting and enriching the theological vision, as well as the modern Christian personal and communal way of life.

As Kierkegaard justly said, all authentic thinking has become in modernity a series of thought-experiments. Indeed, Kierkegaard once observed that if only Hegel had written at the beginning of all his great works "A Thought Experiment," then Kierkegaard too would admit that Hegel was the greatest of modern philosophers. But Hegel—a thinker of totality—could never write such a line. And what do most of us now find in Hegel: fragments of a former totality system. Hegel's vision of totality now seems more like a Piranesi-like vision of multiple fragments of stunning beauty and power; the totality is no more. Whoever enters Hegel's *Phenomenology* begins to fear, as Foucault nicely observed, that Hegel may be waiting for us smiling at the end of our particular journey. For Hegel's extraordinary mind may have already thought our "new" way out. He may have closed that escape-route too in his system—the greatest and most tempting totality-system of modern thought.

As Karl Barth said, Hegel is the greatest attempt and the greatest temptation. Karl Rahner wrote, almost enviously, of the "mad and secret dream of Hegel." We are now all thinkers of infinity, not totality (Emmanuel Levinas). We are now all holders of the fragments of all our traditions trying to discern which fragments can be burst open to the vision of the Infinite God we moderns yearn for.

All thought-experiments help us because they remind us that even the great religious visions responsive to our longings are, for most of us, now aesthetic, metaphysical and contemplative-mystical fragments. All these artistic and spiritual fragments from the highly rich and pluralistic Christian tradition as well as other cultural and religious traditions (Zen *haiku*, Noh theater, African masks, Native American rituals, ancient temples, etc.) may, in fact, burst open as frag-events manifesting healing, artistic, religious, metaphysical and mystical visions of the Real to correlate with a Christian vision and way of life.

Practical theologians are best placed in theology to recover and help others recover the great artistic, metaphysical and mystical fragments: above all, in the diverse Christian traditions (icons, Michelangelo, Rembrandt, Bach, Vivaldi, Dante, Milton, slave narratives, gospel songs, folk tales, Fellini, Bergman, Bresson, Scorcese). Practical theologians are best trained to help people discern the significant moments that occur in each human life that manifest the directions of our lives.

All of us have experienced in everyday life our own revelatory events, our own happenings, our own manifestations, visions and gifts. Most human beings, at one time or another, are en-gifted to fall in love with another person. Notice the language we are driven to use here: we "fall" in love, we do not achieve it; we "are" in love, we do not "have" a person's love. When we are in love, reality seems clearer, cleaner, and more hopeful.

At the very same time that love empowers an ever increasing and disclosive clarity, the beloved seems ever more mysterious. Love, like theology, is both cataphatic and apophatic—ever greater understanding, ever greater mystery. Dante needed the particular person Beatrice to learn how human love also discloses Christian love. In *Paradiso*, Dante—ever more aware of Beatrice's person—knew that she remained a mystery in herself and as manifesting God as "the ever-greater" mystery to all mystics, the ever-greater God. The famous last line of *Paradiso* speaks the Christian truth: *L'amor che muove il sole e l'altre stelle.*

We non-prophets, non-mystics and non-saints can learn from the texts and lives of these exceptional ones: the prophets, witnesses, saints and mystics. As William James observed, the mystics cognitively suggest to the rest of us (i.e., those who do not share their overwhelming visions of God) this much: "something more" may well be more the case than what we presently think possible. James, who insisted that he never experienced the kinds of positive experiences that he read in the texts of the mystics (including those of his Swedenborgian father), nevertheless, found mystical texts illuminating that "something more" available to any open, sensitive seeker. James, as a psychologist and philosopher of consciousness, found that most of us are in touch—through our great gift of reason—with only a part (perhaps even only a minor part) of the full range and depth of consciousness. Perhaps the mystics and prophets were in touch with and expressed in thought and action that "something more." Their texts and the stories of their actions are fully practical resources for practical theologians to read and employ.

The excessive realities of desire and love, the wonder of a seemingly impossible "forgiveness" or reconciliation (South Africa),[1] the reality of such "saturated" phenomena as the gift which breaks through the usual economy of return: all these often forgotten or even repressed phenomena—forgiveness, gift, frag-event, love, excess of the good in many lives (not only those officially called "saints" or "witnesses" or the "elect" or the "just")—are the phenomena needing close study in practical theology. There are good, even "godly" persons who exist in every congregation, every particular setting of practical theology: "attention must be paid" to such persons (*Death of a Salesman*). The practical theologian is the one to whom we rightly turn to help us discern these phenomena: ethically-politically, psychologi-

---

[1] See Cilliers below, pp. 201 214.

cally, aesthetically and spiritually. The more practical theologians learn to reverence and love art, to discern the spiritual realities still alive in our traditions, cultures and ordinary lives, the more concretely practical will theology prove to be.

In some scientists, the same sense of the manifestation of the Real emerges. Albert Einstein was alienated from the revelation of the personal God of his Jewish tradition. Yet it was Einstein who articulated two spiritual realities for the modern scientific mind: first, the fact that the universe is comprehensible is the most incomprehensible thing about it; second, that in the tradition of his spiritual and metaphysical mentor (Baruch Spinoza), this comprehensibility cannot but suggest an impersonal God. For Einstein, like James, intelligible reality itself suggests "something more." Perhaps all these frag-events in our traditions as in our lives and thinking suggest not only "something more" but what Eliot brilliantly named "hints and guesses." What for the Eliot of *The Waste Land* was only "fragments I have shored against my ruins," became for the later Eliot of the *Four Quartets* frag-events of "Hints followed by guesses. . . . The hint half guessed, the gift half understood, is Incarnation" (the Third Quartet).

Like Yeats, Eliot too longed for an overwhelming singular poetic-spiritual vision: not one like Blake's, but one more like Dante's more catholic and Catholic vision. In his own life, Eliot had experienced—in the terrible history of the twentieth century and in his own tortured personal life—his *Inferno* and his *Purgatorio*. As some Eliot scholars suggest, Eliot waited after completing the Third Quartet in hopes that he too, like his mentor Dante, might now experience some glimpse of *Paradiso*. He knew, as Dante did, that he could not merit such a glimpse. It must be pure grace. Eliot hoped, however, that perhaps God would grant his prayer for a glimpse of *Paradiso*. It was not to be. Eliot realized that Dante's manifestation of the Real as love would not come to him save as the healing, manifesting realities available in a pluralistic and secular age so different from Dante's more unified Christian culture. At the end, Eliot admitted this and contented himself—as do so many of us, with "hints followed by guesses." He found his own post-Dante gifts and manifestations: perhaps the only ones available to us moderns; they were and are enough. Indeed, for Eliot, these "hints and guesses" even led him to "the hint half-guessed, the gift half-understood . . . Incarnation" (The Third Quartet).

All these fragments give hope: the hope, above all, that if we learn to listen to these hints and use our best reason to understand them (as in all good practical theology) we may yet sense a way to help ourselves and our contemporaries to name God again in our everyday lives aided by the concrete "hints and guesses" all around us and present with great clarity in the great works of art.

The Return of Spiritual Exercises in Practical Theology

A major difficulty for modern Westerners in reading the texts of the ancient and medieval philosophers and theologians in Western cultures as well as the texts of other great cultures—e.g., not only classical but also contemporary Buddhist texts in East Asian, South Asian and now Western forms—is the habitual belief of modern Western philosophers and even some theologians that theory should be separate from practices, especially practices as specific as what an ancient thinker meant by the phrase "spiritual exercises." The ancients and the monastic medieval schools as well as the great Reformed theologians would have found a separation of theory and practical exercises not merely strange but self-destructive for true philosophy or theology. For the ancients philosophy was, above all, a love of wisdom, a unity of thought and a way of life. Philosophy and theology were eminently practical: theory in the practical service of helping one discern the good life and to live it. For the ancients, the philosopher-theologian was unclassifiable in ordinary life. The unclassifiable character of the philosopher-theologian determined, as Pierre Hadot maintains, all the major schools (Aristotelianism, Stoicism, Epicureanism, Platonism) and the two major philosophic movements (skepticism and cynicism) of the entire Hellenistic period from the third century BCE (when the "sorting out" of the schools as schools occurred) to the third century CE (when the classic neo-Platonism synthesis of Aristotelian and Stoic schools with Platonism was achieved).

Each school maintained itself (and its fidelity to its founding sage) by a specific training in intellectual and spiritual exercises. Each school possessed its ideal of wisdom and corresponding fundamental attitude or orientation. These orientations, of course, differed depending on the ideal itself: for example, a tensive attentiveness for the Stoics or a relaxation or letting-go for the Epicureans. Above all, every school employed exercises to aid the progressive development of its philosophical proponents to the ideal state of wisdom. At that ideal state the transcendent norm of reason ultimately coincides with what functions as God or the Good or the One. Christian theologians of the period also directed their theologies to the theoretical practical task of living a good Christian life (e.g., Augustine as well as all great Cappadocians—Basil, Macrina, Gregory of Nyssa and Gregory of Nazianzen).

Such practical spiritual "exercises" were understood by all the ancient schools as analogous to the exercises employed by an athlete for the body, as well as analogous to the application of a medical cure. In contemporary post-Freudian culture one could expand the analogy to the exercises needed to appropriate one's feelings in therapy and pastoral counseling. Among the ancients, such exercises included intellectual exercises: recall the use of mathematics to help the exercitant to move from the realm of the sensible to the realm of intelligible in Pythagoras and Plato. These exercises also encompassed more obviously spiritual exercises, including the use of images, of memory training, of reflection on the basic doctrines or beliefs of the school as well as exercises of increasing one's attentiveness to the implications of those beliefs for life and thought. Through all such exercises the exercitant can clarify her or his relationship to the ultimate norm, e.g., a Stoic's exercise of attention to one's personal relationship in one's own *logos* to the *Logos* pervading the entire cosmos. The Christian theologian's efforts are in the same direction: to understand God and all other realities—theoretical and practical—as they relate to God. In sum, all reflection among the ancients on the relationship between theory and practice must be understood from the perspective of such practical spiritual exercises, especially but not solely meditation. Even on the very limited basis of this summary of Hadot's analysis of ancient "spiritual exercises" and ancient theory, it is clear that contemporary practical theology explicitly and brilliantly corresponds to the ancient insistence on the role of practical exercises for personal and communal living.

In practical theology we may also recall the ethical, metaphysical and spiritual import of our most quotidian practices. For example, our ordinary human interactions are often our best opportunity both for self-delusion and for spotting those self-delusions as we feel—through the very attractions and confusions of our interaction with others—the magnetic pull of God. A second example: erotic love can wrench us from our usual self-interest to face some other reality as authentically other. A third example, as we argued above in section two: art can, at times, free us to consider the possibility, as Iris Murdoch nicely says, of

> a pure transcendent value, a steady visible enduring higher good, [that] perhaps provides for many people, in an unreligious age without prayer or sacraments, their clearest *experience* of something grasped as separate and precious and beneficial and held quietly and unpossessively in the attention. Good art which we love can seem holy, and attending to it can be like praying. Our relation to such art though "probably never" entirely pure is markedly unselfish (1977, 76-77).

As the ancients insisted, many intellectual practices are also spiritual practices. Mathematics and dialectics direct our attention out of ourselves by their demand that we acknowledge, by intellectually entering a world of pure intelligibility. Indeed, learning anything really well—any genuine painstaking work of scholarship, any careful attention to learning another language well, any organization of a group-project—takes us immediately out of ourselves to a different kind of call and demand (see Murdoch 1992). That call is to a sense of objectivity as our paying virtuous attention to particular realities outside ourselves: a call to the other as other. Moreover, as Simone Weil suggests, explicitly spiritual exercises are available to anyone not only to intellectual elites. Above all, practical theologians can help persons to cultivate moments of tact, silence, attentiveness to the world outside ourselves as ways of decreasing our natural egoism. We can learn to pay attention to nature. Such careful attentiveness to nature can help exhibit the futility of selfish purposes—one of the noble purposes of practical theology.

My hope here for the reunion of thought and spiritual exercises is not focused upon a Kantian abrupt call for the will to abide by duty nor upon a Kierkegaardian leap of faith as a sudden radical transformation or conversion of the self from evil to good. Instead, my hope is more modest and more practical: a slow shift of our attachments, a painstaking education of desire—education in theory and practical spiritual exercises like that which Plato foresaw as our best hope for both living and thinking well. Metaphysics and aesthetics serve not only an intellectual but a spiritual purpose: another great barrier against our natural egoism.

The spiritual exercises now available to practical theologies, therefore, include not only the diverse traditions of Christian spirituality but also the great works of art and the many practices of the good in the ordinary lives of Christians. The very ordinariness of spiritual practices shows that such practices already active (if often too little reflected upon as spiritual practices) can free practical theologians to continue to be in the vanguard of the many attempts by Christians to reconnect theology with spirituality.

Spirituality and Practical Theology
The spiritual situation of our age is marked by an increasingly globalized acknowledgment of double spiritual pluralism: first, the diverse kinds of spirituality at work in both explicitly religious and secular forms; second, the intensely pluralistic character of each major religious tradition. Let me offer some examples. First, the academic work of Gershom Scholem has greatly enhanced the acknowledgment of the mystical-kabbalistic aspect of the "ethical monotheism" of rabbinic Judaism. Second, a profound commitment across Christianity has recovered the many forms of spirituality and theology, especially those forms highlighted by feminist and liberation theologians as prophetic-mystical. Finally, the most developed religious case of uniting spirituality and public, practical theology is Neo-Confucianism—an outstanding example of an explicit, systematic and even institutionalized attempt to integrate the three classical religious traditions of China: the practical, ethical-political tradition of classical Confucianism integrated with the more mystical and metaphysical-meditative traditions of Taoism and Chan Buddhism. The large number of inter-religious dialogues suggest the reemergence of a call for each religious—as well as each theological tradition—to recover the full range of the rich classical traditions of spirituality.

More and more secular persons in Western societies can be heard repeating the refrain (almost by now a cliché) "I am not religious" (shorthand for I am not a practicing member of any institutionalized form of religion), "but I am spiritual." Such declarations should be honored by all theologians and churches as, among other matters, a clear call from the hearts of "secular" seekers for guidance for some vision and way of life beyond secularity. There is, to be sure, always a danger in our consumerist and individualistic modern Western societies that "spiritualities" can become new consumer-goods, new divertissements without ethical and religious demands toward others and the Other.

That is a danger but not a necessity. Sometimes the great works of art are not allowed to challenge one (recall Rilke on his first viewing the Apollo Belvedere: "I must change my life") but only provide a new frisson of purely private experience. So too the plethora of "spiritualities" may not challenge but only fascinate for a moment: some rather thin, at times even trivializing spiritualities (for example, the hollow domesticated "angels" of recent vintage) or vulgarizing uses of some great religious ways. Sometimes, with all the "spiritualities" and third-rate works of art crowding contemporary consciousness, Eliot's *cri de coeur* begins to seem prophetic: art has become today an *ersatz* religion—and so has religion.

A more judicious view would say that sometimes Eliot's words are disturbingly true; at other times, however, profoundly false. In fact, the rediscovery of the classical traditions of spirituality by theologians, especially practical theologians, is liberating. Through the rich and exponentially expanding scholarship of the history of Christian spiritualities, each theologian now has the possibility to learn more deeply the depth and plurality of her own Christian spiritual tradition. For example, Martin Luther's spirituality—thanks to Finnish scholarship—now includes Luther's spirituality of *unio Christi* and even several (thirty-seven to be exact) references to deification in his sermons. A second example: John Calvin's own profound spirituality is related to early modern Christian humanist spiritualities as well as to Bernard of Clairvaux and several patristic writers. A third example: medieval Christian theology is no longer considered by scholars as concentrated only in the Scholastics—wherein theology moved to the universities and began to distinguish between academic theology and personal spirituality but not separate them (Thomas Aquinas and Bonaventure)—as different from the late-medieval nominalist theology wherein a separation of theology and spirituality occurred with deeply unfortunate consequences. Besides Scholastic theologies there are two forms of medieval theology wherein theology and spirituality are integrated: twelfth century monastic theology and mystical theologies, especially of many forgotten (or repressed) medieval and early modern women mystics. As all these contemporary scholarly retrievals testify, theology without spirituality becomes increasingly empty of spiritual substance; without strong fundamental, systematic and practical theology, spirituality can drift off into sentimental and unfocused individualistic piety.

Even after the reunion of theology and spirituality by the Reformers, new orthodox confessional theologies largely divorced from spirituality returned in rationalist neo-Scholastic theologies. These led inevitably to the usually marginalized pietist revolts in Protestant cultures and the similar marginalization of those named "mystics" in

Catholic culture. Michel de Certeau has argued how in seventeenth century France the word "mystique" ceased being a normal adjective for traditional spiritual readings of the scriptures and became a noun for those persons and groups (e.g., Quietists) considered excessively spiritual.

As the scholarship of our own day has made clear (e.g., Bernard McGinn's five volume work in the history of Western Christian mysticism), mysticism is simply a depth awareness of the presence of God to one's consciousness: mysticism is not about "visions," "hallucinations," or "stigmata"— although such may occur. Mystics like Meister Eckhart and John of the Cross were, in fact, deeply suspicious of such "visions." The mystical texts and lives are resources for all Christians, especially practical theologians. All Christians can possess some mystical consciousness. Through "prayer, observance, discipline, thought and action" (Third Quartet), every Christian can become more aware of the presence of God in daily life. All observant Muslims (not only Sufi mystics), for example, call God's presence to mind by their disciplined prayers to Allah five times a day, methodically recalling God's presence through daily prayer. This common Muslim practice is a spiritual practice eminently worthy of becoming incorporated in Christian forms for every practicing Christian.

The deeply practical and contextual nature of contemporary theologies like liberation, feminist and contextual theologies is enriching the attempted reunion of spirituality and theology in our day. Feminist theologies, among other contributions, have helped Christians understand how gendered all Christian spiritual practice is. At times even central Christian spiritual ideals (e.g., love as self-sacrifice) can become, unless reflected on critically, a gendered unloving and unjust (and therefore unChristian) ideological imposition trying to reinforce stereotypical female roles of "self-sacrifice" as a cruel caricature of the common, noble Christian call to authentic Christian love. Moreover, liberation theologies have aided us all (including the elites of academic theology) by enacting liberationist theologies throughout the world. Indeed, more and more formerly marginalized Christian communities (especially communities of the poor) now discover, describe and live new Christian practical theologies and spiritualities. These theologies should find mutually critical correlation with the classical traditions of Christian spirituality.

Art and spirituality should join ethics, politics and social science as conversation partners for all forms of theology, especially for the apex of all theology: contemporary practical theologies.

References:

Browning, Don S., ed. 1983. *Practical Theology: The Emerging Field in Theology, Church, and World*. San Francisco: Harper & Row.

_____. 1991. *Fundamental Practical Theology*. Minneapolis: Fortress Press.

de Certeau, Michel. 1995. *The Mystic Fable: The Sixteenth and Seventeenth Centuries*. Trans. Michael B. Smith. Chicago: University of Chicago Press.

Eliot, T.S. 1950. *The Complete Poems and Plays*. New York: Harcourt, Brace and Company.

Ellmann, Richard. 1954. *Identity of Yeats*. London, Macmillan.

Gadamer, Hans-Georg. 1975. *Truth and Method*. Trans. Garret Barden and John Cumming. New York: Seabury Press.

Gutiérrez, Gustavo. 1973. *A Theology of Liberation: History, Politics, and Salvation*. Trans. Caridad Inda and John Eagleson. Maryknoll, NY: Orbis.

_____. *We Drink from Our Own Wells: The Spiritual Journey of a People*. Trans. Matthew J. O'Connell, trans. Maryknoll NY: Orbis, 2003.

Hadot, Pierre. 1995. *Philosophy as a Way of Life: Spiritual Exercises from Socrates to Foucault*. Trans. Michael Chase, ed. Arnold I. Davidson. Oxford: Blackwell Publishers.

LaCugna, Catherine Mowry, ed. 1993. *Essentials of Theology in Feminist Perspective*. San Francisco: Harper Collins.

McGinn, Bernard. 1991. *The Foundations of Mysticism*. "General Introduction," xi-xx. New York: Crossroad.

McIntosh, Mark. 1998. *Mystical Theology: the Integrity of Spirituality and Theology*. Oxford: Blackwell.

Murdoch, Iris. 1992. *Metaphysics as a Guide to Morals: Writings on Philosophy and Literature*. New York: Viking.

_____. 1977. *The Fire and the Sun: Why Plato Banished the Artists*. Oxford: Clarendon Press.

Schuchard, Ronald. 2001. *Eliot's Dark Angel*. Oxford: Oxford University Press.

Sobrino, Jon. 1988. *Spirituality of Liberation: Toward Political Holiness*. Trans. Robert R. Barr. Maryknoll. NY: Orbis.

Tracy, David. 1981. *The Analogical Imagination: Christian Theology and the Culture of Pluralism*. New York: Crossroad.

_____. 1983. "The Foundations of Practical Theology," in Browning 1983, 61-82.

Yeats, William Butler. 1983. *The Poems: A New Edition*. Ed. Richard J. Finneran. New York: Macmillan.

Empirical Studies

The Case of the Minarets: Swiss Adolescents' Perspectives on Religious Diversity and the Public Presence of Religious Symbols

Aristide Peng, Taylor Christl, Sabine Zehnder, Christoph Käppler, Christoph Morgenthaler

Abstract: *Using the referendum on the ban of minaret construction in Switzerland as a contextual framework, this chapter presents results from a study about Swiss adolescents' perspectives on the public presence of religious plurality, their attitudes towards foreigners, and how these variables are associated with socio-structural factors and personal religiosity. In 2008, 750 adolescents (13-16 years old) in German-speaking Switzerland were surveyed, among other things, about their religiosity and values. Results show that young people are generally open to religious plurality, though these attitudes are moderated by gender, socio-geographical setting, and migration background. Overall, girls were seen to be more tolerant than boys, young people in cities more open than those in rural areas, and adolescents with a migration background showed more approval of religious and cultural plurality than the Swiss adolescents without a migration background. Furthermore, results suggest that young people who are grounded in their own faith (i.e., for whom personal religiosity plays a central role and who feel connected to their religious community) are more open to foreigners and to the public presence of different religions than those for whom personal faith is not important. Finally, these results are used to discuss the valuable contribution empirical research makes to practical theology and to offer suggestions for changes in religious education programs.*

Introduction

"Do you wish to accept the citizen's initiative against the construction of minarets?" This was the question presented to the Swiss public in the vote of November 29th 2009. In the time preceding the referendum the country witnessed an increasingly heated debate about the presence of religious symbols in public. In particular, this debate circled around whether minarets are a symbol of a militant Islam which, among other things, is believed to oppress women. Almost all of the political parties—the large Christian state-supported churches, trade associations, and non-governmental organizations—were against the initiative. Prior to the vote, the poll results suggested a rejection of the initiative. However, on the day of the vote 57.5% of voters (with a relatively high voter participation of 53.4%) showed their support for the initiative. As a result, the following clause is to be included in the Swiss federal constitution: "The construction of minarets is forbidden."[1]

---

[1] Clause 3, Article 72 of the federal constitution, which regulates the relationship between state and religion.

While the right-winged parties celebrated their victory, those opposed to the initiative and disconcerted by the result tried to understand how this could happen. The reactions from many European states showed that they are faced with similar problems. Due to the clause's violation of basic rights, legal practitioners were given the task of deciding whether such a clause would breach the European Convention on Human Rights.

Campaign material from anti-minaret groups which was banned in a number of Swiss cities throughout the campaign.

This referendum is a striking example of how, even in a secular society within a democratic and liberal nation-state, religion can suddenly become politically explosive. In such a situation, religion, diversity and conflict are strongly bound to one another. For this specific reason, long before the 2009 plebiscite, the federal council of Switzerland initiated a national research program (NFP58) in 2003 on "Religion, State and Society." As part of this research program, the processes of religious change in Switzerland were to be investigated scientifically, areas of inter-religious tension identified, and suggestions for how to solve them developed ("Religion, State and Society" 2003, 4; for further information see www.nfp58.ch). Within the NFP58 framework, an interdisciplinary team of researchers was formed to conduct an empirical study from 2007-2010 called "*V*alues and *R*eligious *O*rientations in Relation to *I*dentity *D*evelopment and *M*ental *H*ealth: *A*dolescent *P*erspectives" (the *VROID-MHAP*-Study). The purpose of the VROID-MHAP-Study is to investigate the religious beliefs and value systems of young people from a variety of religious communities living in Switzerland. One focus of the study is to understand the relationship between religiosity, its social context, and attitudes toward the presence of many different religions in Switzerland. What is of special interest for this chapter are the views of adolescents, whose voices were not heard in the plebiscite against minarets but whose attitudes and values will shape how religious and cultural diversity are dealt with in the future, and the corollaries and determinants of these attitudes and values.

Although the questionnaire was developed long before campaigns for the referendum began, one of the items included was "do you think it is right that all religious groups have their own meeting places/places of worship (e.g., church with a steeple, mosque with minaret, synagogue, temple, etc.)?" With the results of this study, it is possible to analyze how young people feel about the same controversy that was voted on by adults and to understand more about the factors influencing their views on religious diversity in Switzerland. How do young people respond to the presence of different religious groups in Swiss society? In what ways are their attitudes towards religious diversity related to religion, gender and social context?

Attitudes towards foreigners
Switzerland, like the rest of Europe, is in the wake of globalization and is witnessing the revival of right-wing, anti-foreign party politics. The anti-minaret movement, initiated and supported by the Swiss People's Party (Schweizerische Volkspartei, SVP), represents just one example of this change. As Hjerm notes, "[such a] situation may be due to insecurity among people in a changing Europe, or to a more general protest about the inability of established political party structures to come up with fresh solutions to the problems salient to voters" (2005, 294).

The individuals who voted for the ban against the construction of minarets seem to be driven by a fear of those or that which is unlike them. This fear is most often referred to as *xenophobia*. Yakushko, who has researched attitudes towards immigrants in the US, defines xenophobia as "a form of attitudinal, affective, and behavioral prejudice toward immigrants and those perceived as foreign" (2010, 43). Researchers from a pioneering study on xenophobia in the European Union made the following observations: "Foreigners are seen as carriers of a different culture with the potential to threaten the integrity of one's own nation. The assumption that the nation embodies culture comes from a belief that the nation is the arena in which critical values and beliefs are transmitted to developing members. Since each culture consists of a unique mix of orientations, foreigners inevitably threaten to alter the domestic culture through the introduction of new orientations" (De Master and Le Roy 2000, 425). Although Switzerland is not part of the European Union, it is reasonable to believe that these beliefs hold true for Switzerland as well.

Xenophobia expresses itself in any number of ways, not all of which lead to conflict. In Switzerland, however, where (part of) the majority group feels that their culture is threatened by a minority group (or several minority groups), conflict between these groups seems inevitable: the majority fights for its right to stay the same, while the minorities fight for their right to bring change.

The literature shows that psychologists and sociologists have been trying to find correlates and determinants of xenophobia for many years. In understanding more about the influencing factors of xenophobia and other more specific related beliefs and behaviors (in this case, voting against the construction of minarets), it is the hope that methods of intervention and changes in (religious) education might be successful in reducing the probability of conflict. At this time, the focus of the analysis will be on a few factors which can be subsumed under two main headings: socio-structural variables and personal religiosity. Specifically, our analyses focus on the following possible correlates for attitudes toward places of worship and attitudes towards foreigners (xenophobia): 1) gender, 2) urban-rural comparison, 3) religious affiliation, 4) centrality of one's own religion in his/her life, and 5) how connected one feels to his/her religious community. In the following section, the individual research questions that guided the analyses will be presented.

Research Questions

The following four research questions guided the subsequent data analysis:

1) How are attitudes towards places of worship moderated by migration background, socio-geographical setting, and gender?

2) How are attitudes towards foreigners influenced by migration background, socio-geographical setting, and gender?

3) What influence does religious affiliation have on attitudes towards places of worship and xenophobic tendencies?

4) In what way are adolescents' feelings towards places of worship and their xenophobic tendencies correlated with each other and with their personal religiosity (i.e., centrality of religiosity, connectedness to a religious community)?

With respect to the first two questions, it is expected that there will be significant differences between male and female responses, between the scores of young people in rural areas and those in urban areas, and between young people with a migration background and those without. In reference to the third question, it is assumed that the religious groups will report different levels of intolerance towards foreigners (xenophobia) and towards the presence of places of worship.

Methods

Study Design: The study follows a cohort-sequence model in which three cohorts of adolescents are surveyed by means of a questionnaire. The adolescents' perspectives are assessed on two occasions, with one year separating the two waves of data collection. During the first wave of data collection (April to July, 2008) the young people were 13-16 years of age, while at the time of the second wave of data collection (April to July, 2009) they were 14-17 years of age. The results presented in this chapter are based solely on data from the first wave of collection.

Participants: In determining the sample, it was attempted to find a balance between the three cohorts, the genders, and the different types of schools (Sekundar- or Haupt-Realschule, Gymnasium and Berufsschule). In order to analyze systematically contextual differences, participants were recruited in both rural and urban areas surrounding Bern and Zurich in Switzerland.

In the spring of 2008, 750 adolescents between 13 and 16 years of age (Mean = 14.94 years; SD = 1.02 years) participated in the survey. The sample consisted of 50.1% girls and 49.1% boys; 48% of the participants did not have a migration background, while 52% did have a migration background. Table 1 shows the religious affiliations of the participants.

Table 1: Sample according to religious affiliation

Religious affiliation	N	%
no religious affiliation	69	9.2
Christian without further specifications	74	9.9
Catholic	191	25.5
Protestant	241	32.1
Independent (free evangelical) churches	21	2.8
Christian Orthodox	22	2.9
Muslim	61	8.1
Hindu	25	3.3
Jewish	17	2.3
Sects	5	0.7
other religious affiliation	8	1.1
unclear religious affiliation	9	1.2
no answer	7	0.9
Total	750	100

Measures: The data presented here were collected through a questionnaire developed specifically for this study which encompasses both standardized instruments and other scales and items for which there were no well-established instruments. In total, the questionnaire comprises of 261 items. The great majority of participants filled out the questionnaire at school with a member of the research team present who followed a standard procedure. A small proportion of participants filled out the questionnaire on their own and mailed it back to the researchers.

In the following, the operationalization of the individual variables discussed in this paper is presented.

Attitudes toward meeting places or places of worship of different religious groups: The attitudes toward places of worship were measured with the following item: "Do you think it is right that all religious communities have their own meeting places/places of worship here (church with steeple, mosque with minaret, synagogue, temple, etc.)?" Participants were to answer this question on a 5-point Likert scale in which strong agreement with this question was understood to show positive attitudes toward different religious groups having their own places of worship.

Xenophobia: In order to access adolescents' attitudes towards foreigners, the participants were presented with the statement, "In the future fewer foreigners should come into this country" and were asked to rate on a 5-point Likert scale whether they agree completely or not at all with this statement. Those with a higher score on this item are considered to be more xenophobic.

Centrality of the religious construct system—Religiosity: The "Structure-of-Religiosity-Test" (S-R-T) (Huber, 2008) was used to measure religiosity. The S-R-T is a well-established instrument that measures five core dimensions of religiosity, i.e., an intellectual dimension, a religious ideology dimension, a public ritual dimension, a private devotional dimension and a religious experience dimension. Each dimension is measured with two questions, which are to be answered on a 5-point Likert scale. The wording in some of the questions of the S-R-T was changed in order to make them more comprehensible for 13-16 year olds, for example: "Are you interested in questions about religion or related topics?" (intellectual dimension), and "How strong is your belief that there is a God or something divine?" (religious ideology dimension). The five dimensions were aggregated in order to calculate a comprehensive centrality score.

Connectedness to a church/religious group: The following item was adapted from Dubach and Campiche (1993) in order to measure the level of connectedness participants feel to a religious community, a construct represented by the following item was formulated: "How connected do you feel to your church/religious community?" As with the other items, this was also answered using a 5-point Likert scale.

The specific comparison groups were defined as follows:

Socio-graphical background: urban vs. rural: Rural areas were defined as villages and small towns which have less than 5000 inhabitants and are at least 20 km from the next city. Urban high-density areas in this case are defined as cities or agglomerations with at least 10,000 inhabitants, at least 50% of whom are immigrants or foreigners.

Migration background: The migration background of the adolescents was determined by their parents' backgrounds. Young people considered to have a migration background are those where one or both of the parents do not have Swiss citizenship or where one or both of the parents were not born in Switzerland.

Results

In the following section a number of results from the VROID-MHAP study will be presented. In a first step, the question of to what extent socio-demographic variables such as gender, migration background and social setting (urban/rural) influence attitudes toward public religious practice (e.g., in reference to the construction of religious places of worship) as well as xenophobic tendencies are displayed. In a second step, the above-mentioned attitudes are examined in view of variations between the different religious groups represented in the sample. Finally, the results of the relationship between these attitudes and their association with centrality of religiosity as well as feelings of connectedness to one's religious community are described.

1) *How are attitudes towards places of worship moderated by migration background, socio-geographical setting, and gender?*

In order to answer the question of how attitudes towards the presence of places of worship of different religious groups are moderated by socio-demographical variables, a three factorial Analysis of Variance (ANOVA) was calculated, including the following factors: gender, setting (urban/rural) and migration background. The results are presented in figure 1.

Figure 1: Attitudes towards places of worship according to migration background, socio-geographical setting, and gender

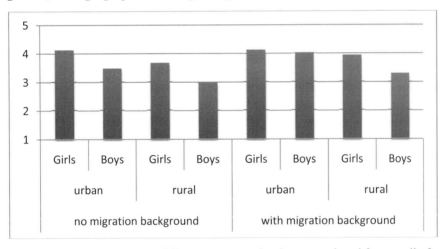

As the graph shows, there are differences among the above-mentioned factors, all of which were found to be significant main effects in the ANOVA. Accordingly, the female adolescents agree with the presence of places of worship for all religious groups to a greater degree than the males ($p \leq .001$; effect size (ES) = .44). The same is true for young people living in an urban setting, who in comparison with those living in a rural setting show greater approval of the question at hand ($p \leq .001$; ES = .51). Lastly, and most likely to be expected is that adolescents who have a migration background agree with the right for all religions to have their own places of worship ($p \leq .01$; ES = .36). Although all three of these main effects were significant, the analysis did not show any significantly relevant interaction effects between the variables.

2) *How are attitudes towards foreigners-xenophobia influenced by migration*
    background, socio-geographical setting, and gender?

In a next step of analysis, a procedure analogous to that presented above was carried
out with regard to xenophobic tendencies. Here, we see a similar pattern of results,
although the findings in this case are even more pronounced (see Figure 2).

Figure 2: Xenophobic tendencies according to migration background, socio-geographical setting, and gender

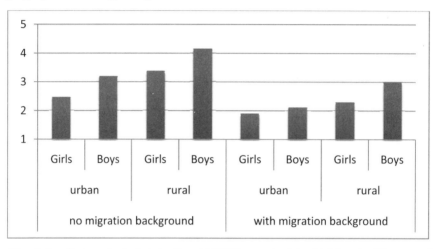

All of the factors included in the ANOVA resulted in highly significant main
effects. It reports that the boys prove themselves to have much greater xenophobic
tendencies than the girls ($p \leq .001$; ES = .44). Furthermore, xenophobia seems to be
more prevalent in rural areas than in urban ones ($p \leq .001$; ES = .78), and as might
be expected less pronounced in the population of young people with a migrant background ($p \leq .001$; ES = .85). Even though the young males in rural areas report the
highest scores on xenophobia (Mean=4.1) and the young females in urban areas the
lowest scores (Mean=1.9), which shows how great the spectrum of the reported
scores is, the interactions between the factors did not reach statistical significance.

3) *What influence does religious affiliation have on attitudes towards places of*
    worship and xenophobic tendencies?

Next, the adolescents' attitudes towards public places of worship for all religious
groups as well as the tendency toward xenophobia were compared according to the
different religious groups represented in the sample. The following graphs summarize the findings.

Figure 3: Attitudes towards public places of worship according to religious affiliation

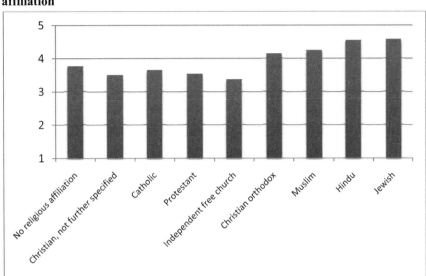

The statistical analysis of the differences between the various religious groups with regard to the right for all groups to have their own places of worship (see Figure 3) exhibits highly significant results (overall effect of the ANOVA, $p \leq .001$). Subsequent calculations of single comparisons show that the religious affiliations can be divided into three groups: the Christian denominations (Catholic, Protestant, independent free, Christian without further specification) together with those without religious affiliation show the least acceptance of public places of worship for all religious groups. Another group, consisting of Muslim, Hindu and Jewish young people, reports the greatest acceptance of public religious spaces; they do not differ significantly from one another but each of them differs significantly from the first group. The young people affiliated with Christian Orthodox are in a group for themselves in between the groups with the lowest and highest scores.

In a next step, the question about whether the xenophobic tendencies would differ between the religious groups was investigated. Here, too, the ANOVA across all groups produces a highly significant effect ($p \leq .001$, see Figure 4).

Figure 4: Tendency toward xenophobia according to religious affiliation

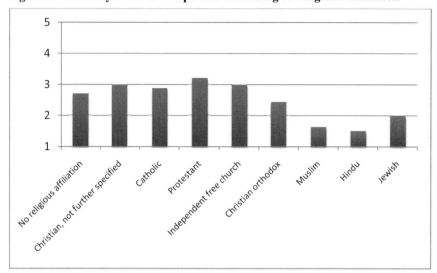

Upon closer analysis of the individual comparisons, it is evident that the picture here is less straightforward than the one previously discussed. On the one hand the Muslim, Hindu and Jewish young people show the lowest scores on xenophobia, and the Christian Orthodox-affiliated young people find themselves once again in a sort of transition area. On the other hand, this time, as well as showing generally higher scores on xenophobia, there are differences within the large group of Christian denominations in which the Protestant young people show significantly more xenophobic tendencies than those affiliated with the Catholic church (p = .03) and those without religious affiliation (p = .03).

4)   *In what way are adolescents' feelings towards places of worship and their*
      xenophobic tendencies associated with each other and with their personal
      religiosity?

In a final group of selected results, the relationships between the most central variables presented here as well as their connection to the centrality of religiosity and the feeling of connectedness with one's religious community are described. In order to do this, correlations between the variables were calculated and the results displayed in Table 2.

Table 2: Correlations between attitudes towards places of worship, xenophobia, connectedness and centrality of religiosity

	Places of worship	Xenophobia	Connectedness	Centrality
Places of worship	1	-0,411***	0,118**	0,186***
Xenophobia		1	-0,166***	-0,200***
Connectedness			1	0,729***
Centrality				1

** = $p \leq 0.01$; *** = $p \leq 0.001$

If one looks first at the relationship between attitudes towards public places of worship and the tendency toward xenophobia, it is clear that the original hypothesis is confirmed through a highly significant negative correlation (r = -.41, ES = .90). More interesting, however, are the correlations of these two variables with the centrality of religiosity and connectedness to one's religious community. Here, for both religious connectedness and the centrality of religiosity, there are clear statistical relationships with xenophobia: the higher the religious connectedness (r = .12, ES = .24) and the greater the centrality (r = .19, ES = .38), the greater the adolescents' tolerance of public places of worship for all religious groups. More pronounced, however, are the relationships with xenophobia: the higher the religious connectedness (r = -.17, ES = .34) and the greater the centrality of religiosity (r = -.20, ES = .41), the lower the tendency towards xenophobia (i.e., the greater the tolerance towards foreigners).

Discussion

To a large extent, the assumptions presented at the beginning of this chapter were confirmed. Both religiosity and the socio-structural variables including urban vs. rural and gender moderate adolescents' attitudes towards the presence of religious spaces in public and towards religious diversity. The girls show more positive thinking toward religious plurality than the boys; the young people living in urban areas show more positive attitudes about plurality than those in rural areas; and finally, the young people who do not belong to the dominant Christian churches are more open to plurality than those who do.

In looking at the role that context plays in attitudes toward religious plurality, it seems that adolescents do not differ greatly from adults, as seen in analyses of the voting behavior of Swiss adults (the so-called VOX-Analyses). Analyses of voting behavior in referendums relevant to minorities in Switzerland over the last 50 years show, consistent with the results from the present study, that older people, those in rural areas, practicing Catholics and Protestants, and males form groups that vote more strongly against minorities than the average Swiss voter (Vatter 2010).

There is, however, one area in which the two sets of results differ greatly from another, and this deserves special attention. If the adolescents' answers to the question about acceptance of religious meeting places are divided into two groups, namely 1) from somewhat disagree to disagree completely and 2) from somewhat agree to agree completely, then we see the following results: 16.4% are somewhat or greatly against all religious groups having their own meeting places or places of worship, 22.0% are right in the middle (neither agreeing nor disagreeing), and 61.6% somewhat or completely agree with every religious group having the right to have its own meeting space. Thus, it seems as if young people, being more tolerant than adults, given the chance may have voted more positively on the question of minaret construction than the adults did.[2]

It should, however, be noted that, although in the present study there was a significant correlation between xenophobic tendencies and attitudes towards places of worship, these represent two separate attitudes. This becomes clear in the VOX-Analyses where we see that among the people who generally feel positively towards foreigners, more than one third (38%) voted for the minaret initiative, i.e., for a ban on the construction of minarets (Hirter and Vatter, 2010). Thus, the mistake must not be made of assuming that individuals who show negative attitudes towards the presence of places of worship for all religious groups are necessarily xenophobic. This emphasizes the need for further research about the connection between general attitudes towards foreigners and specific behaviors (such as voting on foreigners' rights).

The present investigation with adolescents, however, sheds light on one factor which the analyses of voting behavior among adults could not illuminate. The results of the present study are clear: the more central a role religiosity plays in young people's construct system, the more open such young people are to the public presence of other religions and the less xenophobic they tend to be. In reference to the VOX-Analyses of voting behavior among adults, this finding shows that it does not suffice simply to determine whether voters belong to a specific religion or denomination in order to understand correlations between religiosity and openness to a multi-religious society. Rather, the significance of religiosity in one's personal life seems to be a much more important factor.

The present study also sheds light onto a more fundamental question of practical theology: What is the importance of empirical research in practical theology in particular with regard to conflicts that arise in a multi-religious context? According to Grethlein (2004), empirical research represents one branch of practical theology. It contributes to the exploration and understanding of the religious landscape in which practical theology is active. This also holds true for the present study which goes beyond showing how adolescents feel about religious plurality by clarifying the importance of personal religiosity. This is an especially relevant finding for the field of religious education. However, the results of this study alone do not allow us to develop potential guidelines for religious educators. This is where normative reflections come

---

[2] The referendum was only on the construction of minarets; the construction of mosques in general was not up for debate.

into play. Empirical analysis of conflicts and tensions bred by religious diversity, according to Grethlein (2004), must be accompanied by normative reflection based on Christian religious traditions. Both empirical work and normative reflection can then feed into the construction of models of action aimed at dealing with religious conflicts and at improving mutual understanding and respect. In this way, empirical analyses can contribute valuable insights to practical theology. We have chosen to highlight a few such insights from the present study:

Understanding the value of personal and meaningful religiosity. The results of this study have made it clear that the depth of one's own faith has great implications for how tolerant one can be towards those who are different. Furthermore, it is important to consider that personal religiosity is more significant for non-Christian young people with a migration background than for the Christians without a migration background in this study. Both of these findings are important for the discussion of models for religious education. These findings speak in favor of religious education programs offered by the public school system that incorporate both teaching in religion as well as teaching about religion. Such programs would encourage individuals to clarify their own religious beliefs but would also invite young people to learn about religion as a concept and in its multitude of forms.

Identification of specific target groups. Empirical research can also serve to identify specific groups who need special attention when it comes to religious education. The findings of this study show, for example, that male adolescents without a migration background, who are affiliated with the Christian church and who live in rural settings have noticeably more negative attitudes towards religious plurality than the other young people in the study. It is important to ask: What religious education program could be developed in order to increase these young boys' understanding of and appreciation for people with different cultural and religious backgrounds? It would be particularly fascinating to delve further into the results of this and similar studies in order to understand the differences (in needs) between various groups of young people and, in turn, to learn how to make religious pedagogical efforts more fruitful.

Inclusive religious pedagogy: The presence of different religious orientations and traditions among adolescents leads to one of the fundamental questions of religious pedagogy: whose job is it to reflect upon (or represent other groups in) the religious education of adolescents from Muslim, Hindu, Jewish, etc. traditions from a scientific and pedagogical perspective? In the present context it seems that Christian-based religious pedagogy bears this responsibility. But how can the Christian-based religious pedagogical community meet this need with discretion as well as encourage reflective religious pedagogical work in other non-Christian traditions? This will not be possible without a broadening of the current mostly Christian-dominated model of religious education and unless this religious education finds new footing in comparative religious education and theology. A deeper, empirically based understanding of religious diversity and how it is perceived and lived in Western Europe is the key to a differentiated self-understanding of the discipline itself, its capacity to analyze conflict-laden situations and its ability to devise new ways of dealing with the dynamic religious landscape.

When empirical results are integrated into religious pedagogy theory development and practice they can sharpen the perception of religious diversity in Western Europe, can clarify both the related potential and the risks, and can help religious pedagogy recognize opportunities to foster peaceful cohabitation of diverse people and groups in Western Europe.

References:

De Master, Sara and Le Roy, Michael K. 2000. Xenophobia and the European Union. *Comparative Politics* 32, no. 4:419-436.

Dubach, Alfred and Campiche, Roland. 1993. *Jeder (r) ein Sonderfall? Religion in der Schweiz: Ergebnisse einer Repräsentativbefragung.* Zürich: NZN.

Grethlein, Christian. 2004. Praktische Theologie. In *Leitfaden Theologiestudium (UTB)*, ed. Michael Roth, 131-158. Göttingen: Vandenhoeck and Ruprecht.

Hirter, Hans and Vatter, Adrian. 2010. VOX-Analyse der Volksabstimmung vom 29. November 2009. Presentation, Medienkonferenz anlässlich der 100. VOX-Analyse. Bern, Switzerland, January 25.

Hjerm, Mikael. 2005. What the future may bring: Xenophobia among Swedish adolescents. *Akta Sociologica* 48, no. 4:292-307.

Huber, Stefan. 2008. Der Religiositäts-Struktur-Test (R-S-T). Systematik und operationale Konstrukte. In *Individualisierung und die pluralen Ausprägungsformen des Religiösen*, ed. Wilhelm Gräb und Lars Charbonnier, 109-143. Münster: Lit Verlag.

Religion, State and Society: Implementation plan NFP58. 2003. Bern.

Vatter, Adrian. 2010. Tyrannei der Mehrheit? Stimmbürgerverhalten bei minderheitenrelevanten Abstimmungen in der Schweiz: Neue Befunde zu den Wirkungen der direkten Demokratie aus der Basis von VOX-Daten. Presentation, Medienkonferenz anlässlich der 100. VOX-Analyse. Bern, Switzerland, January 25.

Yakushko, Oksana. 2009. Xenophobia: Understanding the roots and consequences of negative attitudes toward immigrants. *The Counseling Psychologist* 37, no. 1:36-66.

No Pluralism – No Diversity? Religious Education's Response to Pluralization in Germany in the second half of the Twentieth Century[1]

Friedrich Schweitzer

Abstract: *This chapter is written on the basis of a research project on the development of religious education in Germany between 1900 and 1975. The focus of the chapter itself is on how pluralism and diversity were addressed in the religious education discussions in major journals between 1945 and 1975. Analyzing the terminology used in these discussions as well as the phenomena addressed in them, the author identifies a clear lack of openness towards pluralism and diversity in these discussions. While the concepts of pluralism and diversity did not come into use before the late 1960s, the phenomena that can be related to these concepts—like cultural or religious diversity—were viewed critically for the most part. Pluralism as a principle did not inform the guiding ideas of religious educators at that time. In another step, different possible interpretations of these observations are suggested, relating them to the churches, to theology, to views of education, to the understanding of culture, and to the contemporary political mindset. Based on his observations and interpretations, the author raises a number of questions which—as lessons from the past—can be related to today's understandings of religious education and practical theology, especially to the role of pluralism and diversity in such understandings. Given the ambivalent legacy of practical theology in this respect, the author argues for a more self-critical attitude.*

Introduction

The questions pursued in the present volume are about *Religion, Diversity and Conflict*. The invitation to the conference that was the starting point for the volume stated a special interest in practical theology's contribution in proposing "paths for dialogue, mutual respect and ethical practices in the face of such conflict." "The conference will explore ways in which the disciplines of practical theology can contribute both to the emerging world dialogue between conflicting religious traditions, as well as addressing parallel issues at the national and local levels."

---

[1] This essay is based on a research project sponsored by the German Research Foundation (*Deutsche Forschungsgemeinschaft*) on the development of religious education as an academic discipline in the twentieth century (1900-1975). The results of the first part of the study (1900-1930) have been published (Schweitzer and Simojoki 2005). A second volume covering the time between 1930 and 1975 is scheduled for publication in 2010 (Schweitzer et al., *Religionspädagogik als Wissenschaft*, Freiburg: Herder). Earlier work together with Richard Osmer (Princeton), comparing the development of religious education in the United States and in Germany (Osmer and Schweitzer 2003), has stimulated the current project in important ways. In addition to F. Schweitzer and Henrik Simojoki, Sara Moschner and Markus Müller are members of the present research team. I am grateful for their comments on this paper.

It is easy to understand that we should be interested in what practical theology can "propose" and how it can contribute to solving social problems. I am also convinced, however, that we must be aware not only of the potentials of practical theology but also of how practical theology has—at least in the past—not been able to address constructively pluralism and diversity, let alone to appreciate such developments in church or society. To a certain degree, we should be aware of how practical theology has even worked against such an appreciation.

I am not saying this because of the rather abstract attitude of humility and repentance that has become fashionable with the increasingly widespread public pleas for forgiveness for failures of the past. Instead I want to show that there is something to be learned here for the future. I want to identify the factors that have worked against an appreciation of pluralism and diversity so that we become capable of asking if these factors are still operative in our field.

My approach is historical in that it relates to developments in the past. At the same time, it is systematic because it traces a general question of current interest. In some sense, it could also be called empirical, not in the sense of doing an empirical survey on today's practical theologians and their attitudes vis-à-vis pluralism and diversity but in the sense of researching the discipline in its actual development.

The Research Project

The basis for my analysis comes from an ongoing research project at the University of Tübingen (see note 1). The main goal of the project is to trace the development of religious education as an academic discipline in the twentieth century in order to reach an understanding of this development that is more descriptive and contextual than the standard accounts of current textbooks (e.g., Bockwoldt 1977, Sturm 1997). The project includes a comparative analysis of Protestant and Catholic religious education. The immediate objects of analysis are the discourses in leading journals of religious education in Germany that are evaluated empirically and analytically. While the project itself equally refers to discourses in Protestant and Catholic journals, especially for purposes of comparison, limited space here only allows for a presentation that, for the most part, is focussed on the Protestant side, with occasional glimpses of the developments in Catholic religious education. It should at least be mentioned that the results for Catholic religious education in Germany are quite similar to those of Protestants in respect to its relationship to pluralism but different in terms of the theological and educational reasons for this non-pluralistic attitude.

It is important to understand what we mean by "discourse" here. Traditionally, most studies of the history and development of religious education have used a different approach. They work by focussing on so-called main representatives, leading scholars, or classics of religious education or practical theology (e.g., Schröer and Zillessen 1989, Meyer-Blanck 2003). In contrast, we are trying to work with a much broader set of data including publications that, following the standard classification, might be considered of secondary importance or quality. Yet while many of these publications have long been forgotten, they may still have played a role at their time—after all, someone assumed that they deserved to be printed—and they may be more indicative of what the majority of the members of the guild were thinking at a particular time. As can be seen from this approach, we are interested in what kind of views of religious education can be considered a common or shared understanding by many or most authors contributing to the ongoing discussions that have found expression in print in major journals of religious education. In this way, we are able to include not only a handful of so-called classical publications but also many different voices that tend to be overlooked and forgotten in later accounts.

The design used in our research project has important implications in terms of the praxis of religious education as well. A broader view of the discourses in religious education and practical theology is not only of theoretical interest but can also bring us closer to the assumptions that have shaped or at least influenced the practice of religious education. While it remains true that it is not possible to make assumptions on this practice by looking at theoretical renderings alone, our attempt of going beyond the standard selection of classics allows for the inclusion of authors that can count as practitioners themselves. Moreover, there are good reasons to assume that the development of any discipline can hardly be understood by only exclusively looking at a few chosen authors and their lasting contributions. Just like in other cases, we should be aware of the so-called scientific community that has been influential in giving shape to religious education as an academic discipline by functioning as a carrier of its development, for example by taking up and thus validating certain ideas—or by not doing so.

While space does not allow for a detailed description of our research procedures here, a few comments are important. The project is based on a model of qualitative content analysis on the one hand and a quantitative statistical approach on the other. The content analysis must be qualitative since its focus is on the theoretical aspects in the materials analyzed. It proceeds by assigning the material to approximately 40 different categories that allow for further interpretation and comparison (e.g., what views of contemporary culture or politics are set forth? How is the relationship to theology, to general education, the social sciences addressed? What model of religious education is pursued? What understanding of children or youth is found in a text? etc.). Quantitative aspects in our study mostly refer to the authors contributing to the discourse (e.g., who is writing in the journals? What is their professional background? What is their institutional and geographical location? etc.). This kind of analysis allows for a better understanding of the different theoretical and practical contexts from which the different contributions emerged (e.g., churches, universities, practical experiences in school or congregation, etc.). Although the quantitative results are quite interesting, for example, in terms of the more and more academic origin of the authors (a tendency that can be characterized as scientification), it is not possible to include them with the present chapter.

The main sources of the project are three journals—on the Catholic side the *Kate-chetische Blätter,* in print continuously throughout the twentieth century (except 1945) and on the Protestant side, first the *Monatsblätter für den evangelischen Religionsunterricht* and then the *Evangelische Erzieher.* In addition to these main sources, we also included a number of other journals that can be considered precursors of our main sources or parallel publications. Since the project covers the period between 1900 and 1975, 150-200 volumes or approximately 60,000-80,000 pages of material had to be examined.

In the context of the present volume and questions of *Religion, Diversity and Conflict,* this chapter may be considered a case study that is of interest in terms of understanding the obstacles encountered by the attempts of practical theology (or of its subdisciplines like religious education) at becoming more open to diversity and pluralism. Corresponding to a section of our research, I will limit my analysis here to the time between 1945 and 1975. At the end of the chapter, however, I will include a number of questions referring to our contemporary situation.

It is obvious that the German situation between 1933 and 1945—the time of National Socialism—requires special analysis and interpretation. In our forthcoming publication (see note 1), we analyze the development of religious education in this period in respect to totalitarianism. Readers should keep in mind that many Protestant religious educators in Germany did not assume a critical stance towards National Socialism (cf. Rickers 1995) and also did not belong to the Confessing Church. While the discourses under study in the project did not, on the whole, follow the ideologies of the Hitler-state in the sense of recommending them to their audience or by replacing Christianity with some kind of Germanic faith altogether, they nevertheless support the acceptance of the state as an authority given by God and to be respected by all good Christians, in many cases, on the basis of the then current understanding of Martin Luther's teaching on the two kingdoms. It is against this backdrop that the situation after 1945 has to be considered, even if I can only hint at it in this essay.

Pluralism and Diversity in German Religious Education between 1945 and 1975
In this section I will try to give a short description of how pluralism and diversity appear in the discourses analyzed by us and how they are addressed by the authors. In a first step, I will use a terminological approach by choosing the concepts or ideas of pluralism and diversity as my lens. Since this lens might be too limited because the same terms have not been used at all times, in a second step I will try to break down the concepts by considering some of the phenomena that, at least from today's perspective, can count as diversity. Both steps, using the concepts and addressing the phenomena related to them, can be distinguished from a third step in which I

raise the question of pluralism as a principle—a principle that may be used, appreciated, and possibly defended by religious education and practical theology.

The Concepts of Pluralism and Diversity in the Discourses
If we ask how the concepts of pluralism and diversity appear in materials under
study, the picture is quite clear. The concepts of pluralism and diversity have definitely not played a central role in the discourse of German religious education for a
long time. It is not before the 1960s, even the late 1960s, that we can observe a
somewhat more widespread use of these concepts.

Moreover, the way in which these concepts are used is telling. Most often, the concepts are not referenced in order to inform the understanding of religious education
itself, i.e., in favor of something like pluralistic religious education or pluralism as
an aim. Instead, pluralism and diversity are considered as a major obstacle and
challenge for religious education. Even in the 1960s and 1970s when references to
pluralism and diversity become more frequent, the concepts mostly refer to what
might be called the context of which religious education must be aware, even if educators do not like it; actually, most of them appear to be quite critical of the pluralization they observe in church and society.

In sum it can be stated that religious education between 1945 and 1975 has not set
forth a pluralistic model that includes a positive relationship to pluralism and diversity. As far as these concepts show up in the discussions, they are used to address
contextual factors jeopardizing the success of religious education. Clearly, pluralism
was not an aim of religious education at that time but was considered a real burden.

How Religious Educators deal with the Phenomena of Pluralism and Diversity
In order to go beyond a purely conceptual or terminological approach, I will now
turn to some of the phenomena that can count as pluralism and diversity. This analysis will be limited to four such aspects that, from today's perspective, certainly
belong to this context: diversity within Christianity, political diversity, religious
diversity and pluralism as a principle.

(1) *Diversity within Christianity*: One of the surprising observations in our material is
openness to international Christian ecumenical perspectives in the late 1940s and
early 1950s. This openness does not include, however, ecumenical relationships between Protestants and Catholics, the two major Christian denominations in Germany
itself. Instead it references openness to Christianity in different countries and within
Protestantism, at least to some degree, openness to different denominations.

This openness did not last very long. In the further course of the 1950s as well as in
the 1960s and 1970s, it no longer plays a major role. The wider international horizon
of Christian ecumenical thinking more or less disappears. Instead we can observe
how Protestant and Catholic religious education move closer together and how they

even begin to actually work together. Major publications from the other denomination are reviewed or even are recommended as important for one's own work as well. Authors from the other denomination are invited to contribute to the journals—something that had never been the case before the 1960s; moving beyond our actual research, this development of mutual awareness and cooperation has continued until today. Since the 1990s, the German *Yearbook of Religious Education* (*Jahrbuch der Religionspädagogik,* Neukirchener Verlag) has been the first and only publication of this kind with an editorial board composed of Catholic and Protestant religious educators.

(2) *Political Diversity*: German religious education and practical theology come out of a history and tradition of non-democratic forms of government. This statement does not only apply to the time of National Socialism. The formative years of these disciplines were strongly influenced by the Prussian monarchy in the nineteenth and early twentieth century. Moreover, political diversity and even democratic forms of government have most often not been welcomed by practical theology. At the founding of the first German democracy in 1918 (the Weimar Republic), many theologians voiced their explicit scepticism vis-à-vis this form of government. They could just not imagine that something like a democracy would really work.

The founding of the second German democracy with the (West) German Federal Republic in 1949, did not immediately lead to a broad appreciation of this form of government within the religious education discussion. Quite often, especially on the Protestant side, political parties were considered ideological while theology and the church should claim what was considered a non-ideological perspective. The introduction of the German constitution in 1949—the so-called Basic Law (*Grundgesetz*) that is still often quoted as a prime example of successful legislation for democracy—went without further comment by religious educators in the journals under study. Nor did these educators see a need to acknowledge or to appreciate the pluralistic system that the new democratic state implied.

That religious educators stayed quiet vis-à-vis the new constitution cannot be explained by pointing out that legislation was not their field of work. In Article 7, the German constitution guarantees Religious Education as an "ordinary subject" in all schools, i.e., although students and parents have the right to opt out of this subject, all schools must offer Religious Education. Moreover, in Article 4 the constitution guarantees the right to religious freedom. In other words, there can be no doubt that much could have been said about the new constitution from the perspective of religious education.

(3) *Religious Diversity*: In the present context, religious diversity also references different religions or, specifically the relationship between Christianity and non-Christian religions. It is easy to see that this topic remained basically untouched in the 1940s and 1950s, and that it received little treatment even in the 1960s. It was

not before the 1970s that different religions started to play a more prominent role in the German religious education discussion; again moving beyond the period under study in our project, it was not before the 1990s that major works on this topic became available. Moreover, most articles referring to non-Christian religions in the journals analyzed are written from a missionary perspective and, consequently, are lacking in dialogical intention and outlook. While such contributions indicate a new awareness of religious plurality, it can hardly be claimed that the pluralism is appreciated by them.

(4) *Pluralism as a Principle*: This aspects is different from the preceding ones in that it does not refer to actual changes in society, culture, or religion—the changes that I have called the phenomena connected to pluralism and diversity. In the present context, the question of pluralism as a principle refers to religious education itself by asking about its intentions and goals. To what degree does religious education recommend a pluralistic outcome for its own practice?

In this respect, I can again be very brief. The idea that pluralism or the appreciation of diversity should or even could count among the guiding theoretical principles for religious education is clearly absent in the material under study. Pluralism appears as a challenge, not as a potential for the future.

Interpretation
There are of course many possible answers to the question why religious education did not appreciate pluralism and diversity during the time in question. I will limit my self to five aspects that play a special role: the position of the Church; the kind of theology in use; the understanding of education; a normative understanding of culture; and the prevailing political mindset. One aspect that certainly plays a role as well can only be mentioned here, not only because of the limitations of space but also because it goes beyond the methodological design of our project. This additional aspect refers to the personal background of the individual authors. Different studies with a more personal and biographical focus remain an important extension of the research presented here (cf., an example from one of our team members, Simojoki 2005).

The Position of the Churches
The position of the Churches was closely related to theological developments. Yet the Churches also are institutions in society and it is in this sense that they play a role for the present context in different ways than theology. Concerning this role, we must be aware of both, internal and external perspectives.

Internally, the Churches did not understand themselves in a pluralistic sense. There certainly are important differences between the Protestant and the Catholic side, especially before the Second Vatican Council. Yet there can be no doubt that neither Church followed the ideal of pluralism in its procedures. The prevailing understanding of the Church in the publications under study views the Church as a unitary institution structured not only by a common creed but also by an understanding of this creed to be shared by all of its members in a uniform manner. This does not imply that, in reality, there were no differences or that such differences would have never been addressed in the periodicals. Yet the image of the ideal church was not affected by these critical observations.

Externally, concerning their position in society, the Churches did not have any use for pluralistic principles. Especially in the years after 1945, many church representatives openly adhered to the idea of a re-Christianization of society that ideally should comprise all members of society. This idea of re-Christianization was closely linked to the task of reconstructing post-war Germany in general, and it is easy to see why many considered education especially important in this context.

Theology
The theology prevailing in Germany after 1945 did not have much space for pluralism. On the Protestant side, religious education was strongly influenced by a mix between Barthian ("Neo-Orthodox") and Neo-Lutheran theologies. Karl Barth's exclusivist position in relationship to other religions is well-known and has received ample criticism in recent debates on multireligious society. Furthermore, beyond the question of the meaning of other religions that has remained difficult for Protestant theology until today, diversity was not appreciated in any sense, not even within Christianity or theology. The one true faith based on the one true revelation in Christ was the guiding ideal that also informed the religious educators writing in the journals under study.

Understanding of Education
It is important to realize that it was not only theology that was lacking pluralistic openness. The guiding ideals in education at that time were far from pluralistic as well. This is not only true for the time immediately following the War or for the period of German Reconstruction in the 1950s. It is also true, although in a different sense, for the new developments following the 1960s. These developments widely favored personal liberty—the contemporary term was "emancipation" —as well as critical attitudes. Yet again, the understanding of critical autonomy itself was not open for different realizations of its goals. The non-pluralistic outlook of education is closely related to the next aspect to be considered, the understanding of culture.

Normative Understanding of Culture
Although the religious educators in our study only rarely address their presuppositions in terms of culture, it is obvious that they clearly presume a normative understanding of culture. According to this understanding, culture means so-called high culture or ideal culture as the aim of education. This culture is not diverse but unitary. It is not open for different influences or backgrounds. Instead it incorporates the "one true meaning of the Western tradition," which is considered the epitome of

human culture altogether. This kind of understanding did not result from some kind of blatantly arrogant Western worldview but, especially after 1945, was closely connected to the immediate need for new orientations after the complete breakdown of National Socialism and of the ideological worldviews connected to it.

Political Mindset
In focussing on the Churches and on theology or on the understanding of education and culture we should not overlook the general political mindset that was not specific to practical theologians or religious educators. A non-pluralistic conservative mindset was characteristic of the German post-war period, and this kind of thinking prevailed well into the 1960s and 1970s; the Cold War situation and its demands on the people was one important factor here. The 1940s and 1950s were no time for radical changes, be it in Germany or in other countries, but a time of political conservatism.

Even in the 1960s and 1970s, Germany did not become a culturally or religiously pluralistic country. As late as in the 1980s and 1990s, the concept of a multicultural society and, even more so, of a multireligious society was highly contested. In both respects, many people seem to adhere to very conservative outlooks. They just cannot imagine that society could be based on something like a pluralistic system of values or on a pluralism of religious traditions, especially if this pluralism should include Islam.

Lessons from the Past: Still no pluralistic Religious Education?
Is there anything to be learned from this analysis that could be important for our contemporary situation? The question to what degree religious education has become more pluralistic since the time covered in our study, must necessarily be left open here. Yet it should not be overlooked that the 1960s and 1970s were the time when many formative decisions were made that have been of major influence until today (for recent accounts of the corresponding developments in German religious education cf. Schweitzer, Elsenbast and Scheilke 2008).

The following three questions deserve special attention in the context of the present volume: 1) We are obviously coming from a tradition of religious education with little openness for pluralism and diversity. Have we really been able to overcome this tradition? 2) Practical theology and religious education have clearly not been among the factors leading to more pluralism, at least not during the time between 1945 and 1975. Is there a need for analyzing contemporary models and understandings of religious education and practical theology in a similar critical manner? 3) Religious education and practical theology have clearly not developed independently from more general tendencies but have been closely related to the parallel developments in the Churches, in theology, in education, and in society or culture in general. To what degree are they related to which tendencies today?

In sum, the historical analysis presented leaves us with the challenge to analyze the guiding ideals and assumptions that inform contemporary religious education and practical theology. It is not enough to introduce a new terminology that is in line with the concepts of pluralism and diversity. Pluralism and diversity can only become integrated to the degree that their constitutive meaning for practical theology can be demonstrated. As can be seen from the past, this would have to include its views of Christian diversity, of religious diversity and of diversity in education. Moreover, this can hardly be achieved without clarifying what I have called above pluralism as a principle. To my knowledge, the corresponding work has just begun—be it in religious education (for example, Nipkow 1998) or in systematic theology (three prominent Protestant examples from Germany are Herms 1995, Welker 1995, Schwöbel 2003). More efforts and more critical scrutiny will be needed if we really are to move beyond our own non-pluralistic heritage. Given the ambivalent legacy of practical theology and religious education in this respect, more self-critical attitudes will be needed.

References:

Bockwoldt, Gerd. 1977. *Religionspädagogik. Eine Problemgeschichte*. Stuttgart: Kohlhammer.

Herms, Eilert. 1995. Pluralismus aus Prinzip. In *Kirche für die Welt. Lage und Aufgabe der evangelischen Kirchen im vereinigten Deutschland*, ed. id., 467-485. Tübingen: Mohr Siebeck.

Meyer-Blanck, Michael. 2003. *Kleine Geschichte der evangelischen Religionspädagogik, dargestellt anhand ihrer Klassiker*. Gütersloh: Gütersloher Verlagshaus.

Nipkow, Karl Enst. 1998. *Bildung in einer pluralen Welt*. 2 vols. Gütersloh: Gütersloher Verlagshaus.

Osmer, Richard and Friedrich Schweitzer. 2003. *Religious Education between Modernization and Globalization. New Perspectives on the United States and Gemany*. Studies in Practical Theology. Grand Rapids: W.B. Eerdmans.

Rickers, Folkert. 1995. *Zwischen Kreuz und Hakenkreuz. Untersuchungen zur Religionspädagogik im „Dritten Reich."* Neukirchen-Vluyn: Neukirchener Verlagshaus.

Schröer, Henning and Dietrich Zillessen, eds. 1989. *Klassiker der Religionspädagogik*. Frankfurt am Main: Diesterweg.

Schweitzer, Friedrich, Volker Elsenbast, and Christoph Scheilke, eds. 2008. *Religionspädagogik und Zeitgeschichte im Spiegel der Rezeption von Karl Ernst Nipkow*. Gütersloh: Gütersloher Verlagshaus.

Schweitzer, Friedrich and Henrik Simojoki. 2005. *Moderne Religionspädagogik. Ihre Entwicklung und Identität*. Religionspädagogik in Pluraler Gesellschaft 5. Freiburg and Gütersloh: Herder and Gütersloher Verlagshaus.

Schwöbel, Christoph. 2003. *Christlicher Glaube im Pluralismus. Studien zu einer Theologie der Kultur*. Tübingen: Mohr Siebeck.

Simojoki, Henrik. 2008. *Evangelische Erziehungsverantwortung. Eine religionspädagogische Untersuchung zum Werk Friedrich Delekats (1892-1970)*. Praktische Theologie in Geschichte und Gegenwart 3. Tübingen: Mohr Siebeck.

Sturm, Wilhelm. 1997. Religionspädagogische Konzeptionen. In *Religionspädagogisches Kompendium*, 5th edition, ed. G. Adam and R. Lachmann, 37-86. Göttingen: Vandenhoeck & Ruprecht.

Welker, Michael. 1995. *Kirche im Pluralismus*. Gütersloh: Gütersloher Verlagshaus.

Religion and Human Rights in a Religious Society: Considerations from a Middle Eastern Context

Raymond J. Webb and Jack Curran

Abstract: *This paper examines the relationship between religious attitudes, beliefs, values and practices and aspects of first generation—secular and religious—civil human rights, drawing on a sample of 532 16-19 year-old urban Middle Eastern students. Gender and parental education are also considered. The mixed-religion (Christian-Muslim) cultural context for this research would aptly be described as religious rather than secular. Societal political unrest and military occupation are also present. The question of how human rights attitudes fare in such a complex and arguably religious context is investigated.*

Background

As Palestinians attempt to build a sovereign state in East Jerusalem, the West Bank (including East Jerusalem) and Gaza, they will face daunting challenges in developing a situation where the rights of all are protected while the religious sensibilities of the citizens are respected. This context provides the opportunity to examine factors affecting attitudes toward human rights in a social setting which can arguably be described as "religious." The Palestinian Arab peoples of the area are under some form of Israeli military and civil occupation and accompanying regulations, as they have been since 1967. Laws imposed in a situation of occupation do not provide inhabitants with a wide experience of human rights. Nevertheless, the Arab societal situation does experience change. This has included a steadily increasing if uneven empowerment of women. The setting also offers an opportunity to explore any contrast in attitudes between the Muslim majority and the decreasing Christian minority. However, we must take note of the fact that the question of religious influence is broader than particular religious affiliation and includes religious characteristics, such as one's claimed influence by one's religion, how much one prays and how much one reads the Bible or the Qur'an.

The area from which the subjects for this research were drawn is perhaps 20% Christian and 80% Muslim. Like all of the Arab world, it is heavily influenced by Islam. However, down through the centuries and including the present time, the Arab world is also influenced by Christian roots and ideas. This influence derives from the original Christians, from those who came during the Middle Ages, from European colonials and from current media. It can be said that almost all of the participants in this research have access to satellite television, to internet and to e-mail.

Research questions

In this context, we investigate several research questions:

1. What evidence is there that the Bethlehem area societal context is religious rather than secular?
2. What is the relationship between living in a "religious society" and support for human rights?
3. What effects do attitudes, practices and characteristics of Christian and Muslim 16-19 year-olds in the Bethlehem area have on their attitudes toward human rights?
4. Does gender affect support for human rights?
5. Does parental education affect support for human rights?
6. Does one's particular religion affect one's support for human rights?
7. Does one's religious practice affect one's support of human rights?
8. How does one's attitude toward interreligious dialogue relate to one's support for human rights?
9. Does the reported influence of religion on one's life affect one's support for human rights?

Focus

Our particular research has focused on the primarily urban area of Bethlehem in the Occupied Palestinian Territories (a.k.a. Palestine). This research attempts to provide empirically-based information from the Palestinian context by surveying the attitudes, behaviors and demographic information of 16-19 year-old students from the greater Bethlehem area.

Human rights

Human rights are anchored in understandings of human dignity. The inhumanity of the death camps, the Holocaust and other atrocities were the immediate background for several significant assertions of human rights and dignity in the last century. We note the United Nations' Universal Declaration of Human Rights (1948), the International Covenant on Economic, Social, and Cultural Rights (1966), the International Covenant on Civil and Political Rights (1966), and the UN Declaration on the Elimination of All Forms of Intolerance and Discrimination Based on Religion or Belief (1981), as well as the Universal Islamic Declaration of Human Rights (1981), the Cairo Declaration (1990) and the Arab Charter on Human Rights (1994).

The Western perspective on universal human rights depends on democratically derived covenants based on reason. It is argued that they no longer can be seen as originating in a relationship to God, with humans as God's creation, but rather from human conscience or from pragmatic grounds (cf. Sachedina 2009, 8-24). However, an Eastern religious society would not have moved away from a supreme being. M. Cherif Bassiouni (2010) notes that Islamic understandings of human rights begin with responsibilities to the community, which has a covenant with God to serve humankind.

Interestingly, the preamble of the amendment of the Palestinian Basic Law (19 March 2003) begins, "In the name of God, the Merciful, the Compassionate." However, the text of the basic law states, "The People is the source of power" (Article 2). This Basic Law of Palestine states that "The principles of Islamic Shari'a are a major source for legislation. Civil and religious matters of the followers of monotheistic religions shall be organized in accordance with their religious teachings and denominations within the framework of law, while preserving the unity and independence of the Palestinian people" (Article 7). Article 20 reads, "Human rights and liberties are binding and must be respected. The state shall guarantee religious, civil, political, economic, social and cultural rights and liberties to all citizens on the basis of equality and equal opportunity. Persons are not deprived of their legal competence, rights and basic liberties for political reasons."

In addition to the documents noted above, we can identify human rights groups related to the Palestinian Territories. Bassem Eid (2008) is the executive director of a Palestinian human rights advocacy group, the Palestine Human Rights Monitoring Group (2009). Among the rights his group emphasizes are the freedom of movement, freedom from torture and unlawful detention, freedom of expression and the right to education. Gaza Dr. Eyad Sarraj is another voice for human rights in Palestine, critically monitoring both Israelis and Palestinians. Israeli human rights groups B'Tselem, Rabbis for Human Rights, Machsom Watch, and Gisha have longstanding records of documenting abuses of the human rights of Palestinians and of mobilizing advocacy as well as legal actions in defense of the human rights of Palestinians, especially focusing on the freedom of movement of Palestinians within their own land.

Christian and Muslim
The relationship between human rights and religion is complex; perhaps it is dialogical. The conversation will not move forward if human rights are *de facto* perceived as an overarching, "conscience based" universal given (from the secular Enlightenment) and then religions, people and practices are measured against this standard. Jürgen Habermas (2001) argues that religions can enter into the post-secular discussion as long as they are able to frame their positions in language (presumably secular) that could be understood and accepted by non-adherents. Religion will want to be a part of the discussion of the meaning and scope of human rights. The drafting of the statement that became *Towards a Global Ethic: An Initial Declaration* at the Council for a Parliament of the World's Religion in 1993 is a significant example of that conversation (cf. Küng & Kuschel 1993).

Irene Oh notes that human rights discussions, though not a religious idea, have become a more common part of the discourse of scholars of Islam, including such diverse voices as Sayyid Qutb and Abdolkarim Soroush (2008, 112). John Witte

(2005) outlines Western support for human rights begun through the work of Catholic scholars but more fully developed by Enlightenment philosophers and the work of the Protestant Reformers. Hermínio Rico (2002, 121) presents the argument concerning the importance of human rights to Catholicism, viewing them as derived from "natural law," but also supported by theological and Biblical warrants. This latter argumentation is highlighted in the *Declaration on Religious Freedom* (1965) of the Second Vatican Council.

Local context

In our research project, we attempted to be particularly sensitive to the political and religious context of the Palestinian population and its various sub-groups. Our respondents—the "future of the society"—were 16-19 year-olds. They had been through continuous and ongoing Israeli military occupation, one (or two) uprisings, sporadic military incursions, periods of martial law, school closings for days and weeks at a time, and regular as well as special military checkpoints. Under military occupation Palestinians live in a situation in which they have very limited rights. Additionally, there are certainly strong internal political tensions within Palestinian society.

Our respondents have lived through violence and external limitations on rights and freedom of self-expression and movement for all of their lives. Given this unique socio-political reality, we recognized that some internationally used research questions might be understood in a unique manner by our respondents. In addition, some academicians and researchers in Palestine are concerned that involvement in broad, international research projects might indicate that there is a "normalization" of the situation of the respondents. They stress that the situation is not "normal," that East Jerusalem, the West Bank and Gaza are under the ongoing effects of continuing military occupation.

Gender

We look briefly at gender in this study. There is a certain "women's revolution" occurring in the society, although its lines may be uniquely drawn. On the one hand, a Muslim woman is much more likely to wear *hijab* (a headscarf) now than a generation ago. Muslim women variously wear austere Muslim clothing (*jilbab*), colorful variants of Muslim clothing, or modern secular dress. Many Christian women emulate European clothing styles. On the other hand, women are much more likely to receive university education and to marry later. Women's work in business and instances of entrepreneurship are increasing. One notes that although the number of men taking the entrance examination at Bethlehem University is approximately equal to the number of women, the student population consists of 70% women and 30% men. We believe that this general perspective is consistent with the work of Amina Wadud (2006), Laetitia Bucaille (2004), and Riffat Hassan (2007) regarding the changing role of women in society. In general, the equality and rights of women are not presumed but are still the focus of a slow evolution, a silent revolution. We note that 17 women were elected to the 132 member Palestinian Legislative Council in 2006, all from general party lists which had a quota requirement. No women were elected to the 23-member Fatah Central Committee in 2009 (the Fatah party effectively governs the West Bank and will lead any PLO peace negotiating team.)

"Religious society"

We contend that there is strong external evidence that the situation in which our respondents live is a "religious society," a context in which religion is of pervasive significance in the public square. In the area, religion seems to be part of daily consciousness. Religion was ranked second only to family in "values important in your life" in the current survey (cf. Appendix 1). The average ranking of religious salience, the importance of religion in daily, thoughts, plans, and action, was "Agree" (4.03 on a 1 to 5 scale). Asked about going to religious services, 15% said weekly or several times a week; 65.4% said on a feast day, now and then, monthly or several times a month; and 18.4% said never. Interestingly, non-attendance at prayers at the mosque is not a negative indicator in regard to religiosity, since one can be a good and observant Muslim and pray elsewhere.

Externally, one hears the five daily calls of prayer of the *muezzin* as well as church bells rung at least once daily. One sees Muslim clothing with a religious significance as well as many Christian men and women wearing crosses as jewelry. Christian and Muslim clerics and female and male Christian religious are always dressed in distinctive religious garb. Many businesses and schools, including the largest employer in the municipality of Bethlehem (Bethlehem University, a Catholic institution) have a significant number of work holidays connected with the Islamic as well as the Latin and Orthodox Christian faiths (e.g., Bethlehem University employees generally have more than 15 religious holidays a year). Religion is taught in government and private schools. Even the identity cards issued to Palestinians by the Israeli government and the passports issued by the Palestinian Authority list one's "Religion."

Methodology

This is an empirical-theoretical exploratory study involving the use of the Human Rights and Religion project survey instrument, developed through Radboud University (Netherlands) and translated into Arabic from English. The instrument is currently in use in an international comparative study. A similar instrument was used in the monumental study of human rights and religion in the context of South Africa by van der Ven, Dreyer and Pieterse (2004). In general, the questionnaire considers actions thought to flow from so-called first generation (civil, political, juridical), second generation (economic, social, cultural) and third generation (environmental, health, development, peace) human rights. Here we consider only those items related to first generation secular and religious civil human rights.[1] In addition

---

[1] While we have included the complete subset of "civil human rights" statements, the authors of this essay hold that abortion and euthanasia are not human rights.

to the "rights" items, questions are asked about religious and secular perspectives and practices, family, education and other attitudes.

The survey instrument was long, producing 192 items of data per protocol. Most questions used a five-point rating scale: "very important" [5] to "not important at all" [1]; "fully agree" [5] to "totally disagree" [1]. Items related to attitudes on human rights were constructed as "concretely formulated norms, connected with concretely formulated situations to which these ... rights apply" (van der Ven and Anthony 2008, 482). The instrument took the participants at least 35 minutes to complete. There were some complaints about length, although some respondents shared comments of appreciation at the end, a gratitude for the chance to express opinions about the matters found in the survey.

Sample

The questionnaire was administered from April to September, 2008 in secondary schools and cultural centers and to some entering first-year university students. 557 protocols were returned; 532 of these were usable. The average age of the respondents was 17.48, with most of the respondents between the ages of 16 and 19. There were no significant effects for age. We did not use the 22 respondents who were younger than 16 or older than 19 in this analysis, because of the possible distorting effect of "outliers."

Our respondents were 31.6% Christian (n=168), 65.8% Muslim (n=350), 2.6% Non-religious (n=14). We did not use the "Non-religious" in our analyses, given their small sample size. 162 of the respondents were male and 370 female.

Findings and Discussion

Table 1: Secular Human Rights Related Statements (beta coefficients)

	Free Lifestyle		Free Assembly		Free Press		Privacy	
	Item 1	Item 2	Item 3	Item 4	Item 5	Item 6	Item 7	Item 8
	Laws should protect personal moral standard	Sexual relations between adults are individual choices	Minority groups free to protest	Strikers can use government offices for meetings	Free to express radical convictions in newspapers	TV journalists with radical ideas have a right to employment	Police may not search homes without a warrant	Police allowed to inspect cars only under strict judicial conditions
Gender	.13				.12		.13	
Parent Univ. educated								
Religion		-.13			-.13			
Praying								
Reading Holy Book								
Inter-religious Dialogue	.10	.19	.25	.20	.21	.14	.11	.16
Religious Salience	.23	.10	.12	.14	.10	.13	.12	
N	472	452	459	457	461	452	460	458
R^2	.091	.068	.093	.061	.087	.054	.057	.043

Only significant (p < .05) betas are shown in the table above.

Means:

	Item 1	Item 2	Item 3	Item 4	Item 5	Item 6	Item 7	Item 8
Christian	3.86	3.65	3.30	3.58	3.47	3.49	3.92	3.49
Muslim	4.08	3.35	3.25	3.63	3.25	3.32	3.96	3.48
Significance	.028	.006			.013	.04		
Male	3.69	3.52	3.28	3.63	3.36	3.32	3.68	3.52
Female	4.14	3.45	3.27	3.60	3.31	3.41	4.05	3.47
Significance	.000						.000	

Table 2: Religious Human Rights Related Statements (beta coefficients)

	Religion and State		Religion and Freedom		Religious Speech		Moral Speech	
	Item 9	Item 10	Item 11	Item 12	Item 13	Item 14	Item 15	Item 16
	Politicians decide on euthanasia irrespective of religious leaders	Politicians decide on abortion irrespective of religious leaders	Politicians not interfere with religious communities	Prayers in public schools should be forbidden	Making fun of religious people is protected	Making fun of atheists is protected	Moral standards critically debated in schools	Morals discussed in class
Gender	-.09			.16				
Parent Univ. educated						-.14		
Religion		-.12		.14				
Praying	-.12		-.11	.12	-.16	-.14		
Reading Holy Book								
Inter-religious Dialogue	.16	.15		-.10			.25	.17
Religious Salience		-.10		.12			.19	.11
N	464	453	462	460	469	450	466	462
R^2	.063	.082	.028	.133	.085	.057	.104	.06

Only significant (p < .05) betas are shown in the table above.

Means:

	Item 9	Item 10	Item 11	Item 12	Item 13	Item 14	Item 15	Item 16
Christian	2.93	2.87	3.66	2.82	2.76	2.80	3.74	3.58
Muslim	2.87	2.50	3.48	2.32	2.48	2.69	3.71	3.65
Significance	.000	.002	.052	.000	.037	.001		
Male	3.21	2.93	3.50	2.99	2.93	3.02	3.66	3.48
Female	2.80	2.53	3.54	2.28	2.47	2.62	3.77	3.69
Significance	.000	.001		.000	.000	.001		.024

General findings

In general, our group of 16-19 year-olds living in what we have argued is a religious society was positive (i.e., above the "neutral" – "I am not sure") about most of the religious and secular civil rights related statements (cf. Appendix 2). While there were significant differences in support for various aspects of human rights based on certain personal characteristics, attitudes and practices, the overall support was nonetheless quite positive. This would counter claims that human rights can only thrive in secular contexts. Statements that were not supported were in three areas: prohibition of public school prayer, free speech allowing ridicule of atheists and religious people, and no religious interference with lawmaking in regard to euthanasia and abortion. The greatest overall support was for laws supporting personal moral standards and for freedom from unauthorized police searches of homes. Moral discussion and debate were also supported. Given that there is significant disagreement that abortion and euthanasia are universal human rights, we find in our group of participants strong support for civil human rights.

Gender

Females were significantly more supportive than males on two statements of secular civil rights (protecting personal moral standards and against home searches), although both groups were supportive of all eight statements regarding secular civil rights. Men were more supportive in five areas of religious civil rights (non-interference with euthanasia and abortion law making, forbidding public school prayer, and freedom of speech regarding atheists and religious persons). A significant difference in direction was found only in two areas. Men were willing to let politicians decide about euthanasia laws; women were not. Men were neutral about a "right" to make fun of atheists; women were opposed. Van der Ven, Dreyer and Pieterse (2004, 133) reported that male South African students were more supportive of civil human rights than female students. Van der Ven and Anthony (2008, 488) found that female gender had a negative effect in the area of civil human rights in India. They attributed this to the position of Indian women, which they described as still being "submission and suppression." We have not found here, in contrast to the South Africa and India data, that men are generally more supportive of civil rights than women, certainly not in regard to secular civil rights and arguably not in regard to religious civil rights. Further analysis of the Bethlehem data on gender is warranted.

University education of parents

Respondents who had at least one parent who had attended university were signifi-cantly more supportive of the secular civil right to express radical convictions in newspapers.

Religion

Christians and Muslims agreed or disagreed with the same items, differing only in the strength of their agreement or disagreement. Both groups were positive toward all areas of secular civil rights. In regard to religious civil rights, they supported neither religious non-interference in political decisions regarding euthanasia and abortion nor a right to ridicule atheists and religious people. Neither group supported forbidding prayer in public schools.

Christians were significantly more supportive of secular civil rights in two areas (sexual freedom and freedom of expression) and Muslims in one (protecting personal moral standards). In regard to religious civil rights, Christians were more supportive in four areas (non-interference in abortion decisions, non-interference with religious communities, forbidding public school prayer, and freedom of speech regarding religious people).

As one considers findings of "non-support" in this context, several points can be noted. Ridicule of others or joking about their beliefs is a strong social taboo in the local culture. Christians are supportive of prayer in public schools, but less so than Muslims. Islam has been a part of the public school curriculum for many years; Christians can opt out. Christians' study of their own religion in government schools has been introduced recently. Both Islam and Christianity have positions opposed to abortion and euthanasia, although there are differences between them and among the different Christian groups. None regard it as a neutral option.

Praying and reading one's holy book
We defined practicing one's religion as praying and as reading one's holy book. There was no significant relationship between how much people read their holy book and their attitude toward secular and religious civil rights. Nor were there any significant relationships between amount of prayer and secular civil rights. However, this was not the case with religious civil rights related statements. Subjects who prayed more were significantly more opposed to ridicule of religious persons and atheists, to politicians deciding about euthanasia without involvement of religious leaders and to forbidding prayer in public schools. Curiously, they were significantly less opposed to politicians interfering with religious communities.

Interreligious dialogue
A positive attitude toward interreligious dialogue was positively correlated with all areas of secular civil rights. In regard to religious civil rights, this positive correlation was significant in many areas. However, those more positive about dialogue did not show significantly more support for the non-interference of politicians with religious communities or for the right to make fun of beliefs of both atheists and religious persons.

Religious salience
Religious salience is a measure of the respondents' opinions of the importance of religion in their daily thoughts, plans and actions. Participants who felt religion guided their lives were generally more supportive of most statements related to

secular and religious civil rights. They were significantly more opposed to banning prayer in schools and to keeping religious influence out of abortion law decisions. In the South African study, religious salience had negative effects (van der Ven, Dreyer and Pieterse 2004, 583).

We believe our evidence indicates that being interiorly directed by one's religion is more related to support for civil human rights than one's particular religious affiliation (Christian or Muslim), yet there may be a more complex assertion. Perhaps interior directedness, together with openness to interaction with the other, is a platform for even stronger support for civil rights in a religious society. The conversation with the other seems to implicitly recognize the rights of the other. Inner-directedness is a "second order" reflective way of living.

The human rights conversation
The religious societal setting does not militate against human rights. In this particular religious, Muslim-majority society there is wide support for civil human rights. Debate in schools and personal moral freedom are supported. There should be no governmental interference with religious communities. The attitudes of respondents do not appear to indicate an implicit acceptance of the privileging of the majority religion over the minority religion. We think the overall response invites a dialogue between religion and the designation of human rights. This brings us back to the issue of religion in the public square as well as a consideration of how human rights are determined. We do not think that it is only for the secular sphere to determine what universal human rights are and then ascertain to what degree religious groups are in accord. The conversation must include religious voices. Our survey's respondents in their religious society implicitly have some expectation that religion will have a place at the table in decisions about the shape of society.

It can be argued that foundational support for human rights from religious sources should not be shunned but rather joined to secular rationales. A convergence of foundational argumentation may be the best way to obtain broad support for human rights in the societal situations of today. Abdulaziz Sachedina develops warrants for human rights from Shari'a and asserts that this religious "complementary" argumentation is important in Muslim contexts. He calls for "simply recognizing the need for dialogue with other claimants of comprehensive doctrines, whether religious or secular. The ultimate goal of this conversation is to reach consensus about human agency linked to human dignity as a special mark of humanness that is entitled to inalienable human rights (2009, 13)." Similarly, arguments for human rights based on understandings of "natural law" theory can promote a shared common good (cf. Rico 2002, 121-122). A secular society, free from any significant public influence of religion, need not be the ideal setting for human thriving. The religious contexts of the Middle East do not seem necessarily to preclude strong support for human rights. While these questions are not the main focus of this research, our findings point us back to them for further investigation and discussion.

The interreligious interests of practical theology have grown greatly in the past ten years. Practical theologians are well positioned to promote the serious examination of empirical data about civil rights attitudes and factors influencing those attitudes in both Western and non-Western contexts. In addition, practical theologians can foster the conversation between advocates of frameworks of civil rights which have grown out of Western intellectual history and traditions and proponents of various other sources of support for human well-being and the common good. These partners would include the developers of human rights documents in the Muslim world as well as scholars, such as Sachedina, who advocate consensus building. Natural law theorists, focusing on rights and obligations while avoiding subverting individual human rights to the common good, may offer a path toward bridge-building. We believe that the religion and human rights discourse in practical theology can contribute to the greater actualization of civil rights in a variety of contexts.

References:

Bassiouni, M. Cherif. 2010. Islam and Human Rights. Chicago: American Islamic College. Unpublished address.

Bucaille, Laetitia. 2004. *Growing Up Palestinian*. Princeton: Princeton University Press.

Declaration on Religious Liberty. *Dignitatis humanae*. 1965. Second Vatican Council. Vatican City.

Habermas, Jürgen. 2001. Faith and Knowledge -- An Opening. Speech. Trans. Kermit Snelson. Frankfurt: Booksellers Convention. http://amsterdam.nettime. org/Lists-Archives/nettime-l-0111/msg00100.html (accessed 3 September 2010).

Hassan, Riffat. 2007. Women in Islam. In *Women in Religion*, ed. Mary Pat Fisher, 234-269. Upper Saddle River NJ: Pearson Longman.

Küng, Hans and Karl-Josef Kuschel, ed. 1993. *A Global Ethic: The Declaration of the Parliament of the World's Religions*. New York: Continuum.

Oh, Irene. 2008. *The rights of God: Islam, human rights and comparative religion*. Washington: Georgetown.

Palestinian Basic Law. 2003. http://www.palestinianbasiclaw.org/2003-permanent-constitution-draft

Palestinian Human Rights Monitoring Group. 2009. About Us. http://www.phrmg. org/profile.htm (accessed 4 September 2010).

Rico, Herminio. 2002. *John Paul II and the Legacy of Dignitatis Humanae*. Washington: Georgetown University Press.

Sachedina, Abdulaziz. 2009. *Islam and the Challenge of Human Rights*. New York: Oxford University Press.

Sarraj, Eyad. 2008. The grief counselor of Gaza, *The Link* 41, no. 3. http://www. ameu.org/page.asp?iid=281&aid=597&pg=1 (accessed 4 September 2010).

van der Ven, Johannes A., Jaco S. Dreyer and Henrik J. C. Pieterse. 2004. *Is there a God of human rights? The complex relationship of human rights and religion: a South African case*. Leiden: Brill.

van der Ven, Johannes A. and Francis Vincent Anthony. 2008. Impact of Religion on Social Integration from an Empirical Civil Rights Perspective (Part Two). *Salesianum* 70: 463-489.

Wadud, Amina. 2006. *Inside the gender Jihad: women's reform in Islam*. Oxford: Oneworld

Witte, John. 2005. Rights in the Western Tradition. Emory University School of Law: Public Law & Legal Research Paper Series, Research Paper 05-21, n.d. Prepared for the *Encyclopedia of Christianity*. Grand Rapids-Leiden: Wm. B. Eerdmans and E. J. Brill, vol.4. http://ssrn.com/abstract=753484 (accessed 4 September 2010).

Appendix 1: What respondents value

	Mean	Std. Deviation
My family	4.58	.815
My religion or world view	4.54	.809
My study	4.45	.867
My friends	4.32	.829
Having time for myself	4.27	.860
My career	4.25	.912
My partner or intimate friend	4.25	.826
Sharing time with acquaintances	3.90	.895
Sports	3.74	1.073
Importance of politics	2.81	1.252

Appendix 2: Civil Rights Related Statements

Our laws should protect a citizen's right to live by any moral standard he/she chooses.	4.01
Police searches of private homes without a search warrant are prohibited.	3.94
The community's moral standards should be critically debated in schools.	3.74
Children should be free to discuss all moral ideas and subjects in schools, no matter what.	3.63
A cabinet minister should allow his striking officials to meet in a ministerial building.	3.61
Politicians are not allowed to interfere with religious communities.	3.53
Prayers in public schools should not be forbidden.	3.50
The police are only allowed to inspect people's cars under strict judicial conditions.	3.48
Any form of sexual relations between adults should be their individual choice.	3.47
TV journalists with radical ideas have a civil right to employment.	3.38
Newspaper columnists should be free to express radical convictions.	3.33
Minority groups should be free to use the town hall to hold protest meetings.	3.27
In regard to euthanasia, politicians should decide irrespective of any religious leader's will.	2.92
Making fun of atheists in public meetings is permissible.	2.74
In regard to abortion, politicians should take decisions independently of religious leaders.	2.66
Making fun of religious people in cabarets is a legally protected right.	2.61

Out-group Attitudes in the Context of Religious and Cultural Diversity: The Impact of Religiosity, intercultural Competences, Religion and a Curriculum on Gender

Hans-Georg Ziebertz and Barbara Flunger

Abstract: *Can religion be understood as a resource of values and valuable principles or must religion be evaluated as a cause of tension and conflicts? These two options are not so easily answered. Religiously motivated people could be assumed to take care of others, to take part at the social life, to be integrated and to behave peacefully. At the same time, religion seems to stimulate thinking in terms of superiority, creating constraints between people and causing conflicts, legitimizing differences between sexes and functioning for non-religious violent goals. In this paper, we assume that the out-group attitudes are dependent upon religious convictions. More precisely, we expect that people believing that there is only one truth and that this truth is purely represented in their own religion will have difficulties with diversity and will tend to be more rigid toward out-groups than people who basically accept religious diversity. The problem does not stem from religious truth claims; it is rather the conviction that denies there can be other and different religions with access to truth. That was the theme of a curriculum carried out in schools to develop interreligious and intercultural learning in the project "Gender in Islam and Christianity." In the following we focus on the question of whether out-groups attitudes were changed by the curriculum, whether Muslim and Christian adolescents differ in their out-group attitudes and we explore whether three religious perspectives on truth-claims moderate the effects. The results can help to identify the role of religious attitudes for cohesion or conflict.*

Theoretical Background

The curriculum

The curriculum "Gender in Religion: Christianity and Islam" was developed by Ziebertz, Remmlinger and Herbert. The curriculum is built on the presumption that religions promote people's ideas in which gender is legitimated religiously (Ziebertz, Remmlinger, Herbert 2010). To implement the curriculum, a quasi-experimental design was used. The curriculum was taught in 43 classes in 2008 during five weeks (two hours each week). In the curriculum, the students read texts on the theological reflections and doctrinal positions of both Christian Churches and Islamic schools on the behaviour of men and women. Based on a communicative pedagogical concept (value communication), students were challenged to argue rationally on the arguments of different positions. Therefore they were repeatedly urged to reflect on their I-perspective, to reconstruct You-perspectives and to reflect on the wishfulness of a We-perspective (see Ziebertz 2010). It was hypothesized that the curriculum would contribute to a better understanding of the habits of different religions. Thus, it was expected that the curriculum would have a positive impact on out-group attitudes (Ziebertz, Remmlinger, Herbert 2010).

Religion
Religion can be considered both a social and a cultural category (Roccas and Brewer 2002; Ziebertz, Kalbheim, Riegel 2003) and relates to the experiences of group membership. The perception of sharing characteristics with other individuals in contrast to individuals who are members of a comparable group results in the sense of belonging to a common group: the in-group. People who can be differentiated according to their group identity belong to the out-group. There is consistent evidence from research that mere social categorizations create in-group favouritism (Brewer 1979; Tajfel 1982; Kalin and Berry 1996). Another consequence of social categorizations for intergroup behaviour and attitudes is explained by social-identity theory. In-group members tend to display uniform attitudes towards out-groups and out-group members are seen as a homogeneous group with similar attributes (Tajfel 1982). This unified perception results in the social stereotyping of out-groups (Tajfel 1982). We therefore expect that religion has an effect on out-group attitudes and that the direction of the effect differs depending on the religious denominations. Our research is undertaken in Germany where the majority of the believers are Christian. Thus, differentiations in religious denominations are also related to status differentials and to differences in group size. According to that, we expect that the Christians in Germany have lower ratings in out-group attitudes than members of other religious groups.

Intercultural competences
There are various models of intercultural competences. In most conceptualizations, intercultural competences refer to capabilities and certain behaviors (Bender-Szymanski 2008). In particular, intercultural competences are defined as "the ability to think and act in intercultural appropriate ways" (Hammer, Bennett, Wiseman 2003, 422). In this study, because intercultural competences can be understood either as culture-specific, cross-cultural or general social competences (Rathje 2006), we focus on general social competences. In particular we studied the concepts perspective-taking and independence (Bourjolly et al. 2005).

Findings from former research provided insight that the attainment of intercultural competences is essential for the amelioration of the relations between cultures (Hammer et al. 2003, 422; Bender-Szymanski 2008). Perspective-taking could be shown to have a positive impact on group-based judgements through reducing cognitive biases and altering representations of out-groups (Finlay and Stephan 2000; Galinsky and Moskowitz 2000). Perspective-taking can promote a greater insight in the consequences of prejudices (Coke, Batson, Mc Davis 1978). Independence relates to the trait "openness to change" (Sagiv and Schwartz 1995). Openness to change has a positive effect on the out-group attitudes as it encompasses a tendency for exploration (Sagiv and Schwartz 1995). Thus, we expect that the intercultural competences, perspective-taking and independence have a positive impact on the out-group attitudes.

Mono-, Multi- and Interreligiosity
The tensions between different religious traditions in Germany lead to the potential for conflicts. In the context of dealing with diversity, religious plurality is an important topic. In the conceptualization of this study, there are three models of attitudes toward religious pluralism: individuals can favor a monoreligious, a multi-religious and an interreligious mindset (Van der Ven and Ziebertz 1994). The three models can be seen as differences in the way to react to the existence of different religions. The monoreligious model considers the tendency to refer to the convictions of one's own religion in judging other religions (self-reference). The multireligious model encompasses a different mindset in dealing with religious plurality, namely, a rather distant relation to the absolutism of one religion and the promotion of the idea that all religions and religious convictions are equal. The interreligious model embraces the principles of perspective taking and the consequent belief that different religions should engage with each other.

The three models are in a way interdependent and they are rated independently as individuals can differ in their ways of coping with religious diversity. The mono- and the multireligious model are expected to be antipodes, as their handling of the assertions that one religion can claim the one truth is opposed.

With regard to out-group attitudes, we expect different impacts of the three concepts. A monoreligious perspective is often hypothesized to be connected with fundamentalism, xenophobia and a negative evaluation of diversity (Gross and Ziebertz 2009; Ziebertz 2010). Thus, we expect a negative effect of monoreligiosity on out-group attitudes. In the multi- and the interreligious model, pluralism and diversity are approved. Accordingly, we expect a positive impact of multi- and interreligious convictions on out-group attitudes (Gross and Ziebertz 2009; Ziebertz 2010).

Summary and Research question
We assume direct effects on out-group attitudes by the curriculum implemented in the study, religion, intercultural competences and mono-, multi- and interreligiosity. In this contribution, we want to explore whether intercultural competences and mono-, multi- and interreligiosity can be moderators of the effects of the independent variables (the curriculum and religion) on the out-group attitudes. We did not develop specific hypotheses on the directions involved.

The basic question of this study is whether the curriculum on "Gender in Islam and Christianity" has an effect on the out-group attitudes of adolescents. The curriculum, the religious denomination, intercultural competences and mono-, multi- and inter-religiosity are the independent variables. The dependent variables are the out-group attitudes. In addition, the moderating impact of intercultural competences and mono-, multi- and interreligiosity on the effects of religion and the curriculum on out-group attitudes is explored (see figure 1).

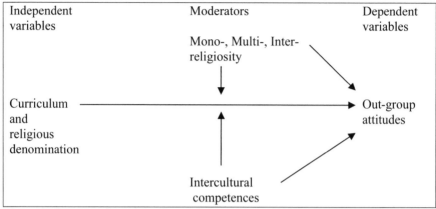

Figure 1: Conceptual model: effects of the curriculum and possible moderators

The study

The study was conducted as part of the project "Religion, Interkulturalität und Identität" ("religion, interculturalsm and identity") supported by the German Research Foundation (DFG). The project was pursued in order to investigate possibilities for improving intercultural communication in religious education. A basic aim was to test a curriculum that introduced the conflict-ridden topic how gender is authorized by the two religions Christianity and Islam.

Sample

Initially, 1790 students of the secondary schools (*Realschule*) from 31 schools (84 classes) in cities or at least regional main centers of the German federal states Bavaria, Baden-Wuerttemberg, North Rhine-Westphalia and Hessen were surveyed. 43 classes were assigned to the experimental group and 41 classes to the control-group. Religious diversity was a requirement to be able to take part in the study. Thus, the criterion for selection was that the schools had a bigger proportion of Muslim students (min. 15%). Regarding the Christians, 30.6% are Roman Catholics (n=547), 26.9% Protestant (n=481) and another 4.1% belong to Christian-Orthodox Churches (n=74). The group of the Muslims comprises 208 Sunnite (11.6%), 14 Shiite (0.8%), 42 Allevit adolescents (2.3%) and 108 (5.1%) pupils who identified themselves simply as "Muslim." 151 (7.2%) students were non-religious.

The drop out quote was large, only 1144 students could be questioned a second time. The sample consists of 639 female and 497 male adolescents. The majority of the students (46.2%) were 15 years old (M=15.10; SD=0.86). The participation of both Christian (n=707; 61.8%) and Muslim students (n=243; 21.2%) declined. 654 students who took part in the curriculum and 490 students of the control group could be studied twice. 78.9% (n=869) of the Christian and 82.1% (n=124) of the non-religious students consider Germany their home; 114 students (10.4%) without denomination are German by nationality, like 857 (77.8%) members of the Christian group. 570 Christian adolescents were German, the majority of the Muslim adolescents were Turkish (n=148), the share of other nationalities was 19%.

Method

The students were queried by questionnaires. The measures were adapted and partly developed for the study. The applied instruments were mostly scales and several single items. If interval scales were used respondents replied on a 5-point Likert scale anchored by 1 (I do not at all agree) and 5 (I definitely agree). The questionnaires also gathered information on gender, religious denomination and other background information.

Instruments

For the reported analyses, the concepts mono-, multi- and interreligiosity were applied; regarding intercultural competences, the constructs perspective-taking and independence were used. The out-group attitudes were measured by discrimination, acceptance and tolerance. The instruments were tested by factor analyses with promax rotations; the reliability was explored by investigating the internal consistencies. The measures are depicted in table 1.

Table 1: Overview of the applied measurements

Construct	Example of an item	Number of items	Reliability (Cronbachs Alpha)
Monoreligiosity	Only in my religion do people have access to true redemption.	4	.92
Multireligiosity	There is no difference between religions, they all stem from a longing to God.	4	.72
Interreligiosity	The real truth can only be discovered in the communication between religions.	3	.65
Perspective-taking	It is hard to see the world through the eyes of someone else.	4	.65
Independence	I decide if I tell my parents about my problems.	7	.65
Discrimination t1 (t2)	I think members of other cultures commit more crimes.	6	.86 (.88)
Acceptance t1 (2)	I think people from other nations are fascinating.	4	.80 (.81)
Tolerance t1 (t2)	People from other cultures are more open.	2	.65 (.66)

Results

The description of the results is ordered in three parts. First, the descriptive results are presented; next the direct effects of the independent variables curriculum, religion, and intercultural competences are reported; finally the effects of mono-, multi- and interreligiosity are reported. In the following, the exploration of the interactions between the independent variables religion and curriculum and the possible moderators intercultural competences and mono-, multi- and interreligiosity are presented.

In table 2, the ratings on all measures used in the study are depicted separately for the participants of the experimental group and the control group referring to their religious denomination.

Table 2: Descriptive Results regarding the different religious groups and the participation in the curriculum

| | Experimental group | | | | Control group | | | |
| | Christian | | Muslim | | Christian | | Muslim | |
	M	SD	M	SD	M	SD	M	SD
Independent variables								
Independence t1	4.25	.58	3.84	.67	4.23	.61	4.01	.83
Perspective-taking t1	3.41	.82	3.25	.75	3.49	.79	3.42	.86
Monoreligiosity t1	2.25	.91	3.47	1.14	2.26	.91	3.58	1.15
Multireligiosity t1	3.31	.79	3.05	.90	3.29	.82	2.99	.99
Interreligiosity t1	2.93	.80	2.97	.74	2.87	.78	2.91	1.01
Dependent variables:								
Out-group attitudes								
Discrimination t1	2.21	.92	1.54	.54	2.19	.85	1.44	.68
Discrimination t2	2.32	.93	1.74	.61	2.29	.87	1.83	.71
Acceptance t1	3.18	.87	3.48	.73	3.10	.82	3.81	.82
Acceptance t2	3.11	.89	3.55	.80	3.13	.81	3.45	.85
Tolerance t1	2.78	.83	2.88	.93	2.66	.84	3.27	1.10
Tolerance t2	2.71	.85	2.81	.89	2.72	.81	3.10	1.03

Legend: t1/t2= first and second measure

In table 2 first, the ratings on the independent variables are listed. In the lower section of table 2 out-group attitudes, the dependent variables are shown, the out-group attitudes assessed at the first test interval (t1) and the second test interval (t2) are listed. The differences between the participants are objects of further analyses, as the significance of the descriptive results has to be tested.

The effects of the independent variables
The effects of each independent variable were tested independently by an analysis of variances (ANOVAS) with repeated measures and regressions. The regression analyses were made with a data set consisting only of Muslim and Christian adolescents. As two–time point data was analyzed, the independent variables of the first test interval (t1) were used to predict the out-group attitudes (t2) at the second testing (simple prediction model; Cohen, Cohen, West, Aiken 2003).

Effects of the curriculum and religious denomination on out-group attitudes
The ANOVAS with repeated measures revealed that the participants of the curriculum did not differ from the students of the control group regarding discrimination and

acceptance. Significant differences were found regarding tolerance (F (1/978) = 5.26; p<.05; η^2<.01), but this effect is statistically not meaningful because of the low effect size. The religious groups differed in discrimination (F (2/987) = 46.35; p<.01; η^2=0.08), acceptance (F2/982) = 18.00; p<.01; η^2=0.04) and tolerance (F (2/978) = 5.97; p<.01; η^2=0.01). Post-hoc Tests (Scheffé) yielded significant differences between Muslim and Christian or Non-Religious adolescents (p<.01). There were no significant differences between Christian and Non- Religious students.

Effects of the intercultural competences and mono-, multi-, and interreligiosity
The out-group attitudes discrimination, acceptance and tolerance were regressed on the variables perspective-taking, independence, mono-, multi- and interreligiosity.

Perspective-taking predicted discrimination (ß=-.06; p<.05; R^2=.01; n=1100) and acceptance (ß=.07; p<.05; R^2=.01; n=1094). There were no significant relations of perspective-taking to tolerance. Independence had no significant effects on dis-crimination and acceptance, but a negative effect on tolerance (ß=-.09; p<.01; R^2=.01; n=1093). The hypotheses could only partly be confirmed, because uniquely the relations of perspective-taking to discrimination and acceptance were consistent to the assumptions.

Monoreligiosity predicted discrimination (ß=.13; p<.01; R^2=.02; n=1063) and acceptance (ß=-.09; p<.01; R^2=.01; n=1059). Multireligiosity predicted all three out-group attitudes (discrimination ß=-.18; p<.01; R^2=.03; n=1064; acceptance: ß=.21; p<.01; R^2=.05; n=1060; tolerance: ß=.08; p<.01; R^2=.01; n=1057). Besides, interre-ligiosity predicted discrimination (ß=-.12; p<.01; R^2=.02; n=1059), acceptance (ß=.20; p<.01; R^2=.04; n=1055) and tolerance (ß=.10; p<.01; R^2=.01; n=1052). The directions of the effects were according to the hypotheses. Accordingly, the assumptions could be confirmed with the exception to the relation of monoreligiosity and tolerance.

Exploration of interactive effects
In order to explore whether intercultural competences or mono-, multi- and interre-ligiosity strengthen or weaken the impact of the independent variables curriculum and religious denomination on the out-group attitudes, the interactions between the effects were tested by regression analyses. The continuous variables were centered by subtracting their mean values. The two religious denominations Muslim and Christian were represented through a nominal variable coded as a dummy variable, Code 0 represents the Christian, Code 1 the Muslim adolescents. Thus, product terms representing the interaction effects between the independent variable religious denomination and the possible moderators were computed. First, the out-group attitudes were regressed on the religious denomination. Next, for discrimination, acceptance and tolerance, the interactions between each intercultural competence and religious denomination and the interaction between the three religious models and religious denomination were added (see table 3). The testing of the moderation of the effect of the curriculum was excluded as there was no significant effect by the curriculum.

Table 3: The moderating effect of the intercultural competences and mono-, multi- and interreligiosity

		Step 1					Step 2				
		B	S	β	t	R²	B	SE	β	t	R²
Discrimination	Religion	.54	.06	-.27**	8.40	.07	.54	.07	.27**	8.26	.07
	perspective-taking	-.07	.04	-.06*	-1.99		-.04	.07	-.04	-.54	
	Interaction effect						-.04	.08	-.03	-.47	
	Religion	.60	.07	.30**	8.98	.08	.58	.07	.29**	8.65	.08
	independence	-.16	.05	-.12**	-3.64		-.11	.08	-.08	-1.44	
	Interaction effect						-.08	.10	-.05	-.85	
	Religion	.85	.07	.42**	11.78	.15	.70	.08	.34**	9.04	.18
	Monoreligiosity	.27	.03	.34**	9.64		.07	.05	.09	1.53	
	Interaction effect						.29	.06	.27**	4.99	
	Religion	.56	.06	.28**	8.79	.12	.56	.06	.28**	8.80	.14
	multireligiosity	-.25	.03	-.24**	-7.44		-.04	.06	-.04	-.68	
	Interaction effect						-.31	.07	-.24**	-4.30	
	Religion	.50	.07	.24**	7.51	.07	.52	.07	.25**	7.72	.08
	interreligiosity	-.11	.04	-.10**	-3.09		.01	.07	.01	.15	
	Interaction effect						-.16	.08	-.13*	-1.96	
DV acceptance	Religion	-.40	.06	-.20**	-6.23	.04	-.40	.07	-.20**	-6.15	.04
	perspective-taking	.05	.04	.05	1.38		.04	.07	.03	.48	
	Interaction effect						.02	.08	-.01	.21	
	Religion	-.40	.07	-.20**	-6.03	.04	-.40	.07	-.20**	-5.86	.04
	independence	.02	.05	.02	.48		.00	.08	.00	.06	
	Interaction effect						.03	.10	.02	.28	
	Religion	-.64	.07	-.32**	-8.86	.09	-.61	.08	-.31**	-7.74	.09
	Monoreligiosity	-.20	.03	-.26**	-7.23		-.16	.05	-.21**	-3.27	
	Interaction effect						-.07	.06	-.06	-1.09	

Predictor	B	SE	β	t	R²
Religion	-.44	.06	-.22**	-7.03	.10
multireligiosity	.27	.03	.26**	8.13	
Religion	-.36	.06	-.18**	-5.55	.07
interreligiosity	.20	.03	.19**	5.75	
Religion	-.20	.07	-.10**	-3.11	.01
perspective-taking	.00	.04	.00	-.09	
Religion	-.16	.07	-.08*	-2.39	.02
independence	-.11	.05	-.08*	-2.30	
Religion	-.25	.08	-.12**	-3.22	.01
Monoreligiosity	-.03	.03	-.03	-.89	
Religion	-.24	.07	-.12**	-3.65	.03
multireligiosity	.13	.04	.12**	3.63	
Religion	-.20	.07	-.10**	-2.99	.02
interreligiosity	.12	.04	.11**	3.18	

DV tolerance

Predictor	B	SE	β	t	R²
Religion	-.44	.06	-.22**	-7.01	.11
Multireligiosity	.17	.06	.17**	2.94	
Interaction effect	.14	.07	.11*	1.99	
Religion	-.35	.07	-.18**	-5.43	.07
Interreligiosity	.22	.07	.21**	3.23	
Interaction effect	-.03	.08	-.03	-.40	
Religion	-.20	.07	-.10**	-3.08	.01
perspective-taking	.00	.08	.00	-.05	
Interaction effect	.00	.09	.00	.00	
Religion	-.17	.07	-.09*	-2.52	.02
Independence	-.05	.06	-.04	-.64	
Interaction effect	-.09	.10	-.05	-.89	
Religion	-.27	.08	-.14**	-3.30	.01
Monoreligiosity	-.06	.05	-.01	-1.20	
Interaction effect	.05	.06	.05	.85	
Religion	-.24	.07	-.12**	-3.63	.03
Multireligiosity	.06	.06	.06	.93	
Interaction effect	.10	.07	.08	1.36	
Religion	-.23	.07	-.11**	-3.37	.03
Interreligiosity	-.06	.07	-.05	-.77	
Interaction effect	.23	.08	.18**	2.74	

Note: ** p<.01; *p<.05

The contents of table 3 are the slopes (B), the standardized regression coefficients
(ß), the standard errors (SE) and the t-values that report the significance of the coefficients. In the first row, the effect of religion is reported. The coefficient B=.54
indicates the difference between the reference group (the Muslims) and the Christians. The finding suggests that the Christian students have a higher value regarding
discrimination than the reference group of the Muslim students. In the next row, the
effect of perspective-taking is reported. The coefficient is negative, that means that
the value of discrimination decreases as a function of perspective-taking. The
explored interaction effect is depicted in row three, the coefficient is negative, but it
is not significant.

The results in Table 3, Step2, show that the product of monoreligiosity with religion
predicted discrimination. The interaction between multireligiosity with religion also
predicted discrimination and acceptance. The interaction of interreligiosity and religion was a predictor of discrimination and tolerance. The explained variance got
higher through the inclusion of the interaction effects, the change of the R squares
was significant (p<.01).

The interactions were interpreted by plotting the simple slopes for the relationships
between the different religious models and religion, religion was effect coded (-1=
Muslim, 1= Christian). The coefficient of the interaction effect between monoreligiosity and religion was positive; the simple slopes indicated that higher discrimination in the Christian group was associated with the approval of monoreligiosity.
Lower monoreligiosity was related to lower discrimination (see figure 2). The coefficient of the interaction effects between multi- religiosity and religion was negative;
figure 3 demonstrates that lower multireligiosity was associated with higher discrimination in the Christian group. A similar pattern could be found regarding the
interaction effect between interreligiosity and religion (see figure 4). The simple
slopes for acceptance suggested that higher multireligiosity seems to be connected
with higher acceptance and lower multireligiosity with lower acceptance (see figure
5). The simple slopes revealed that in the case of the Christian adolescents, the
reported higher interreligiosity was positively associated with slightly higher tolerance (see figure 6).

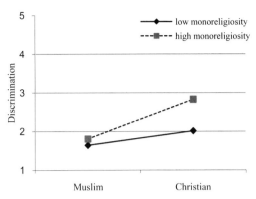

Figure 2: regression slopes for the interaction
between monoreligiosity and religion

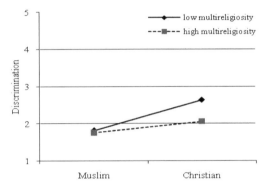

Figure 3: regression slopes for the interaction
between multireligiosity and religion

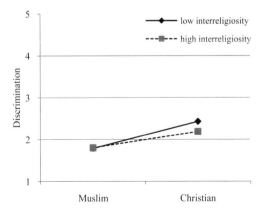

Figure 4: regression slopes for the interaction
between interreligiosity and religion

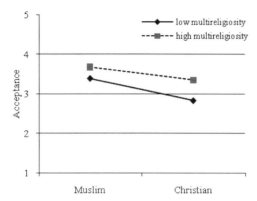

Figure 5: regression slopes for the interaction
between multireligiosity and religion

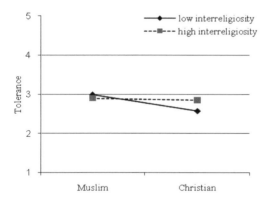

Figure 6: regression slopes for the interaction
between interreligiosity and religion

Summary and discussion

Four hypotheses were tested. The curriculum had the aim to affect positively the out-group attitudes of both Christian and Muslim adolescents. Therefore, the participants of the curriculum were expected to have lower ratings in discrimination and higher ratings in acceptance and tolerance than the students of the control-group. The assumed impact of the curriculum could not be confirmed as the experimental group and the control group did not differ significantly in discrimination and acceptance, and the significant difference in tolerance was statistically not meaningful according to the effect size. Several reasons can explain the missing effect of the curriculum.

Maybe the requirements of the curriculum were too demanding for the students of a secondary school or for the age-group in target. Another reason could be the design of the study as quasi-experimental. In that design, the control of intervening variables is hardly feasible. A possible explanation can also be the preparation of the contents in the curriculum. The students had to reflect the positions of the Islam and the Christian belief that possibly were contrary to the attitudes of the students. Furthermore, the accentuation of the different conceptions of gender could have contributed to the awareness of group categories, and thus, could have provoked negative attitudes towards out-groups. Perhaps, the confrontation with the chosen contents did undermine the designated positive effect.

Religious denominations are social categorizations (Roccas and Brewer 2002) and social categorizations have been shown in former research to affect out-group attitudes (Brewer 1979; Turner 1981; Tajfel 1982; Kalin and Berry 1996). Therefore, it was assumed that religion had an effect on out-group attitudes. The Christian adolescents as members of a higher status group were expected to devalue out-groups more than Muslim adolescents. Thus, it was hypothesized that the Christian adolescents would rate higher on discrimination and lower on acceptance and tolerance in comparison to the Muslim students. The assumptions could be confirmed and provide further support of social identity theory.

Intercultural competences could be shown to affect the relations between cultures (Hammer et al. 2003, 422). Perspective-taking can be expected to have a positive impact on out-group attitudes as it relates to the insight in the effects of stereotypes and prejudices (Coke, Batson, Mc Davis 1978; Finlay and Stephan, 2000; Galinsky and Moskowitz 2000; Bender-Szymanski 2008). Independence can also be expected to affect out-group attitudes positively, as the concept independence is closely linked to openness to change that has positive relations with out-group attitudes (Sagiv and Schwartz 1995). The assumptions could be partly confirmed: perspective-taking was shown to have a negative impact on discrimination and a positive impact on acceptance. There was also a significant negative relation of independence to tolerance that was contrary to our assumptions. The findings regarding perspective-taking support the notion that intercultural competences seem to be related to processes of social exclusion and integration (Hammer et al. 2003; Bender-Szymanski 2008). This has major implications for religious education. For example, it could be an important reflection to be responsive to ego-centric views.

There is evidence from research that monoreligiosity is negatively associated with out-group attitudes and that multi- and interreligiosity are positively connected with out-group attitudes (Ziebertz 2009; 2010). Thus, a positive effect of monoreligiosity on discrimination and a negative relation between discrimination and multi- or interreligiosity was expected. It was also hypothesized that monoreligiosity had a negative impact on each acceptance and tolerance, whereas positive effects of multi- and interreligiosity on both positive out-group attitudes were expected (Ziebertz 2009; 2010). The assumed linkages could be confirmed: monoreligiosity had a positive effect on discrimination and a negative effect on acceptance; multi- and interreligiosity had a negative impact on discrimination and a positive impact on acceptance and tolerance.

To gain further insight in the relationships involved, we explored whether the intercultural competences and the mono-, multi- and interreligiosity could be moderators of the effect of religion on out-group attitudes. The analysis of the significant interaction effects revealed that monoreligiosity had a relation to the higher approval of discrimination especially in the Christian group, still the Muslim adolescents rated lower on discrimination than the Christians. The favoring of multi- and interreligiosity was related to a lower discrimination tendency in the Christian group. Multireligiosity was related to higher acceptance in both groups, but the difference was larger in the Christian group. The reported higher interreligiosity was positively associated with higher tolerance in the Christian group.

These findings suggest that the effect of religion on out-group attitudes could be strengthened by the conviction that one's own religion is the only access to truth and weakened by a conviction that approves other religions. This assumption is, for example, supported by the finding that multireligiosity weakens the effect of religion on discrimination and strengthens the impact of religion on acceptance. Further research is needed to explore the effects of mono-, multi- and interreligious convictions, especially regarding the Christian group.

References:

Bender-Szymanski, Dorothea. 2008. Interkulturelle Kompetenz bei Lehrerinnen und Lehrern aus der Sicht der empirischen Bildungsforschung. In *Interkulturelle Kompetenz und pädagogische Professionalität*, ed. Georg Auernheimer, 201-28. Wiesbaden: Verlag für Sozialwissenschaften.

Bennett, Milton. 1986. A developmental approach to training for intercultural sensitivity. *International journal of intercultural relations* 10, no 2:179-196.

_____. 1993. Towards ethnorelativism: A developmental model of intercultural sensitivity. In *Education for the intercultural experience,* ed. R. Michael Paige, 21-71. Yarmouth ME: Intercultural Press.

Bourjolly, Joretha, Roberta Sands, Phyllis Solomon, Victoria Stanhope, Anita Pernell-Arnold, Laurene Finley. 2006. The Journey toward Intercultural Sensitivity. *Journal of Ethnic and Cultural Diversity in Social Work* 14, no. 3:41-62.

Brewer, Marilynn. 1979. In-group bias in the minimal intergroup situation: A cognitive-motivational analysis. *Psychological Bulletin* 86, no. 2:307-324.

Cohen, Jacob, Patricia Cohen, Stephen G. West, Leona S. Aiken. 2003. *Applied Multiple Regression-Correlation Analysis for the Behavioral Sciences*. Mahwah NJ: Lawrence Erlbaum Associates.

Coke, Jay S., C. Daniel Batson and Katherine McDavis. 1978. Empathic mediation of helping: a two-stage model. *Journal of Personality and Social Psychology* 36:752-766.

Finlay, Krystina and Walter G. Stephan. 2000. Reducing prejudice: The effects of empathy on intergroup attitudes. *Journal of Applied Social Psychology* 30:1720–1737.

Galinsky, Adam and Gordon Moskowitz. 2000. Perspective-taking: Decreasing stereotype expression, stereotype accessibility, and in-group favoritism. *Journal of Personality and Social Psychology* 78, no. 4:708-724.

Gross, Zehavit and Hans-Georg Ziebertz. 2009. Religion and xenophobia. In *Youth in Europe III*, ed. Hans-Georg Ziebertz, William K. Kay, Ulrich Riegel, 181-198. Münster: LIT Verlag.

Hammer, Mitchell, Milton Bennett and Richard Wiseman. 2003. Measuring intercultural sensitivity: The intercultural development inventory. *International journal of intercultural relations* 27, no. 4:421-443.

Kalin, Rudolf and John W. Berry. 1996. Interethnic attitudes in Canada: Ethnocentrism, consensual hierarchy and reciprocity. *Canadian Journal of Behavioral Science* 28, no. 4:253-261.

Karcher, Michael and Kurt Fischer. 2004. A developmental sequence of skills in adolescents' intergroup understanding. *Journal of Applied Developmental Psychology* 25, no. 3:259-282.

Rathje, Stefanie. 2006. Interkulturelle Kompetenz-Zustand und Zukunft eines umstrittenen Konzepts. *Zeitschrift für interkulturellen Fremdsprachenunterricht* 11, no. 3:15-36.

Roccas, Sonia and Marilynn Brewer. 2002. Social identity complexity. *Personality and Social Psychology Review* 6, no. 2:88-106

Sagiv, Lilach and Shalom H. Schwartz. 1995. Value priorities and readiness for outgroup social contact. *Journal of Personality and Social Psychology* 69, no. 3:437-448.

Tajfel, Henri. 1982 [1981]. *Gruppenkonflikt und Vorurteil*. Bern-Göttingen-Seattle-Toronto: Verlag Hans Huber.

Van der Ven, Johannes and Hans-Georg Ziebertz, eds. 1994. *Religiöser Pluralismus und Interreligiöses Lernen*. Weinheim-Kampen: Deutscher Studien Verlag and KoK.

Ziebertz, Hans-Georg, Boris Kalbheim and Ulrich Riegel, eds. 2003. *Religiöse Signaturen heute. Ein religionspädagogischer Beitrag zur empirischen Jugendforschung*. Gütersloh: Gütersloher Verlagshaus.

Ziebertz, Hans-Georg, ed. 2010. *Gender in Islam und Christentum. Theoretische und empirische Studien*. Münster: LIT Verlag.

Ziebertz, Hans-Georg, Barbara Remmlinger and Markus Herbert. 2010. Konzeption des Curriculum Gender und Religion. In *Gender in Islam und Christentum*, ed. Hans-Georg Ziebertz, Münster: LIT Verlag, 137- 167

Expanding the Boundaries
of Practical Theology

Sharing a Place and Sharing the Divine:
An exploration of the (im)possibilities of living peacefully together in a pluralistic society

Riet Bons-Storm

Abstract: *Under which conditions can it become possible that people of different religions share a place in a salvific way? Place as "territory" is closely linked to a person's identity. One's religious affiliation is an important feature of one's identity. In this article I focus on* Sulha, *an old Arabic method of reconciliation and conflict handling. Important in this method are notions human dignity, identity, everyday life, concreteness and power. My supposition is that the way to be able to share a place as people of different religions is to literally see "the other" and to see "the other" not only as somebody who represents another religion, but as a believer. While learning to know each other better as believers, it may become possible to acknowledge that the Divine, never to be grasped or known fully, can be shared, while the ways to worship this Divinity may be different. This shared Divinity can be a "shared religious envelope," encompassing the different religions, making living and working together possible.*

> "Allah, OHM, Father/Mother,
> Eternal One, Adonai – I Shall Be.
> Face without a name.
> Who is, without proof.
> King without land.
> Who cannot be grasped, cannot be understood,
> Who has no name and still...
> You are known in many countries, loved by
> Many who seek You." (Jan Bosman, unpublished)

The situation and the question

My practical-theological research question is: how can people from different religions live together in a salvific way? In my country people of different faiths have to share our small country. Most of the immigrants are Muslims. An outrageous right-wing politician kindled the sparks of fear for "others," meaning Muslim immigrants, the more the economy collapsed and jobs became scarce. This politician, a true demagogue manipulating the media, called Islam "a stupid religion," "anti- modern" and "the breeding place for terrorism." The result is that the *street,* as a metaphor for the whole public domain, becomes more and more the place where people fight the "other," resulting in fear, threats and violence (see Gopin 2002: 21ff.). Indigenous Dutch people claim their street. But "strangers"—people of color and women wearing headscarves—claim the street as well. Many of them came to the

Netherlands in the 1980s, when they were needed by the Dutch economy. Others came when the former colonies of the Netherlands became independent. Many of these former immigrants have Dutch citizenship. They rightly want to share the territory of the indigenous Dutch people. The violence that smoulders in numerous places in society erupts. Even murders happen.

Many indigenous Dutch people have a deep attachment to their small country. The narratives of national history tell them that in the sixteenth and seventeenth century they fought the big country Spain to gain their freedom to choose their own religion. In those days this meant choosing one of the forms of Christianity. Today the Netherlands is a secularized country; nevertheless, many Dutch people sing heartily the sixth verse of the national anthem: *Mijn schild ende betrouwen zijt Gij, o God mijn Heer* ("You are my shield and trust, O God my Lord"). In the media politicians, who do not practise any form of Christianity themselves, write about their fear that the Netherlands will no longer have Christianity but Islam undergirding its culture. In these secularized times one could consider Christianity a part of the Dutch folklore, but during conflicts and heated discussions people of all parties become more conscious of their religion and their God or Allah.

In this paper I shall contribute some thoughts about the question: how can it become possible that people of different religions can work towards the possibility of living together with fewer conflicts? I focus on the non-hypothetical case of plans to build a mosque in a neighborhood of a Dutch town, whose church spires are visible from afar.

An example: *Sulha*
We can learn from peacemaking methods used with positive results in other parts of the world. I focus here on the method of *Sulha* as an example of systematic conflict handling. I experienced *Sulha* used by Jews, Muslim and Christian Palestinians who are working for peace in Israel and Palestine, and I was impressed by the results (http://www.sulha.org; Gopin 2002, 135ff; Bons-Storm 2008).

Sulha is a traditional Arab form of mediation and reconciliation. In Arabic *Sulha* means "peacemaking" or "settlement." *Sulha* was already used long before the birth of Islam. The method is traditionally used in solving concrete problems between tribes or families. A livable situation must be attained. Its main characteristics are the following:

The formation of listening groups
Sulha can take various forms. In most cases people come together in "listening circles" to listen to each other's stories; sometimes these tales of suffering due to conflict extend back in time for many generations. Each party tells the other party and the mediator how they and their interests are damaged by the other party during the conflict. This means that the participants give each other the opportunity to be known in their own context. *"Context"* is used here in the sense of "context-

symbolism." In context-symbolism "context" means more than just the social-cultural-religious environment or the background of a life story. What counts is *the meaning* the person gives to their own socio-cultural-religious environment. In this sense, "context" can be understood as a product of a human agent in their relatedness and search for meaning (Nagy 2009, 6-7). In listening circles the (history of the) experience of the conflict by both parties has to come into the open. When that happens it becomes evident that the participants in the group, from both sides, are directed by conscious but also by many unconscious fears, needs and hopes—these being the main motivations for human conduct. Nobody is allowed to take exclusively the role of victim. All participants are invited to take responsibility for their situation and to see themselves as "actors."

There is always a mediator
In a concrete conflict situation an impartial mediator is called. This mediator guards the self esteem of everybody in the groups. They have to have the ability to understand both conflicting viewpoints. Often this is not easy. The Palestinian Lucy Talgieh is a Christian theologian, who participates as mediator in the Wi'am Peace Program in Bethlehem, working along the lines of *Sulha*. She said, "I had to take courses in mediating for three years before I could bring myself to sit at the same table with Jews." The Nakba of 1948, the loss of her family home and the ongoing humiliation are trauma's that still haunt her (Bons-Storm 2008, 42-43; Van der Veen 2009).

The preservation of dignity and sense of self
A key concept in *Sulha* is the preservation of *self-esteem and dignity* of everybody involved in the conflict. Dignity is the preservation of a positive sense of self. I prefer to use "sense of self" over "identity" because in Sulha the emphasis lies on the *personal experience* of life and self, not on "identity" as a philosophical or psychological concept in general. This sense of self is obtained in "context," that means in the meanings given by a person to the self in relation to others in their environment, and to an Ultimate Point of Reference, which in many cases is Divine, according to the leading stories of one's culture and religion. Moreover, a sense of self is always linked to a certain relationship to a territory.

In analyzing this point the following theories can be useful. A territory is that part of the *physical or cultural space* a person feels entitled to inhabit with dignity. One needs justification for this entitlement and finds it, for instance, in the sacred texts of a religion, or in the narratives of history, all told and retold from generation to generation. The Dutch-North American psychologists C.B. Bakker and M.K. Bakker-Rabdau contend, "Territoriality permeates every aspect of human existence. Constantly a person divides everything in categories of possession: mine and yours, his and hers, ours and theirs. This territorial index helps one to evaluate themselves in relation to others and serves them in times of conflict" (Bakker and Bakker-Rabdau 1973, 50). Immigrants—at least when newly arrived in their new country—

are de-territorialized persons. The anthropologist Nestor Garcia Canclini defines "de-territorialisation" as "the loss of the natural relation of culture to geographical and social territories" (Nestor Garcia Canclini 1995, 229; quoted in Nagy 2009, 48). De-territorialization is often a threat to one's sense of self: what is the place one can claim as their own?

All human beings develop strategies to occupy a territory. Human beings, their sense of self linked to a territory, define and guard its boundaries. They feel entitled to defend themselves against invasions. Aggression is often seen as the best form of defense. The smallest territory one can inhabit is one's own body. Rape is invasion and annexation of that minimal territory and consequently reduces a raped person to nobody. Most of the conflicts between persons can be understood as battles about the boundaries of their territories.

Josselyn stresses the importance of *eye-to-eye contact* across the boundaries of territories. Literally *seeing* the other challenges the prejudices that grow out of fear for the other and the threats to one's own territory (Josselyn 1996).

The Spanish theologian Mercedes Navarro (2003), speaking about territories, contends that "liminal space" is possible. At boundaries, where confrontation, competition and violence so easily occur, a virtual no-man's-land can be imagined. This liminal space gives people of competing territories the possibility to think about their own sense of self and see the other. Here the importance of a competent mediator can become evident: mediators create a liminal space between the opponents, give them the possibility to see and hear each other, in order to create gaps in the walls that defend the territories.

The goal: re-establishing working relations between the opposing parties and reaching a settlement
The goal of *Sulha* is not to establish who is right and who is wrong, but to reach a solution to a concrete problem between the parties. Zoughbi, the founder of Wi'am, the Palestinian Conflict Resolution Center in Bethlehem that uses *Sulha*, speaks of reaching "relative justice" or "a simple portion of integrity" (http://www.gbgmc.org/NWO/99ia/wiam.html). This settlement will nearly always be a *compromise.*

Bitter coffee
When a solution, at least a compromise, or a cease fire is reached, there is always a ritual: bitter coffee drunk together, a symbol of suffering. Then the participants shake hands, a seal to the contract to act differently than they did before (Gopin 2002, 135ff).

Looking for a shared religious envelope
In one Dutch neighborhood Muslims and indigenous Dutch people with a Christian background come together to solve the problem of a new mosque. Guided by a

competent mediator the participants seek to find a "shared religious envelope," however small (Gopin 2002, 14), a basis upon which the disagreeing parties can find each other. The mediator has to make it clear that the goal of the meetings is not to find out which is the one true religion with the one true Divinity, but to solve a particular problem: the building of a mosque. When the group meetings begin there are usually many prejudices, resulting in feelings of insecurity. It is my experience in working with interreligious groups that more knowledge about the religion and the founding texts of the other helps not only to lessen the power of false prejudices, but can also give mutual *recognition*. In the liminal space, carefully created by the mediator, participants start to see each other with new eyes. The awareness dawns that both Muslims and Christians have something in common: both are "sincere believers," who try to live their faith in God or Allah. This is a crucial point in the negotiations.

It is impossible to create a fruitful liminal space between believers who take all their founding texts literally, and stress the texts that testify that God or Allah destroys all those who do not serve Him in the one true way. "Where we think we are right, flowers cannot grow" (Jehuda Amichai quoted in Oz 2006, 54).

If the participants are willing to listen to what the others, as sincere believers, narrate about their everyday life with their God or Allah, they become aware of *the particular understanding of the source-texts* each participant has, sometimes looking further than an a-historic or an a-cultural exegesis that takes all texts at face value. Both Muslims and Christians believe that the Divinity reveals the Divine-self in the texts. The Muslim scholar Asma Barlas points to the fact that often Qu'ran as revelation (divine discourse) and Qu'ran as text (a fixed discourse in writing by humans interpreted in history) are confused (Barlas 2002, 10). The same confusion often occurs among Bible-reading Christians. Reading Bible and Qur'an with an open mind, acknowledging that both sacred texts consist of *experiences* of revelations written down in a specific time and place, one can find much common ground between Christians and Muslims. A Muslim tells about the way she lives her life with Allah, the Just and Merciful, who guides and comforts her. The need for a place of worship for this Allah becomes evident. A Christian tells the same about life with the God of the Bible and his half-conscious idea that the Dutch culture must be, as such, based upon the Jewish-Christian tradition. Fears can come into the open.

On the basis of increasingly acknowledged common ground, guided by a skilled mediator, participants may become more and more conscious of the impossibility of defining the Divine, *qualitate qua*. This is a crucial step. It is impossible to draw boundaries around (the idea of) the Divine. The Divine, Allah, God can only be acknowledged in faith. God and Allah can never be known fully. Both Christianity and Islam believe that they reveal the Divine-Self to us in the source-texts. Qur'anic and biblical texts can be found that preach hostility and even violence to believers in other faiths, as well as texts that testify that God's or Allah's love includes "the others." Listening to the way people talk about their life with their faith, in their own context, it can become clear that people *choose* which texts are the most important for them, in their life and its history. In a safe liminal space a good mediator can lead the participants to re-think these choices. The Palestinian Muslima Safa' Abu Assab bases her efforts to make peace between the people of different faiths in her country on Sura 49:13, "O people, We have created you from man and woman, We have made you into nations and tribes, in order that you come to know each other" (Bons-Storm, 2008, 91). In the Bible we find texts about God's house with many dwellings. Cautiously the belief can be admitted that the God of the Bible and the Allah of the Quran could refer to the same Godhead: both could be glimpses given to us of the Indefinable Divinity, God/dess and Allah, never fully known or possibly defined by humans. What binds Jews, Christians and Muslims together—their common ground—is faith in the Oneness of God, *Tahwid* in Arabic, the Justice of God and the Incomparability of God (Barlas 2002, 13).

Different traditions on the common ground

Every religion has its own "narratives" or, as Burton Mack calls it, its own "myth." "Myths are more than fascinating phantasies, fuzzy memories, misguided science, or collective deceits. Myths acknowledge the collective gifts and constraints of the past and create a space for thinking critically about the present state of a group's life together" (Mack 2003, 69). Marc Gopin uses myth "in the sense of a story that contains some ultimate truth and enduring truth, and in a way makes sense of amorphous reality, for those who believe it. Whether the myth is believed to be literal history, approximate history, or simply didactic legend, depends on the believer" (Gopin 2002, 8). The myth of every religion—the corpus of narratives, confessions and directions for a good and just life—develops over centuries and consists of efforts to construct (with the help of images, tales, and metaphors) a certain communicable and coherent form for the inexplicable longing-inkling-faith that humanity can have a relationship with a Supreme Being. This "myth" is recorded in the tradition of a religion: the narratives of its sacred texts and dogmatics.

To solve the dilemma about the building of the mosque it is not necessary to merge the different narratives or myths into one. Believers may live by their religious narratives, based on their own sacred texts. Each religion can be honored in its unique way to create a way to worship the Divine and to live with this Divinity every day. In these different narratives the Divine One plays a distinctive role (see Sundén, 1966) revealing the Divine character. In Judaism, Christianity and Islam the common ground is that the Divinity is Creator, Giver of Blessings, Companion in life and death, fount of morality, but also the Merciful One forgiving sins.

Stumbling blocks

In most conflicts the parties do not have equal power. In the Netherlands the conflict about the building of the mosque occurs between indigenous Dutch people and people who are originally immigrants. Even secularised Dutch people tend to see their country exclusively as *their* territory, linked to the God of the Bible, who helped them to obtain it. Immigrants, as de-territorialized persons, are dependent on the indigenous Dutch to grant them a territory, necessary for their positive sense of self. Dorottya Nagy stated, "For many migrant groups religion lies, next to politics and ethnicity, at the basis of identity and community formation" (Nagy 2009, 59). Many indigenous Dutch people see their country as a Christian country, giving to their faith the claim of *exclusivity*. In that case the building of a place of worship to Allah on Dutch soil is an abomination. Many Dutch people feel they are entitled to forbid the building of "strange," un-Dutch places of worship on their territory, as the Swiss—as secular as the Dutch—felt entitled to forbid the building of minarets in their country in 2009. A mediator takes this situation into account and creates an atmosphere where the less powerful feel safe to speak uninterrupted and without consequences for their safety afterwards.

"Texts of terror" (Phyllis Trible 1984) can be found in both the Bible and Qu'ran. In misogynic texts the Bible and Qu'ran are certainly each other's match. I agree with Asma Barlas who writes: "This is why we need to make another crucial distinction that patriarchal readings of Islam do not make: between Islam in theory and Islam in practice, thus also between Islam and already existing patriarchies on the one hand and Islam and Muslim history and practices on the other" (Barlas 2002, 11). The same is true about patriarchal texts in the Bible. However, the actual texts of the Bible and Qur'an, although both patriarchal, are less misogynist than their reception in the centuries of their exegesis. Dominant traditions are even more misogynist than the source-texts of both religions (see for instance Kecia Ali 2006).

Often one of the breaking points in the negotiations is the biblical texts that say that Jesus is the only way to God. Christianity's dominant "myth" focuses on the role of Jesus as Son of God who by the shedding of his blood removed the obstacles of sins between God and humanity, paid the price, absolved the debt (although God is called "gracious"); this often goes to the very core of Christian identity. For many believers it is difficult to see the official dogmas of Christology, of cross and blood, as episodes in a particular myth that was created *in faith* in a particular culture, place and time, expressing how a relationship to the Divine can be understood, true for its believers, but without universal claims of objective truth. Listening to the ways the participants in the meeting live with their faith often removes the sharp edges of the official dogmas.

What has to be done: orthopraxis

Part of the shared religious envelope can be the fact that both religions stress the importance of *orthopraxis*, based on love for the Divine. In the Bible we find this in Amos 6:1-8 and Matthew 25, in the Qur'an in Sura 2:177, where is written that not piety, but giving one's possessions to surviving relatives (widows), orphans, travellers and the oppressed makes a person just and faithful. As always in *Sulha*, it is the praxis of everyday life that counts. If the possibility that Muslims and Christians try to live sincerely according to their longing for the same Divine, who can be worshipped in various ways, comes to prevail during the meetings of the group, then the mosque can be built.

Rituals to remember the pain of the conflict and its causes and to celebrate new possibilities of harmony are important to implant the experiences of conflict and healing deeply in the participants' consciousness.

References:

Ali, Kecia. 2006. *Sexual Ethics and Islam. Feminist Reflections on Qu'ran, Hadith and Jurisprudence.* Oxford: Oxford University Press.

Bakker, C.B. and M.K. Bakker-Rabdau. 1973. *Verboden Toegang. Verkenning rond het menselijk territorium.* Antwerpen: De Nederlandse Boekhandel.

Barlas, Asma. 2002. *"Believing Women" in Islam. Unreading Patriarchal Interpretations of the Qu'ran.* Austin: University of Texas Press.

Bons-Storm, Riet. 2008. *Vertel onze verhalen verder. Ontmoetingen met Joodse en Palestijnse vrouwen.* Gorinchem: Narratio.

Garcia Canclini, Nestor. 1995. *Hybrid Cultures: Strategies for Entering and Leaving Modernity.* Stanford: Stanford University Press.

Gopin, Marc. 2002. *How religion can bring peace to the Middle East.* Oxford: Oxford University Press.

Josselyn, R. 1996. *The Space between Us: Exploring the dimensions of human relations.* Thousand Oaks, CA: Sage Publications.

Mack, Burton L. 2003. *The Christian Myth, Origins, Logic and Legacy.* New York-London: Continuum.

Nagy, Dorottya. 2009. *Migration and Theology. The Case of Chinese Christian Communities in Hungary and Rumania in the Globalisation-Context.* Zoetermeer: Boekencentrum.

Navarro, Mercedes. 2003. Women and Religions. Visibility and invisibility in society in Southern Europe. Unpublished lecture, given at the European Women's Synod in Barcelona.

Oz, Amos. 2006. *Hoe genees je een fanaticus.* Amsterdam: De Bezige Bij.

Sundén, H. 1966. *Die Religion und die Rolle.* Berlin: Töpelmann.

Trible, Phyllis. 1984. *Texts of Terror.* Philadelphia: Fortress Press.

Van der Veen, Freek, ed. 2009. *Nakba. Verhalen over een ramp die niet voorbijgaat.* Gorinchem: Narratio.

Spiritual Resistance in the Native American Renaissance

Lynn Bridgers

Abstract: *This article examines spiritual resistance in the writings of a group of authors known collectively as the Native American Renaissance. These authors include N. Scott Momaday, Leslie Marmon Silko, Joy Harjo and Linda Hogan. After reviewing the semiotics of Ferdinand de Sassure and Clifford Geertz's development of symbolic anthropology, the article adopts the comparative symbology approach utilized by Victor Turner. This allows for the combination of literary and anthropological perspectives and the utilization of the works of these authors as a form of thick description. Examination of that description employs both Foucauldian analysis and insights from postcolonial theory. The article then explores the questions of whether the spiritual resistance found consistently in the writers of the Native American Renaissance could be considered a form of practical theology, given that it can be seen as a form of spiritual practice, a process grounded in experience, one that fosters a formational process and ultimately results in the construction of spiritual identity. Finally, the author reflects on the insights gathered in light of her own experience living in the postcolonial setting of contemporary New Mexico.*

Introduction

It has been estimated that in 1500 the Native American population in North America stood at 12 million. Four centuries later their population had been reduced by 95%, to only 237,000. That decline represents what one historian called a "vast genocide…the most sustained on record" (Churchill, cited in Lewy 2004). By the beginning of the twentieth century, as historian David Stannard concludes, Native Americans had suffered the "worst human holocaust the world had ever witnessed, roaring across two continents non-stop for four centuries and consuming the lives of countless tens of millions of people" (cited in Lewy 2004). It was not until the late 1960s that Native American voices decrying this history of devastation reached a wide audience. In the decade and a half that followed N. Scott Momaday's 1969 Pulitzer Prize winning *House Made of Dawn,* the voices of a vibrant group of Native American writers emerged. Literary critic Kenneth Lincoln first used the term "Native American Renaissance" to describe these authors in 1983 (1983). They included such notable figures as N. Scott Momaday, Leslie Marmon Silko, Joy Harjo and Linda Hogan.

This article combines literary and anthropological perspectives with Foucauldian analysis in interpreting their cry of resistance. Ferdinand de Saussure's semiology initially explored the sign processes by which meaning is generated. Semiology helped to give rise to symbolic anthropology, which Clifford Geertz saw as "a system of inherited conceptions expressed in symbolic forms by means of which people communicate, perpetuate, and develop their knowledge about and attitudes toward life" (Geertz 1973, 89). From these perspectives, the writers of the Native American Renaissance struggle to impose meaning on their own harsh legacy, and by doing so to give voice to their own resistance.

Using Geertz's symbolic anthropology as a springboard to Victor Tuner's comparative symbology, one can explore the power dynamic and spiritual resistance, finding in the literary work of the Native American Renaissance a form of thick description. Only then can one consider whether this resistance actually serves as a form of practical theology, bursting forth in response to the sustained genocide of Native American populations, educating and transforming the lives of millions in their wake.

Semiotics and Symbolic Anthropology

The anthropologist most commonly associated with the term "thick description" is Clifford Geertz. In fact, Geertz goes so far as to say that "ethnography is this description" (Geertz 1973, 9-10). Geertz considers thick description, which looks not only at surface phenomenon but at the context of the practices and discourse in societies, as central to the task of the anthropologist. For Geertz, the core task of the anthropologist is to provide thick descriptions (Geertz 1973, 3-30).

A broader perspective is provided by anthropologist Victor Turner. While both men's work grew out of semiotics, Turner saw semiotics as a broader field of study than the comparative symbology and comparative anthropology that he utilized in his own work. Semiotics, from Geertz's perspective was "a general theory of signs and symbols, especially in the analysis of the nature and relationship of signs in language, usually including three branches: syntactics, semantics, and pragmatics" (Turner 1982, 20-21). Comparative symbology, in Victor Turner's view, was not as connected to the technical aspects of linguistics, but incorporated the non-verbal aspects of culture, including ritual and art. "Its data are mainly drawn from *cultural genres* or *sub-systems* of expressive culture. They include both oral and literate genres, symbolic actions, such as ritual and drama, as well as *narrative* genres, such as myth, epic, ballad, the novel and ideological systems" (Turner 1982, 21).

Turner believed that comparative symbology was a broader field of study than comparative anthropology, for it moved beyond the mere study of ethnographic materials. Rather, "this broader perspective forces it to come to terms with the methods, theories, and findings of specialists and experts in many disciplines which most anthropologists know all too little about, such as history, literature, musicology, art history, theology, the history of religions, philosophy and so forth" (Turner 1982, 23). Thus a perspective grounded in comparative symbology moves beyond a strict reading of the work of the Native American Renaissance grounded in semiotics, or the limitations of one focused purely on examination of ethnographic elements, to one based on the utilization of a broader range of disciplines. The latter seems far more appropriate to an examination of the symbols and thick description found in the literature of the Native American Renaissance.

Power and Spiritual Resistance in the Native American Renaissance

Central to any real understanding of Native American spirituality and the role of resistance is some recognition of the special relationship between humanity and nature. The vital connection to the land, to the natural world, deserves particular attention. Accordingly, N. Scott Momaday begins his seminal work, *House Made of Dawn,* with a description of the sacred site in which his story is rooted, the Jemez Valley (Momaday 1968, 1). Momaday is a member of the Kiowa tribe, plains Indians most often associated with neighboring Oklahoma. Since both his parents accepted teaching positions at Jemez Pueblo, Momaday grew up amid the red rocks of the Jemez Valley, in north central New Mexico. His novel begins with a description of the rugged land: "There was a house made of dawn. It was made of pollen and of rain, and the land was very old and everlasting. There were many colors on the hills, and the plain was bright with different colored clays and sands. Red and blue and spotted horses grazed in the plain, and there was a dark wilderness on the mountains beyond. The land was still and strong. It was beautiful all around" (Momaday 1968, 1).

Chickasee poet and novelist Linda Hogan clarifies the importance of the land to the Native American in her description of what she calls places of power. She writes, "There are places of power on the earth. They have meaning not just because humans associate meaning with them, but because they resonate. They are designated sacred places not only because of stories humans tell about them, but because of the energies of the places themselves. They are alive....They may be mountains, they may be a bend in a river, but they are sacred sites" (Hogan 2001, 149). The land itself becomes a character in many of the works of the Native American Renaissance.

In Leslie Marmon Silko's *Ceremony,* for example, this happens quite literally. The mountain that shelters Laguna Pueblo, where Silko grew up, is called Mount Taylor by Anglos. In the novel it becomes embodied in a beautiful young woman, Ts'eh, with the transparent last name of Montano. Her traditional ways of living, high on the mountain, becomes a refuge for the exhausted wanderer at the heart of her story (Silko 1977).

In Momaday's *House of Dawn* the novel's main human character, Abel, is a veteran, a common theme in the novels of the Native American Renaissance. Returning to his grandfather's house after combat service in World War II, Able seeks to find his place in the conflict between two worlds and two worldviews: the traditional world of his grandfather and the pueblo, and the outside, white world of progress, development and science. This division of self is also a central theme in the writers of the Native American Renaissance. The self is divided between the traditional world, passed down through the generations in stories and rooted in the land, and the modern world, where the white man demands Native American must live.

In Silko's novel *Ceremony,* the main character is another returning veteran, recovering from the horrors of the Pacific in World War II. The Laguna elders send the veteran to a Navajo Medicine man, Betonie, to see if he can cure him of his horrific memories.

What is the source of his illness, according to Betonie? "It was everything they had seen—the cities, the tall buildings, the noise and the lights, the power of their weapons and machines. They were never the same after that: they had seen what the white people had made from the stolen land" (Silko 1977, 169). The illness Tayo suffered was directly related to his exposure to the white man's war and to the loss of the land. "Every day they had to look at the land, from horizon to horizon, and every day the loss was with them; it was the dead unburied, and the mourning of the loss going on forever. So they tried to sink the loss in booze; and silence their grief with war stories about their courage, defending the land they had already lost" (Silko 1977, 169).

For the medicine man Betonie, the white man's war and the loss of the land are symbolic of a greater evil, which he calls "the witchery." "'That is the trickery of the witchcraft,' he said. 'They want us to believe all evil resides with white people. Then we will look no further to see what is really happening. They want us to sepa-rate ourselves from white people, to be ignorant and helpless as we watch our own destruction. But White people are only tools that the witchery manipulates; and I tell you, we can deal with white people, with their machines and their beliefs'" (Silko 1977, 132). The way for the Native American to deal with both the white people and the witchery is to reclaim tradition, to develop new ceremonies and once again sing the songs of their elders. As Tayo finally comes to understand, "The witchery would be at work all night so that people would see only their losses—the land and the lives lost—since the whites came; the witchery would work so that people would be fooled into blaming only the whites and not the witchery. It would work to make the people forget the stories of the creation and continuation of the five worlds; the old priests would be afraid too, and cling to ritual without making new ceremonies as they always had before, the way they still made new Buffalo Dance songs each year" (Silko 1977, 249).

Similarly, for Linda Hogan, the reconciliation of the divided self comes through acceptance, through the transcendence of a destructive dualistic perspective. Her returning veteran reflects on the destructiveness and the personal legacy of his own military service. "He had been wrong, and he was not wrong. I killed, he thinks, but I saved. I ended up loving and then hating myself for it. It was a world of double-ness. There are no clear lines between evil and good. He is both. This is the slow dawn of his knowing" (Hogan 2008, 136).

Repeatedly in these works, true spiritual resistance is grounded in the return to tra-ditional belief, in the stories passed on by one's ancestors, in the reconnection with the land and transcendence of dualistic division. We find the same elements in the poetry of Joy Harjo. In "Reconciliation, A Prayer," she writes: "O sun, moon, stars, our other relatives peering at us from the inside/ of god's house walk with us as we climb into the next century/ naked but for the stories we have of each other. Keep us from giving/ up in this land of nightmares which is also the land of miracles" (Harjo

2002, 89). Overcoming the difference between the sacred and the secular becomes not only an act of spiritual resistance but an experience of grace. In an earlier poem, entitled "Grace," Harjo wrote:

> ...one morning as the sun struggled to break ice and our dreams had found us with coffee and pancakes in a truck stop on Highway 80, we found grace.
>
> I could say that grace was a woman with time on her hands, or a white buffalo escaped from memory. But in that dingy light it was a promise of balance. We once again understood the talk of animals and spring was lean and hungry with the hope of children and corn.
>
> I would like to say, with grace, we picked ourselves up and walked into the spring thaw. We didn't; the next season was worse. You went home to Leech Lake to work with the tribe and I went south. And Wind, I am still crazy. I know there is something larger than the memory of a dispossessed people. We have seen it (Harjo 2002, 67-68).

The "memory of a dispossessed people" haunts the works of all the authors of the Native American Renaissance. As Linda Hogan reminds us in her memoir, *The Woman Who Watches Over the World,* "Few people outside our cultures can comprehend the depth of the pain, despair, and for many of us Native peoples, anger. To other Americans, this history, if thought of at all, belongs to the far past, but in truth these events are recent and remembered. We have not forgotten the past so quickly and easily" (Hogan 2001, 79).

Insights from Postcolonial Analysis
While the devastation suffered by the Native American peoples in the centuries since 1500 certainly cannot be equated with the forms of oppression suffered under various colonial rules, many of the concepts that have developed in postcolonial thought can applied to their contemporary situation. One of the theorists most frequently utilized in postcolonial critique is French poststructuralist Michel Foucault. Foucault himself never directly addressed the postcolonial context, but his work on the nature and pervasiveness of power have made his theoretical work applicable to the examination of how power shapes and modifies the relationship between colonizing Western Europeans and the indigenous Other.

One of the first to systematically apply Foucault's thought to postcolonial settings was Ashis Nandy in *The Intimate Enemy.* As Leela Gandhi explains:

> Nandy's book builds on an interesting, if somewhat contentious, distinction between two chronologically distinct types or genres of colonialism. The first, he argues, was relatively simple-minded in

its focus on the physical conquest of territories, whereas the second
was more insidious in its commitment to the conquest and occupation of minds, selves, cultures. If the first bandit-mode of colonialism was more violent, it was also, as Nandy insists, transparent in
its self-interest, greed and rapacity. By contrast, and somewhat
more confusingly, the second was pioneered by rationalist, mod-
ernists and liberals who argued that imperialism was really the
messianic harbinger of civilization in the uncivilized world
(Gandhi 1998, 15).

For the writers of the Native American Renaissance, the first form of colonialism is
clearly *fait accompli.* It reverberates in their writings, in the legacy of lives lost and
land stolen. But it is the second dimension that consistently haunts these writers, that
leaves them with a sense of a divided self, in which both the traditional world and
the world of the whites co-exist. It is, as Linda Hogan described above, the "world
of doubleness" where "there are no clear lines between evil and good." The deepest
forms of resistance are rooted in resistance to "the conquest and occupation of
minds, selves, cultures" (Gandhi 1998, 15).

Postcolonial thought recognizes something like this "doubleness" in the concept of
hybridity. Homi Bhabha saw hybridity as "the negotiation of contradictory and
antagonistic instances that open up hybrid sites and objectives of struggle, and
destroy those negative polarities between knowledge and its objects, between theory
and practical political reason" (Bhabha 1994, 22). Susan Abraham notes how this
concept of hybridity dismantles reigning polarities. "As it is enunciated to discursive
spaces, cultural difference makes problematic temporal binaries such as past and
present, historical ones such as tradition and modernity, spatial ones such as East
and West, and value categories such as pure and impure or civilization and barbar-
ism" (Abraham 2008, 382).

Franz Fanon locates hybridity not in the world of temporal discourse, but in the
consciousness of the colonized, noting "the challenging of the very principle of
foreign domination brings about essential mutations in the consciousness of the
colonized, in the manner in which he perceives the colonizer, in his human status in
the world" (Fanon 1965, 69). As Leela Gandhi so clearly notes, "The grim polarities
of the colonial encounter…are necessarily bridged by a 'third space' of communication, negotiation and, by implication, translation. It is in this indeterminate zone, or
'place of hybridity' where anti-colonial politics, first begins to articulate its
agenda…" (Gandhi 1998, 130-31). As the colonized absorbs and internalizes the
values of the colonizer, so too does the colonizer absorb, to some extent, the values
of those colonized; in effect, both experience hybridity.

The writers of the Native American Renaissance have, by necessity, engaged in a form
of hybridity that allows them to use the English language and modern publishing

houses to give voice in their own quest for transcendence of inner divisions. They do not do so, however, in a neutral landscape, but in a landscape marked by enormous discrepancies in cultural validation and power. In Foucault's work, power is not limited to the political or militaristic power that enabled the developing US to conquer and confiscate Native American lands. It is far more complex than that. Tom Beaudoin elaborates, "Foucault's account of power defies simple categorization. As constant expressions of 'elementary' force relations in society, 'power is everywhere,' but not as a seamless, total macro, undifferentiated presence. It is instead to be understood as viscous, a 'dense web, an ambiguous, always local, polyvalent, shifting, 'enigmatic,' and 'ubiquitous,' unstable permanence in human relations...." (Beaudoin 2008, 4). By transcending any simple binary relationship between the powerful and the powerless, in Foucault's thought power becomes a neutral force that can be both creative and destructive, that can elude human control and intention.

So it is perhaps unsurprising that so many of these novels feature Native American veterans as their main characters (Momaday 1968; Silko 1977; Hogan 2008). In the aftermath of their combat experiences each of these protagonists struggles with their sanity, trying to construct some sense of meaning out of both personal and universal suffering. Each of them struggles with some form of madness, trying to achieve some level of sanity in a world that has clearly gone insane.

In his early work Foucault would suggest that branding these young veterans insane would, in fact, reflect Western culture's need to identify the deviant other. In an early work, *Mental Illness and Psychology,* he writes:

> If Durkheim and the American psychologists have made deviancy and departure the very nature of mental illness, it is no doubt because of a cultural illusion common to both of them: our society does not wish to recognize itself in the ill individual whom it rejects or locks up; as it diagnoses the illness, it excludes the patient. The analyses of our psychologists and sociologists, which turn the patient into a deviant and which seed the origin of the morbid in the abnormal, are, therefore, above all a projection of cultural themes (Foucault 2008, 63).

This leads Hubert Dreyfus to conclude, "Foucault thus switches from an account of the social conditions that cause mental illness to the cultural conditions that lead us to treat madness as mental illness" (Dreyfus 2008, xi). Foucault proposes "to show that the root of mental pathology must be sought...in certain relation, historically situated, of man to the madman and to the true man" (Foucault, cited in Dreyfus 2008, xi).

The quest of the returning veterans in the novels of Momaday, Silko and Hogan is to discern their own relationship to both the madman and the true man, to reconcile division and determine who they really are in relation to white society—madmen in a sane culture, or true men in a culture gone mad. For Tayo in Silko's *Ceremony,* that reconciliation comes at the conclusion of the story. "He cried the relief he felt at finally seeing the pattern, the way all the stories fit together—the old stories, the war stories, their stories—to become the story that was still being told. He was not crazy, he had never been crazy. He had only seen and heard the world as it always was: no boundaries, only transitions through all distances and time" (Silko 1977, 246).

Resistance as a Form of Practical Theology

These reflections lead us to a final question: Is the spiritual resistance found in these works actually a form of practical theology? It does at least mirror some of the central tasks of practical theology. It can be seen as a form of spiritual practice, a process grounded in experience, and one that fosters a formational process and ultimately results in the construction of spiritual identity. As a spiritual practice, the spiritual resistance found in these works confronts one of the basic questions that has always plagued Christian theologians: the question of dualism. Repeatedly, healing is found when the dualisms of good and evil, of Native and non-Native, of human and nature are transcended.

This resistance is also grounded in experience. The writers of the Native American Renaissance begin with the assumption that the experience of the Native American, and the Native American writer, is in some way distinct or different from the prevailing forms of experience in modern Western culture. These experiential perspectives are shaped by a different way of living, different world views, and different belief systems that all find their way into this body of work.

Spiritual resistance is also a formational process. As the wounded veterans come to a greater sense of wholeness through their return to ceremony, tradition and homeland, so too does the reader accompany them in what Joy Harjo termed "the epic search for grace" (Harjo 2002, 65). Harjo acknowledges this. She closes her book *How We Became Human* with the simple words, "all acts of kindness are lights in the war for justice" (Harjo 2002, 236).

Most importantly, spiritual resistance in the work of Native American Renaissance celebrates the establishment or *re*-establishment of spiritual identity. As N. Scott Momaday remarked in an interview reproduced in his *House Made of Dawn*, "From birth, I grew up being in touch with sacred matters." He later concludes, "I saw people who were deeply involved in their traditional life, in the memories of their blood. They had, as far as I could see, a certain strength and beauty that I find missing in the modern world at large. I like to celebrate that involvement in my writing" (Hagar 1988, 189). Momaday's work not only celebrates the traditional spiritual life of that he witnessed growing up in Jemez Pueblo but communicates that spirituality to the reader, passing it on to another generation. The work of a writer such as Momaday, with its critical and popular acclaim, fosters understanding and acceptance of Native identity not only for himself as author, but for other Native Americans and for the non-Native reader as well.

Conclusion

The soil of New Mexico sustains a legacy of loss. Challenges of religion, conflict and diversity preceded the coming of the first Europeans, five centuries ago, and continue to this day. I recently bought a small piece of that land in a village called San Ysidro, New Mexico. Founded as a Spanish settlement in 1699, it currently has a population of 230. According to official records, the land previously belonged to Severo Montano. Before that, however, it belonged to the people of Jemez Pueblo, which lies lodged above it in the foothills of the Jemez Mountains. I have not yet discovered just how the land was wrested from the people of Jemez Pueblo and become part of the Montano family holdings, nor how it left the Montano family and became available for purchase by a *gringa* like me. It seems somehow strange that an Anglo like me could ever be considered its rightful heir.

There are arguments in my favor. After all, I was born in New Mexico and raised on the food that came out of its soil. In the light of some Native American beliefs, this genealogy means that I have achieved a kind of kindred status. We are products of the same soil, sun and sky, and some Native Americans would contend that the land itself has laid claim to my soul. For others, however, my fair skin and green eyes mark me irrevocably as an outsider and my purchase of the land is the appropriation of the worst kind.

There is some evidence to support that view as well. Recently, through genealogical research completed by my cousin through the Smithsonian Institute we have learned that our earliest American ancestor, on my father's side, was General Joseph Bridger. Originally an English Cavalier, he left Britain after King Charles was decapitated by the Puritans, fled to Virginia and established himself near the Chesapeake Bay in the 1650s. He promptly made a name for himself through the efficient extermination of Native Americans in the area, in what are now known as the Indian Wars. When he died in 1680 he was the largest landholder in what is now Virginia.

Learning of my descent from Joseph Bridger sparked conflicting emotions. The first was my surprise that my family's roots were sunk so deep in American soil. While my father often assured us that we had a "fine Southern heritage," it never occurred to me it extended prior to the late 19th century. On the other hand, I was also forced to recognize the divided heritage of being a descendent of someone who gained his reputation through military campaigns against the Native peoples of his area, and as such a large landholder was undoubtedly a slaveholder.

This is the personal context that spurred this exploration of the role of religion, diversity and conflict in the work of this remarkable group of Native American writers. Recognizing the hybridity and ambivalence that comes with a history such as my own, I have explored themes of division and healing, of historical legacy and contemporary identity, of spiritual resistance and acceptance. These foundational questions shape not only the lives and writings of these astonishingly articulate figures. They shape my own soul as well.

References:

Abraham, Susan. 2008. "What does Mumbai Have To Do With Rome? Postcolonial Perspectives on Globalization and Technology." *Theological Studies* 69:376-393.

Bhabha, Homi K. 1994. *The Location of Culture.* New York: Routledge.

Beaudoin, Tom. 2008. "Foucault Teaching Theology." *Witness to a Dispossession.* Maryknoll, NY: Orbis Books.

Churchill, Ward. 2004. Cited in Guenter Lewy, "Were American Indians the Victims of Genocide?" George Mason University, History News Network. http://hnn.us/articles/7302.html (accessed 19 January 2009).

Dreyfus, Herbert. [1987] 2008. Forward to the California Edition. In *Mental Illness and Psychology* by Michel Foucault. Trans. Alan Sheridan. Berkeley: University of California Press.

Fanon, Franz. 1965. *A Dying Colonialism.* Trans. Haakon Chevaiar. New York: Grove Press.

Foucault, Michel. [1987]. 2008. *Mental Illness and Psychology.* Trans. Alan Sheridan. Berkeley: University of California Press.

Gandhi, Leela. 1998. *Postcolonial Theory: A Critical Introduction.* New York: Columbia University Press.

Geertz, Clifford. [1973] 2000. *The Interpretation of Culture.* New York: Basic Books.

Hagar, Hal. 1988. N. Scott Momaday. In *House Made of Dawn* by N. Scott Momaday. New York: Harper & Row.

Harjo, Joy. 2002. *How We Became Human.* New York: W. W. Norton & Company.

Hogan, Linda. 2001. *The Woman Who Watches Over the World.* New York, London: W. W. Norton & Company.

Hogan, Linda.2008. *People of the Whale.* New York, London: W. W. Norton & Company.

Lincoln, Kenneth. 1983. *Native American Renaissance.* Berkeley—Los Angeles: University of California Press.

Momaday, N. Scott. 1966. *House Made of Dawn.* New York: Harper & Row.

Silko, Leslie Marmon. 1977. *Ceremony.* New York: Penguin Books.

Lewy, Guenter. 2004. Were American Indians the Victims of Genocide? George Mason University, History News Network. http://hnn.us/articles (accessed 19 January 2009).

Turner, Victor. 1982. "Liminal to Liminoid in Play, Flow and Ritual." In *From Ritual to Theatre,* 20-60. New York: PAJ Publications.

New Directions in Interfaith Spiritual Care

Leah Dawn Bueckert and Daniel S. Schipani

Abstract: *The authors of this essay present the results of their work on interfaith spiritual care together with a number of specific suggestions for further exploration. They begin by mapping the area of interfaith care with a brief discussion of several main findings related to the changing landscape of spiritual care, conceptual clarity, theoretical consideration and practical integration of recent developments in intercultural counseling and psychotherapy, and theological foundations. They make the case for further development in both the broader field of pastoral care and the discipline of pastoral theology in particular. In part two of the essay the authors present a picture of excellence in interfaith spiritual care as a window to the fruits of their research. Their "emerging profile of professional wisdom" consists of the interconnection of core competencies pertaining to the domains of knowing, being and doing. The profile highlights a number of core specific competencies respectively associated with understanding, presence and companioning. They conclude by identifying key dimensions of theological education and ministerial formation— academic, personal-spiritual, and vocational-professional—and corresponding pedagogies.*

Introduction

Our recent and ongoing research focuses on the foundations and the dynamics of interfaith spiritual care as a work of practical and pastoral theology (Schipani 2009, 407-414). In the course of our own practice of spiritual care and in collaboration and conversation with others, we have identified reliable guidelines for the competent and duly contextualized caregiving practice as provided primarily but not exclusively in health care institutions (Schipani and Bueckert 2009). This essay presents a view of the present situation in the field together with challenges and opportunities for the years ahead. First we discuss a number of research findings related to current understandings of interfaith care and the way forward for further research in the field. In the second part we introduce an emerging profile of professional wisdom consisting of core competencies pertaining to the domains of *knowing*, *being* and *doing,* necessary for effective care in interfaith situations.

A Brief Overview of Key Findings

There is no general agreement in the field concerning semantics. We continue to prefer the term "interfaith" while other writers employ the concept "interreligious," which is more widely accepted in Western Europe (Weiss 2009, 239-258). In other contexts such as Latin America, "inter-confessional" and "inter-spiritual" are sometimes used but not yet in a systematic way.

Our proposed way of integrating the three constructs—spirituality, faith and religion—is as follows. We adopt the understanding of *faith* as a human universal as
articulated by James Fowler (Fowler 1981). So understood, faith may or may not
find expression in terms of specific religious traditions and content. *Spirituality* in
this light is the overarching construct connoting a fundamental human potential as
well as a need or longing for meaning, value and hope, and a disposition for relationship with a transcendent power. According to Richards and Bergin, "[r]eligious
expressions tend to be denominational, external, cognitive, behavioral, ritualistic and
public. Spiritual experiences tend to be universal, ecumenical, internal, affective,
spontaneous and private" (Richards and Bergin 1997, 13). The category "faith" is
employed to connote, as in Fowler, developmentally patterned kinds of construals:
patterned knowing (beliefs), patterned valuing (commitment, devotion), and patterned constructions of meaning (usually in the form of an underlying narrative;
Fowler 1987, 54-57). Both faith and religion are considered subsets of "spiritual,"
i.e., we are fundamentally spiritual beings.

Intentionality in addressing the social realities of spiritual and religious diversity and
particularity is crucial yet long overdue in the field of pastoral care and counseling
and in the discipline of pastoral theology. Recently there have been promising developments regarding spiritual care in health care institutions (Koenig 2007; Taylor
2007) and particularly in chaplaincy (Anderson and Fukuyama 2004; Bueckert and
Schipani 2006; Schipani and Bueckert 2009) that can enrich the larger field of pastoral and spiritual care and the discipline of pastoral theology. New resources are
available in the area of psychotherapy which may also be critically considered and
creatively appropriated. For instance, the American Psychological Association
(APA) now embraces a sustained focused concern on spirituality and religious diversity. In recent years the APA has published a number of valuable works on psychotherapy and spirituality (e.g., Richards and Bergin 1997; Miller 1999; Richards
and Bergin 2000). Furthermore, contributions linking spiritual direction and pastoral
care (Stairs 2000) are also helpful for interfaith care situations.

A significant shift is occurring away from a monoculture approach and from what
many consider the "monopoly" of *Christian* pastoral care. This shift is reflected in
the change in terminology, from *pastoral* care to *spiritual* care. The latter is becoming the preferred term in reference to caregiving settings other than Christian
(Driedger 2009, 138-141). In recent years representatives of other faith traditions
such as Jewish and Muslim have made significant contributions to the theory and the
practice of interfaith care by focusing on the specific nature of those traditions
(Friedman 2005; Ansari 2009; Isgandarova 2005; Lahaj 2009). Others propose a
more inclusive multifaith approach to spiritual care that includes equality of professional status and complementary participation among caregivers representing a plurality of religious and nonreligious (e.g., Humanist) traditions and perspectives (Pergola 2009; van Buuren, Kaya and ten Broek 2009; Walther 2009).

It is very helpful, indeed necessary, for both practitioners and theoreticians in the field to pay attention to existing research and reflection on intercultural care and counseling because, in principle, interfaith spiritual care can be viewed and approached as a special form of intercultural care. This can be documented, for example, concerning *core competencies* identified as essential for effective practice, as articulated in the pioneering work of David Augsburger (Augsburger 1987, 17-47) and Emmanuel Lartey (Lartey 2003, 163-177) regarding pastoral counseling, and Derald Wing Sue and David Sue (Sue and Sue 2008, 42-52) in the broader field of counseling. At the same time, the uniqueness of interfaith spiritual care must not be underestimated to the extent that visions of reality, life and death, suffering, healing, wellness and the good life, tend to become more readily and explicitly the focus of attention in the caregiving relationship. Therefore, in the near future practitioners and theoreticians focusing on intercultural care will in turn likely benefit from the systematic contributions of and engagement with those who work on interfaith spiritual care.

Our research reconfirms the assumption that the caregiver's theology matters clinically, and especially in interfaith situations. That is true because such conceptual and inherently normative frameworks significantly condition the form and quality of care made available to careseekers. For example, chaplains who hold an exclusivist Christian view of faith and salvation are often seriously limited in their ability to care well for patients of other faith traditions. At the same time, we have also documented ways in which caregiving practices, duly reflected upon, can correct, revalidate and reshape the caregiver's theology. Indeed, spiritual caregivers have a unique opportunity, professional duty and ethical imperative to flourish as reflective practitioners and pastoral theologians (Bueckert and Schipani 2006b; Schipani and Bueckert 2009b). They can also do so with explicit reference to their religious tradition and theological convictions (Peterson 2009) while upholding the professional, legal, ethical and institutional standards which safeguard carereceivers' rights and the very integrity of the relationship of care in any given setting.

Interfaith spiritual care looks different in diverse regional and cultural contexts. Recent writings document significant variations represented, for example, in Brazil and the Netherlands. Not unlike most other places in Latin America, interfaith care in Brazil has not yet been intentionally and systematically implemented and developed; it rarely exists on formal, institutional and ecclesiastic levels and tends to be personal and informal and spontaneous (Farris 2009). At the other end of the spectrum, spiritual care in the Netherlands deliberately addresses the multifaith social realities of the country; it seeks to make spiritual care accessible to people of diverse religious traditions and faith or philosophical orientations, and calls for specialized training on the part of caregivers also representing diverse spiritual identities and viewpoints (van Buuren, Kaya and ten Broek 2009).

Finally, our research suggests that progress in understanding and practicing inter-faith spiritual care is transferable in several ways. Insights we have gained in the practices of interfaith pastoral counseling and chaplaincy as well as in supervision received and given in those two forms of care can be mutually beneficial. For their part, Christian caregivers soon discover that the very attitudes, knowledge and skills necessary to care well for people of different religious traditions are indispensable for quality care of Christian carereceivers whose beliefs, values and practices stem from a different theological stream or denominational background. Further, Chris-tian and other caregivers soon realize that ultimately all relationships of care can be viewed as both intercultural as well as interfaith interactions. As presented in the next section, training in interfaith care always enhances the caregivers' general competence and professional wisdom.

Wise Interfaith Spiritual Caregivers: An Emerging Profile
The following paragraphs present a picture of excellence or *professional wisdom*, inspired in part by John Patton's view of pastoral wisdom in pastoral care (Patton 2006, 7-38). Wisdom in interfaith care involves not only what we know but also who we are and what we do. In other words, professional wisdom for quality inter-faith care may be viewed as the integration of three interconnected domains: *know-ing*, *being* and *doing* (fig. 1). This is the case concerning both the "clinical" (i.e., attitudes, knowledge and skills that define expertise) as well as "ministerial" (i.e., vocational identity, philosophy of care and consistent practice) dimensions connoted in *professional*. We propose that a portrait can be drawn by focusing on a number of core competencies within each of those domains. The resulting profile of wise spiritual care consists of three sets of core *competencies* which we have identified in the course of our own spiritual care practice, research, and extensive consultations and collaboration.

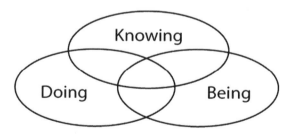

Competencies are those dispositions and capacities necessary to care well in inter-faith situations. Core competencies correlate with professional *standards* normally articulated by organizations such as the Association for Clinical Pastoral Education and the Canadian Association for Spiritual Care, or by governmental or ecclesiastic institutions. The standards embody key values and vocational commitments; they also identify certain legally binding professional and ethical requirements for effec-tive care giving. In sum, competencies are those personal and professional qualities or assets with which care givers meet the standards of practice in a wide variety of care giving settings.

A number of practitioners and researchers in the wider field of care and counseling have similarly presented three sets of core competencies. This is the case, for example, with Derald Wing Sue and David Sue concerning multicultural competence in counseling practice. These authors discuss fourteen competencies under the categories of *awareness* (e.g., being aware of and sensitive to one's own cultural heritage and to valuing and respecting differences); *knowledge* (e.g., becoming knowledgeable and informed on a number of culturally diverse groups, especially groups with which therapists work); and *skills* (e.g., being able to generate a wide variety of verbal and nonverbal helping responses; Sue and Sue 2008, 42-52). Other authors have integrated the contribution of Sue and Sue and others in their own three-fold characterization in terms of 1) caregivers' awareness of their own values and biases, 2) understanding of the clients' worldview, and 3) developing culturally appropriate intervention strategies and techniques (Corey, Corey and Callanan 2007, 141-148). Some government organizations also present a tripartite view of core competencies as "the essential knowledge, skills and attitudes necessary for the practice of …care" (Public Health Agency of Canada 2008, 1).

We find those considerations very useful and, in principle, transferable with regard to interfaith care giving. At the same time, we believe that the larger categories of *being, knowing* and *doing* can help us to present a more complete view of professional wisdom. That is especially the case regarding the "being" dimension, because in it we include competencies definable in terms of virtues (viewed as values embodied in the moral character of the caregiver) and faith development, which are not usually explicitly considered in current discussions and writings in the field.

Competencies of knowing (*understanding*)
In order to grow in pastoral wisdom, spiritual caregivers participate in what we might call "circles of learning" that include four dimensions: 1) actual experience of being cared for and caring for others (learning by "feeling"); 2) observation and reflection on care provided by others (learning by actively "seeing" and "hearing"); 3) systematic analysis of those practices of care (learning by "thinking"); and, 4) active experimentation with new ways of caring well for others (learning by "doing"). The more intentionally and consistently we participate in the four dimensions of the "circle," the more likely that our knowledge about interfaith care will increase. Supervision, seminars and consultation groups are fertile settings for developing knowledge and understanding related to spiritual care in interfaith

situations.[1] A sample of indicators of professional wisdom directly connected with this domain (*knowing*) include:

- a philosophy of spiritual care, including a view of human wholeness, truth, the good life, excellence in professional work (as seen especially in an ethic of care), grounded in one's faith tradition;
- optimal theoretical integration of spirituality, human science and theological perspectives;
- understanding of the complexities, dynamics and richness of interfaith situations, with appreciation for human and spiritual commonalities and due consideration to gender, culture, religious, family and social and political contexts;
- theological assessment that includes revisiting the validity of certain absolute, normative doctrinal claims, a selective reappropriation of theological and religious convictions, and rediscovery of the simplicity and beauty of core spiritual clues for interfaith care, etc.;
- linguistic-conceptual and "multilingual" competency (knowing a variety of psychological, theological and spiritual languages) born out of theological and human science perspectives and resources; and,
- clinical ways of knowing, such as interpretive frameworks (psychodynamic, systemic, etc.) that enhance understanding, communication, and ministerial practice of spiritual care.

Such comprehensive ways of *knowing* must always be closely related to the *being* and *doing* dimensions of professional wisdom, as briefly considered below.

Competencies of being (*presence*)
Professional wisdom is also a matter of "being" as well as "being with" that defines *presence*. Caregiving in interfaith situations involves special sensitivity and self-awareness regarding what one feels and experiences in the relationship. It also involves the sense that one represents not only a religious tradition and community but also, somehow, healing grace. We deem such embodiment essential to remind carereceivers that a caring Presence is available. Therefore, a sense of personal and professional (ministerial) identity is an essential component of being and presence. It is indispensable to engage the carereceiver in a relationship characterized first of all

---

[1] The writers co-led a year-long seminar group (2006-7) jointly sponsored by the Associated Mennonite Biblical Seminary and the Pastoral Care Department of Lutheran Hospital of Indiana. They have also presented numerous workshops on interfaith spiritual care in different settings in Canada, the US and Europe. Concerned with increasing the theoretical and practical-clinical knowledge of interfaith spiritual care, these events included actual caregiving practice, preparation and analysis of spiritual care situations, group and individual supervision of caregiving practice, discussion of readings and special topics of concern, and engagement in conversation and study with other health care professionals.

by respectful attending and listening. Such relationship allows the spiritual caregiver to be a witness, not primarily to "tell" carereceivers how to cope with or fix their situation, but rather to "admire," to behold with love and hope the mystery that is the stranger. Among the traits related to the *being* dimension of professional wisdom, we find the following essential:

- self-awareness and other indicators of emotional intelligence including: acknowledgment of strengths and limitations; movement beyond preoccupation with one's "ministerial-therapeutic" self (while maintaining clarity regarding identity as spiritual caregiver); and recognition of ways in which that ministerial self influences the interfaith encounter;

- moral character that integrates a plurality of attitudes and virtues such as: a capacity for wonder and respect in the face of the stranger; sensitivity and receptivity; courage to risk and to be surprised; freedom to be vulnerable and open to learning and growth; a disposition to recognize, accept and honor those deemed to be different; hospitality grounded in compassion, humility, and generosity; passion to care and creative energy to transform the inherent violence of separation, prejudice, and alienation into a way of being with (empathy) and for (sympathy) the other as neighbor and partner in care and healing; etc.;

- spirituality defined in part in terms of a "conjunctive faith" which informs ministry style. We have adopted the concept of *conjunctive faith* as presented by James Fowler (Fowler 1981, 184-98; Fowler 1987, 71-4, 92-8) which denotes a desirable level of faith development, as briefly characterized here in terms of: an ability to embrace ambiguity and paradox; a sense of truth that is multiform and complex; post-critical receptivity ("second naiveté") and readiness to participate in the reality expressed in symbols, myths and rituals of one's own tradition; genuine and disciplined openness to the truths of communities and traditions other than one's own (not to be equated with relativism); movement from the prevalence of certainty to the centrality of trust;

- a sense of personal and spiritual wellbeing, integrity and growth. While being aware of their own woundedness, wise spiritual caregivers normally experience holistic wellness of body, soul and spirit and an existentially fruitful and fulfilling life journey;

- a connection with a transcendent Source of love and grace. Christian spiritual caregivers often define such connections as a partnership with the Spirit of God or Holy Spirit to whom they attribute the power to heal even in the face of suffering and death.

Competencies of doing (*companioning*)

Accompaniment and *guidance* are words that name well what we actually do in spiritual care. On the one hand, spiritual caregivers are responsible for attending to and guiding the actual caregiving process as such. Guidance is a form of leading which includes setting appropriate boundaries of time, space, contact, and remaining fully aware of what is going on in the caregiving process. Guidance may include gently probing questions, encouragement and support, instructing, confronting and mediating. On the other hand, except in emergency or crisis situations, spiritual caregivers will not be directive and try to resolve the problems and struggles faced by carereceivers. Especially in interfaith situations, wise caregivers will rather help patients and others to use the specific spiritual resources that have been part of their lives or that may be now available for them. In short, accompaniment and guidance will optimally be a practice of wisdom—knowing how to relate and act in order to care well in interfaith situations. There is actually an interesting etymological connection between *wisdom* and *guidance*. In English, the words *wisdom* and *wise* derive from the Indo-European root *weid-*, which means *to see* or *to know.* They are related to the Greek *eidos* (idea, form, seeing), to the Latin *videre* (to see), and to the modern German *wissen* (to know). The word *guide* comes from an ancient Romanic word *widare*, which means to know. The words *wise*, *wisdom*, *wit*, and *guide* all share the same origin. Therefore, among other competencies and skills, effective caregivers will be able to:

- relate to care-seekers, their relatives, and colleagues in ways that engage their spirituality and facilitate spiritual assessment, including the skill to articulate desired outcomes of spiritual care;

- internally monitor ongoing caregiving practice so as to remain carereceiver-centered, avoiding cultural and spiritual invasion or intrusiveness, and open to receiving manifold gifts from carereceivers even as caring well for them; actively listen and discern the appropriateness and timeliness of specific caregiving gestures, use of language and action. Fittingly provide opportune responses in a variety of caregiving modes (e.g., probing, supporting, encouraging, comforting, guiding, confronting, mediating, reconciling, evoking, advocating; praying, blessing, anointing, and others);

- reflect pastorally-theologically on ministerial practice on an ongoing basis and continually develop a practical theology of interfaith care;

- actively partner with the Spirit of God while anticipating and participating in caregiving ministry (e.g., by privately praying for oneself and for care-seekers, engaging in contemplation and meditation, and other spiritual disciplines); and

- maintain patterned practices of self-care with adequate attention to physical, emotional and relational needs and to spiritual nourishment.

Holistic professional formation

It has become more and more apparent that the education of interfaith spiritual caregivers in professional wisdom requires that theological education and ministerial formation be holistic and comprehensive. For example, as articulated in the standards of the Association of Theological Schools, such formation must include three equally important and interrelated aspects: academic, personal-spiritual and professional. Further, such education must include specific pedagogies of interpretation, contextualization, formation and performance.

The *academic* formation of interfaith caregivers is indispensable because, among other things, it includes learning about one's own (religious or nonreligious) faith tradition or heritage and as much as possible about other traditions. Philosophies, theoretical frameworks and other resources stemming from the human sciences are also indispensable. Academic formation further includes learning about the social, cultural and institutional contexts of caregiving work. Therefore, this dimension of education and ministerial formation must focus primarily, although by no means exclusively, on learning and developing competencies of *knowing* for wise caregiving as highlighted above.

Personal-spiritual formation focuses on the identity and integrity of interfaith spiritual caregivers primarily but not exclusively as representatives of a given tradition. Personal-spiritual formation primarily involves attending to oneself as a human and spiritual being and to nurturing one's moral character and particularly one's vocation. Hence, this dimension of education and ministerial formation is concerned primarily with fostering and nurturing the competencies of *being* for wise ministry practice. Indeed, those competencies will directly inform the content of specific curricular learning goals towards personal-spiritual formation.

The *vocational-professional* formation of wise spiritual caregivers centers on the development of those clinical and other habits, skills, methods and approaches necessary for caring effectively and faithfully. Therefore, the third aspect of theological education and ministerial formation of interfaith spiritual caregivers must focus primarily on the development and practice of competencies of performance—i.e., the *doing* dimension of the profile—as the main curricular goal.

These three resulting sets of goals of theological education and ministerial formation must be duly integrated and approached through appropriate, mutually complementary pedagogies. Recent reflection on pedagogies for educating clergy can be helpfully applied to the formation of wise spiritual caregivers as described below (Foster, Dahill, Golemon and Tolentino 2006, 67-186).

Pedagogies of interpretation focus the attention of caregivers as interpreters on their interaction with their tradition and with other sources of knowledge, particularly their relationship with careseekers. They especially seek to foster the abilities to "read" adequately and analyze human situations, and to think and reflect critically and creatively. They are aimed at expanding and deepening *understanding* through interpretive practice. Pedagogies of contextualization are closely related, as they seek to develop the spiritual caregivers' consciousness of context, the ability to participate constructively in the encounter of diverse contexts and to engage in the transformation of contexts.

Pedagogies of formation aim at fostering personal integrity and professional identity. Specific strategies that contribute to the formation of ministering caregivers, especially those representing certain religious traditions, may include: awakening students to the presence of God; practicing holiness, i.e., nurturing those dispositions and habits that embody religious commitments integral to the identity of ministering persons; and practicing religious leadership whose very *presence* communicates grace and wisdom.

Pedagogies of performance focus on the interaction of academic and religious expectations for effective leadership in ministerial practice. They seek to prepare caregivers to be adequately proficient in meeting a wide variety of expectations for excellence in interfaith care. In sum, they are learning strategies aimed at equipping caregivers for the ministerial art of *companioning*.

References:

Anderson, Robert G. and Mary A. Fukuyama, eds. 2004. *Ministry in the Spiritual and Cultural Diversity of Health Care: Increasing the Competency of Chaplains.* New York: The Haworth Pastoral Press.

Ansari, Bilal. 2009. Seeing with Bifocals: The Evolution of a Muslim Chaplain. *Reflective Practice: Formation and Supervision in Ministry* 29:170-177.

Augsburger, David W. 1986. *Counseling Across Cultures.* Philadelphia: Westminster Press.

Breitman, Barbara Eve. 2005. Foundations of Jewish Pastoral Care: Skills and Techniques. In *Jewish Pastoral Care: A Practical Handbook from Traditional and Contemporary Sources*, 2nd ed., ed. Dayle A. Friedman, 95-124. Woodstock VT: Jewish Lights Publishing.

Bueckert, Leah Dawn and Daniel S. Schipani. 2006a. Interfaith Spiritual Care: The Case for Language Care. In *Spiritual Caregiving in the Hospital; Windows to Chaplaincy Ministry,* eds. Leah Dawn Bueckert and Daniel S. Schipani, 245-263. Kitchener ONT: Pandora Press.

_____. 2006b. The Chaplain as Reflective Practitioner and Pastoral Theologian. In Spiritual *Caregiving in the Hospital; Windows to Chaplaincy Ministry,* eds. Leah Dawn Bueckert and Daniel S. Schipani, 205-218. Kitchener ONT: Pandora Press.

van Buuren, Ari, Mualla Kaya, and Bart Ten Broek, 2009. The Junction of the Seas: Interfaith Spiritual Care in the Netherlands. In *Interfaith Spiritual Care: Understandings and Practices,* eds. Daniel S. Schipani and Leah Dawn Bueckert, 279-313. Kitchener, ONT.: Pandora Press.

Corey, Gerald, Marianne Schneider Corey and Patrick Callanan. 2007. *Issues and Ethics in the Helping Professions.* Belmont CA: Brooks-Cole-Thomson Learning.

Driedger, Patricia Morrison. 2009. Different Lyrics but the Same Tune: Multifaith Spiritual Care in a Canadian Context. In Interfaith *Spiritual Care; Understandings and Practices,* eds. Daniel S. Schipani and Leah Dawn Bueckert, 129-142. Kitchener ONT: Pandora Press.

Farris, James R. 2009. Interfaith Spiritual Care: A View from Brazil. In *Spiritual Caregiving in the Hospital; Windows to Chaplaincy Ministry,* eds. Leah Dawn Bueckert and Daniel S. Schipani, 171-190. Kitchener ONT: Pandora Press.

Foster, Charles R., Lisa E. Dahill, Lawrence A. Golemon and Barbara Wang Tolentino. 2006. *Educating Clergy: Teaching Practices and Pastoral Imagination.* San Francisco: Jossey-Bass.

Fowler, James H. 1981. *Stages of Faith: The Psychology of Human Development and the Quest for Meaning.* San Francisco: Harper and Row.

_____. 1987. *Faith Development and Pastoral Care.* Philadelphia: Fortress Press.

Friedman, Dayle A., ed. 2005. *Jewish Pastoral Care: A Practical Handbook from Traditional and Contemporary Sources.* 2nd ed. Woodstock VT: Jewish Light Publishing.

Isgandarova, Nazila. 2005. Islamic Spiritual Care in a Health Care Setting. In *Spirituality and Health: Multidisciplinary Explorations*, eds. Augustine Meier, Thomas St. James O'Connor and Peter L. VanKatwik, 85-104. Waterloo ONT: Waterloo University Press.

Koenig, Harold G. 2007. *Spirituality in Patient Care: Why, How, When, and What.* 2nd ed. Philadephia and London: Templeton Foundation Press.

Lahaj, Mary. 2009. Making Up as I Go Along: The Formation of a Muslim Caregiver. *Reflective Practice: Formation and Supervision in Ministry* 29:148-153.

Lartey, Emmanuel Y. 2003. *In Living Color: An Intercultural Approach to Pastoral Care and Counseling.* 2nd ed. London-New York: Jessica Kingsley Publishers.

Miller, William R., ed. 1999. *Integrating Spirituality into Treatment: Resources for Practitioners.* Washington DC: American Psychological Association.

Patton, John. 2006. *Pastoral Care: An Essential Guide.* Nashville: Abingdon Press.

Pergola, Michael. 2009. Nurturing Inter-Spiritual Hearts and Interfaith Minds. *Reflective Practice: Formation and Supervision in Ministry* 29:119-127.

Peterson, John. 2009. A Lutheran Chaplain's Nine Thesis on Interfaith Care. In *Interfaith Spiritual Care: Understandings and Practices*, eds. Daniel S. Schipani and Leah Dawn Bueckert, 69-80. Kitchener ONT: Pandora Press.

Public Health Agency of Canada. 2008. *Core Competencies for Public Health Service in Canada.* Ottawa: Ministry of Health.

Richards, P. Scott and Allen E. Bergin. 1997. *A Spiritual Strategy for Counseling and Psychotherapy.* Washington DC: American Psychological Association.

_____. 2000. *Handbook of Psychotherapy and Religious Diversity.* Washington DC: American Psychological Association.

Schipani, Daniel S. 2009. Interfaith Pastoral Care in the Hospital: A Project in Pastoral and Practical Theology. In *Secularization Theories, Religious Identity and*

Practical Theology: Developing International Practical Theology for the 21st Century, eds. Wilhelm Grab and Lars Charbonnier, 407-414. Berlin: Lit Verlag.

Schipani, Daniel S. and Leah Dawn Bueckert. 2009. *Interfaith Spiritual Care: Understandings and Practices.* Kitchener ONT: Pandora Press.

_____. 2009b. Explorations I: Applying an Interpretive Framework, and Explorations III: An Exercise in Pastoral Theological Imagination. In *Interfaith Spiritual Care: Understandings and Practice,* eds. Daniel S. Schipani and Leah Dawn Bueckert, 89-98, 105-112. Kitchener ONT: Pandora Press.

Stairs, Jean. 2000. *Listening for the Soul: Pastoral Care and Spiritual Direction.* Minneapolis: Fortress Press.

Sue, Derald Wing and David Sue. 2008. *Counseling the Culturally Diverse: Theory and Practice.* 5th ed. Hoboken NJ: John Wiley and Sons.

Taylor, Elizabeth Johnston. 2007. *What Do I Say? Talking with Patients about Spirituality.* Philadelphia-London: Templeton Foundation Press.

Walther, Tabitha. 2009. Interfaith Formation for Religious Leaders in a Multifaith Society: Between Meta-Spiritualities and Strong Religious Profiles. *Reflective Practice: Formation and Supervision in Ministry* 29:128-134.

Weis, Helmut. 2009. Interreligious and Intercultural Pastoral Care and Counseling: Notes from a German Perspective. In *Interfaith Spiritual Care: Understandings and Practice.* eds. Daniel S. Schipani and Leah Dawn Bueckert, 235-258. Kitchener ONT: Pandora Press.

Doing Theology in a Globalized World: Religion, Diversity and Conflicts in Films

Wilhelm Gräb

Abstract: *This essay refers to God-Talk as reflection about lived religion in a media age. Three film—"Cast away," "As it is in Heaven," and "Babel" —are analyzed in order to illustrate forms of God-Talk in modern media. Watching films may stimulate spiritual experiences and theological reflections. If it is true that because of a spiritual need and a need for God-Talk every human being is motivated to theological reflection—because the quest about the last unconditional meaning of life is imposed on all of us—films open up a wide range of theological thinking. The question is whether the framework of Christian tradition provides sufficient room for theological reflection. Popular culture has developed its own reflective framework and basic thinking about fundamental human issues. Films may create a new understanding of these topics. The pluralism that confronts the cinema-goer differs from the uniformity of the belief-system which the traditional church-goer faces. To be in dialogue with others' world views, cultures, languages and theological frameworks of thinking is one of the most compelling challenges in the globalized world of today.*

Theology as reflection about lived religion in a media age

God-Talk is reflection about the deepest interests of human life: how one can discover meaning and coherence in the course of life, and which aspects of one's biography are worth acceptance in spite of all contingency and irrationality. Theology is reflection on the thinking about God. In our human language the word "God" embraces an ultimate reality and gives it a significant interpretation. As Christian theologians we know the biblical interpretation of God's word. It is the word of God as the creator and redeemer in Jesus Christ.

Doing theology in a media age does not mean that the biblical interpretation of the word of God is left behind. It is directed much more to investigate the continuance and the transformation of God-Talk in the wider context of a Christian influenced but at the same time post-Christian, secular and in some aspects also post-secular society. Doing theology in a media age means tracing the reflection on the deepest human interests like love and justice, sin and grace, creativity and fulfilment in works of popular culture. As one example, films are increasingly important for theological thinking because they talk often about God and stimulate theological reflection in the spectators' minds (Marsh 2007).

We begin with the Hollywood film "Cast Away" (directed by Robert Zemeckis, USA 2000) with Tom Hanks as the leading character. This film narrates the story of a manager of a large transport company who is the only survivor of an airplane crash. After more than 4 years on an island in the Pacific Ocean during which he is personally transformed he is rescued and finds his way back home. When he comes back, however, his wife is remarried. He has to find his way in a new life. The story of this film motivates the viewer to ask, "What does it mean to be thrown back on to myself, to look for things which enable me to carry on living, to reflect on the meaning and the final destination of my life, to look after relationships which give me support?"

The film demonstrates how a person finds new strength in a life crisis. Attention is drawn to the fact that life is not a personal achievement but a gift from outside. What is my relationship to this mysterious dimension which I cannot control but upon which I depend in an absolute sense? In a life crisis it can become obvious that life is a gift, but also that we have to live it in a new and more reflective way—but in which direction and with which goal? Discussing the film "Cast Away," perhaps with a group in your congregation, may draw people into a conversation about the goals of their lives, about crises in their own lives and how to deal with them.

In some parts of the film we can also find traditional religious symbols, for example wings of an angel that the protagonist finds on a parcel which was originally in the airplane and which he returns to its sender after he has been rescued. Such traditional religious symbols have the function of underlining the message of the film in general. The message is exactly a religious or spiritual one and it tells us that we do not have everything in our own hands. We live under a higher power which determines our fate. We cannot recognize what it is but we believe that it is there. There are good reasons to believe in this divine power because it is the ground of self-confidence in the world. God is the ground of our ability to act. The Bible speaks about this God, identifying him with the power of love and unity, forgiveness and creativity, describing him as concretely human in Jesus Christ, as present in those who believe in Jesus Christ through His activity in the Holy Spirit. The film does not explicitly suggest this kind of theological interpretation of the transcendent power that provides human beings with confidence in their life course, but viewers of the film are capable of such interpretations of this transcendent dimension in their life.

The film motivates viewers to be aware of how contingent life is, how fragmentary it is and yet still related to a higher power outside of us. They are motivated to talk about their own experiences of crises and more, as the film also hints that this higher power is a God of love who provides the strength to survive in hard situations. It further shows that crises have a particular power to help people realize the importance of good relationships to the divine as well as to other persons whom they trust.

Watching films may stimulate spiritual experiences and theological reflections. There is also an emotional dimension to this practice. Watching a film may become a ritual-like practice with a symbolic value. If we do not want to constrain theology to the church's dogmatic reflection and to its function for Christian communities in a narrower sense, analyzing films and other aspects of popular culture should enrich the theological discussion. If it is true that because of a spiritual need and a need for God-Talk every human being is motivated to theological reflection; the quest about the last unconditional meaning of life is imposed on all of us. Films open up a wide range of theological thinking.

In terms of traditional systematic theology, a theology of film is the continuation of the theology of the word of the triune God in consequence of a postmodern und post-secular society. In the theology of the word of God developed by Karl Barth under the condition of the post-enlightenment-situation, the word of God and there-fore his human presence stands for the communicable human word. The presence of this God who is the redeemer in Jesus Christ is communication in the Christian community which is fulfilled with the presence of the Holy Spirit. Yet, in Barth's theology this specific theological topic has a universal significance. God makes us understand each other. Reconciliation is nothing else but communication, as Karl Barth points out in Part IV of the *Kirchliche Dogmatik*, written in the early 1960s. The basis of communication and understanding between human beings who are in struggle against each other is Jesus Christ the incarnated and crucified God. At the core of his work Karl Barth always intends to explain that proclaiming Jesus Christ as the redeemer means explaining how communication can take place among human beings who are struggling against each other. Reconciliation is just the biblical expression for the principal conditions of human communication and understanding.

The continuation of this post-enlightenment theology of the word of God under the socio-cultural conditions of the media age is a theology reflecting the quest of meaning and God-Talk in the popular media culture, especially in films.

Theological reflection in films
Thinking about what it means to be a human being engages a whole range of issues. We are asking how our identity and our destination as human beings have been formed, how we relate to others, how we relate to nature, what value we attach to the material world, what we think a human being is, how we respond to evil (in ourselves and in the world around us), which groups we attach ourselves to and why, and what will happen when we die.

The consideration of such basic human issues is part of the belief-system of a relig-ion. The Christian tradition gives specific answers to these questions. Continuing to think about these basic human issues from a Christian perspective is a challenge to the church. The churches and Christian congregations are, indeed, still present in the public sphere in terms of bringing people together and educating them to understand the Christian faith and what it means to live in a Christian community. Nevertheless, in what Charles Taylor calls this *Secular Age* there is an enormous gap between the traditional doctrine of the Christian faith on the one hand and the practiced spiritual-ity or ordinary folk on the other hand. Sociological research in the field of religion shows us that in the broader society, outside the institutionalized Church and tight-knit Christian communities, there is hardly a notion or confident acceptance of the topics of Christian doctrine and its God-Talk. Consequently there are two fields of modern theology. On the one hand, theology is still reflecting on the Christian tradition and on God-Talk within the framework of the Christian tradition. On the other hand, there is a notion of spirituality as a lived experience of a personal relationship with the divine around fundamental human issues in the more private sphere of individual lives. Most important here is the realization that popular culture has developed more effective forms of reflective frameworks for basic thinking about fundamental human issues than Christian theology has. There is also the word of God outside the church. Karl Barth called these traces of reflection "beams of light" into the world which indicates the presence of God's love and the work of His redeeming acts.

Films in cinemas, on television or available on DVDs produce for the broader society what theology (in its usual form) provides for the institutionalized Church and for the Christian community. Films stimulate the reflection of basic human thinking about what it means to be a human being, about human flourishing and destination, destruction and error, fulfilment and meaning. Films also refer to a broader theological framework but in a way which, in the perspective of the church, may seem heretical. This is the theologically interesting point. Films retell the Christian story and they also reflect theologically but in strange and odd forms. They talk about God by using new and unusual images. They confront us with sin and redemption but by doing so provide us with a new perspective unlike traditional Christian doctrine.

For example, in the Swedish film "As it is in Heaven" (directed by Kay Pollak, Sweden 2005) we cannot only find many spiritual motives but also a new formulation of the Christian doctrine of sin and redemption. The Lutheran minister in this film is preaching the doctrine of sin as a moral condemnation of human freedom. In his view sin is not the loss of God who is love and fulfilment of life but a lack of a narrowly defined and traditional morality. With the image of this Lutheran minister the film shows a cold, uninviting church producing a dark and unhappy form of Christianity. However, under the veneer of this theology of sin the real evil in the community and hypocrisy among the people is happening. Eventually a redeemer from outside is able to show the community how to recognize the true misery among them, the real sin. He shows the community how to escape evil and how to experience grace, love and unconditional acceptance. Here the experience of love and partnership is identified with the relationship to the divine. Those who live their relationship with God and, therefore, feel His love can become self-confident human beings. The redeemer from outside helps the villagers to discover their inner voice, to perceive the value of their personal lives, to realize their destination and to find a supportive community. There is the example of a woman which suffers under domestic violence and who rediscovers her own human dignity.

The redeemer is the famous conductor Daniel Dareus (Michael Myquist). He returns to his childhood village in search of peace and rest. Yet, he stirs up painful memories and jealousies when he takes on the role of the choir master in the tiny community. The choir is a platform for bringing characters together but also for revealing the chasms within the village and its relationships. The rural setting underlines the isolation of the village, focusing the drama on its core elements: the nature and the danger of community.

The danger ranges from domestic violence to intolerance of all kinds, often seething under the surface of genteel neighbourliness. The screenplay digs even deeper still when the pastor's wife Inger (Ingela Olsson) confronts her husband (Niklas Falk) with her buried secret of 20 years: she doesn't believe there is sin ... it's an invention by the church, she says, which has an interest in offering absolution. The confrontation is triggered by the sweeping changes that Daniel's passion for music has brought to the community, and feelings about religion are not the only kind of emotions Inger has been repressing.

The title embraces the basic human need for happiness and its spiritual equivalent, themes with which the film deals in subtle but powerful ways. The movie stimulates the viewer to pose questions regarding the place of the established religion, the Lutheran Church standing for law and order, violence and masks. The answer offered by the film seems to lie in mustering up the personal courage needed to confront one's personal hypocrisy, to strive for authenticity and for a community which strives for peace and justice, in which each person can find their personal identity, dignity and integrity.

The film "As it is in Heaven" corresponds to many other films, especially those directed by the Swedish director Ingmar Bergman. In his films Bergman, son of a Lutheran pastor in the Swedish State-Church, reflects on the gap between the essence of the Christian faith—the belief in God who is love and mercy—and a Church that represents law and order based on a narrow understanding of God's will. These films have to be understood as a critique of the Church but they also try to indicate that in secular societies in which people become distanced from the church there is still a religious and spiritual need, a search for human destination and for a deeper meaning of life. There is a need to find God who stands for the fulfilment of life, the recognition of the highest good. The point of God-Talk is the search for a social and cultural environment in which the dignity of each human being can be acknowledged.

Today there are many films which engage religious thinking of that kind. We can observe that films can address ethical issues, e.g., helping someone to die in "One Million Dollar Baby" (directed by Clint Eastwood, USA 2004), environmental matters in "Jurassic Park" (directed by Steven Spielberg, USA 1993) or regarding the quest for peace and justice in several critical films about war and totalitarian regimes. Through films religious topics in their Christian understanding are made manifest in the public sphere and even in the minds and hearts of people who are not involved in Christian communities and their ritual practices.

Today religions find themselves in a situation of pluralism, confronted with different and sometimes conflicting world-views and religious affiliations. Individuals as well as different communities are confronted with this pluralism but they still need to find some ways of working out who they are and where they think they are heading. We have to look to film-watching, the part of people's leisure in which religious practice is also located for many. Watching films in cinemas or at home on TV or on-line is a kind of activity which often provokes critical reflection without being intended as such. This is how philosophical and theological reflection often occurs: in response to the practice of living and the search for meaning as a constitutive dimension of this practice. Film is part of the "package" of available media that people access in order to create meaning. Film primarily functions through emotions, while at the same time it influences the senses. It has the capacities as a medium to get viewers experientially involved in the subject matter of the narratives it presents.

Viewers are introduced to a realm of possibilities for developing their own interpretations of their lives and their worldviews, which are theological interpretations in the sense that they reflect on the quest for an ultimate reality. By doing so, they have the freedom to use the images and the stories in their own way, to find their own voice.

In considering film and theology together, the discipline of theology is reminded that it is itself a multi-dimensional discipline. Theology is more than just ideas and beliefs based on biblical texts. It relates to a wide range of human practices and life experiences. Theology must see itself as a discipline that takes account of the affective, aesthetic and ethical aspects of being human, as well as the cognitive side. And all of these aspects of being human occur in embodied form. We feel, sense and act, as well as think as embodied beings. By watching films theologians become involved in all these aspects of human life. So the quest of meaning and the way theology deals with these questions become concrete.

How God Talk can happen in a disrupted world
The Christian framework of thinking based on the biblical issues of creation, sin and redemption embedded in a community of practice embraces all the religious issues: meaning, purpose, how to live and the nature of reality. Therefore it can be argued that cinema and film-watching function in a "religion-like" way. Cinema is religion-like because it is based upon an understanding of the power of stories and the extent to which human beings need stories in order to create meaning. The dramatic visual and aural form in which films present stories makes their narratives more accessible and compelling. At the same time cinema is unlike religion in so far as one is not presented with a single story or a set of stories. In films made for public consumption multiple world-views and ideologies are explicitly and implicitly conveyed. This illustrates the

extent to which a contemporary western person is confronted with a diversity of options and concepts of life. The pluralism with which the cinema-goer is confronted differs from the uniformity of the belief-system which the traditional church-goer faces. This is one of the most important reasons why film-watching is also essential for theologians. It helps to put the Christian story and the frame for thinking theologically in dialogue with others' world views and it also contributes to disclosing the Christian tradition in other stories. To be in dialogue with others' world views, cultures, languages and theological frameworks is one of the most compelling challenges in today's globalized world.

One film that deals with these challenges in a Christian framework is the film "Babel" (directed by González Iñárritu, Japan, Mexico, Morocco, and USA 2007). "Babel" is based upon a handful of verses in the 11th chapter of Genesis which illustrate, among other things, the terrible consequences of unchecked ambitions. As a punishment for trying to build a tower that would reach the heavens, human beings were scattered over the face of the earth in a state of confusion—divided, dislocated and unable to communicate. In the globalized world of today we find ourselves more or less in a similar situation. The film "Babel" tells four distinct stories, disclosing bit by bit the chronology and causality that link them and emphasizing the linguistic, cultural and geographical distances between the characters. The movie travels—often by means of abrupt cuts and tone shifts—from the barren mountains of Morocco where the dominant sound is howling wind, to fluorescent Tokyo where the natural world has been almost entirely supplanted by a technological environment, to the anxious border between the United States and Mexico. Each place has its own aural and visual palette. The languages used by the astonishingly diverse cast include Spanish, Berber, Japanese, sign language and English. The misunderstandings multiply accordingly, though they tend to be most acute between husbands and wives or parents and children, rather than between strangers. Surely, something must hold this world—or, at any rate, this film's vision of the world—together. What is it? "Babel" tells stories which represent a world full of differences, misunderstandings and violence. It tells stories of sin but at the end it gives also hints to something that can be understood as redemption.

What is it that produces differences, misunderstanding, fear and anger, suffering and hopelessness, desire and despair? What are the faces of sin? What makes sin so dominant? The film "Babel" reveals the nature of sin and therefore the reason why the world is so disrupted. Sin is grounded on the inability to see the other human being as a person like oneself with the same basic needs for acceptance, love and mercy. Sin is the loss of the human dimension. Sin is the hubris which does not see the needs of the other as it only realizes one's own need for recognition. Sin is the inability to listen to the other and consequently the inability to understand the other.

There is no God-Talk in "Babel" but allusions to the biblical story of the tower of Babel as a symbol of the human sin are always present. The end of the film opens up a Christian framework for thinking which makes it possible to identify the inability to communicate with the loss of contact with God, who is the common ground of unity between all human beings and between human beings and the world. In this film sin ultimately damages the possibility to be or become human, while the tension between unity and difference can only be relieved by God.

The film does not explain the doctrine of sin in a scholarly manner. The film narrates different stories that, at first viewing, do not have any connection which each other. In this way the film raises questions about what it is that separates people from each other. If we look to the different languages, cultures and finally to political situations—the dangerous borders between nations, the enormous gap between rich and poor countries, between economically developed areas and those which are less developed—we see nothing else but deep differences and causes of misunderstanding, social distance and hatred between people. Nevertheless, just looking to what makes people different does not reach the core of their feelings, emotions, needs, desires, fears and hopes. The film also gives some hints about what brings people together, that there is something that can grow inside and between individuals that connects them in spite of their differences in language, culture, gender, power and social positions.

"Babel" uses impressive images of human faces to depict the inner feelings of love which bind them together. I think its thesis is that the disrupted world is held together by the non-verbal language of emotions, love and the experience of (physical) proximity. All four stories in "Babel" start with a conflict based on an inability to communicate rooted in some past injury. A past event makes man and woman, father and daughter, father and sons strangers to each other. There is a deep gap between them based on misunderstandings and the unwillingness to listen to each other. Most painful is the inability to listen. The characters in this film are not able access the feelings and the thinking of the other, as though a wall separates the characters in the different stories.

What is the case on the level of personal encounter also occurs between the different cultures, nations and races. The stories play in different parts of the globalized world. What makes these parts of the world—the desert in Morocco, the big city in Japan, the border between the USA and Mexico—so different from each other? Not the behavior and the reactions of the human beings, not the feelings and the thinking of the people, not their desires, their anxieties and hopes. What disrupts the world and divides it into pieces are the national borders, the political statements of power, the differing achievements of civilizations, and the differing levels of economic development. Yet, if we take a closer look the film shows us that human beings in different parts of the world with their different civilizations share the same experiences and the same difficulties in understanding each other. They have the same needs for love and human touch but the same difficulties in recognizing this because they are not in contact with their feelings. They are not in contact with themselves. In Morocco and Tokyo, in San Diego and Mexico live people with the same inability to listen to each other. They have the same problems in understanding each other because they do not know the language of their emotions; they share the desire for love and acceptance but they do not recognize that. At the end there are some signs that people begin to recognize their equivalent needs for emotional nearness, love and acknowledgement of their human dignity. This is the first step towards reconciliation.

What holds the globalized world together? It is not global travel or the connectivity of international news on television or the World Wide Web. The divided world is unified by human faces with their anger and fear, their tears and laughter. In all the stories which "Babel" narrates we can detect signs of redemption in the unexpected non-verbal movements toward (physical) proximity. The way to reconciliation is through sensitivity for the emotions of others. The feeling of love is the ultimate human reality and symbol of the presence of God in the world.

Some of the pieces of "Babel" are attached to one another by the banal lingua franca of television images as, for example, events in North Africa make the evening news in Tokyo. However, director González Iñárritu's own visual grammar tries to go deeper, to suggest a common idiom of emotion present in certain gestures and expressions that can immediately be recognized. We may not be able to read minds or decipher words, he suggests, but we can surely decode faces, especially when we see them at close range and in distress. Loss, fear, pain, anguish—none of these emotions, it seems, are likely to be lost in translation.

Can it be that human beings are deeply connected by basic nonverbal emotions? Is, therefore, a theology of basic human feelings the Christian interpretative key for finding a way to overcome what makes us different and to realize what holds the world together and connects all human beings? Is the possibility of understanding each other at the level of feelings a glimpse of how divine redemption works?

What is sin? If sin is the inability to communicate then the first step to redemption is recognizing our need for love, acceptance and nearness and thus creating a better understanding of what human beings have in common. "Babel" suggests that our feelings of love enable a deep connectivity. Hatred or other forms of distance between human beings is a result of culturally performed desires. Basic human emotions such as love and the human need for touch are older than culture or civilization. Those emotions and needs emerge in the early relationships between mother and son or daughter and father—one of the last images of this film. Emotions of hatred and animosity produced by different cultures and religions can be overcome. The basic feelings which all human beings have in common can be recognized. This is the first step that leads to understanding and therefore to redemption. People become able to read between the lines and they realize that listening to the other is the beginning of being understood.

References:

Marsh, Clive. 2007. *Theology goes to the movies: an introduction to critical Christian thinking.* London and New York: Routledge

Peace Building
and
Reconciliation

Cultural Wars, Systematic Fear, or Lack of Trust? Different Perspectives on Congregational Conflict

Rein Brouwer

Abstract: Conflict, a mixture of cooperation and competitiveness between interdependent people, is endemic to congregational life. Consequently, Christian faith communities should improve their ability in dealing openly with conflict. In order to enhance the comprehension of conflict within congregations, this article compares three different approaches to congregational conflict: the sociology of organization approach from a new institutionalism perspective by Penny Edgell Becker; the systemic work of church consultant Speed Leas; and the pastoral/ethical-contextual approach developed by the Hungarian American family-therapist Ivan Boszormenyi-Nagy. These different theoretical and practical approaches to congregational conflict are compared and interpreted. Their interconnectedness is discerned against the background of Richard Osmer's communicative model of rationality. These three approaches are presented as complementary, with a slight inclination to the contextual approach, because the root metaphor of "balance of trust" resonates with the theological discourse in Scripture and tradition.

Introduction

Ecumenical ecclesiology perceives Christian communities of faith "to be God's instrument in the reconciliation of human division and hatred" (WCC 2005, 40). Nevertheless, the church is not free from division. God's gift of communion (*koinonia*) is threatened by heresies and schisms, as well as by dissent and indifference. That is why Christian communities "are called to work untiringly to overcome divisions, to prevent legitimate diversities from becoming causes of division, and to live a life of diversities reconciled" (WCC 2005, 63). Overcoming violence, resolving conflict, and reconciling division is not easy, especially when such fights are religiously charged. Furthermore, the record of accomplishment of faith communities in dealing constructively with conflicts is not encouraging. "Congregational conflict is a near fact of life" (Roozen 2007, 20), according to Dave Roozen, director of the Faith Communities Today (FACT) project. The FACT 2005 survey showed that a majority of US congregations (57%) reported either a minor or a major conflict in the two years prior to the survey. More than two thirds (69%) reported a loss of members, one quarter (25%) a pastor leaving, and just over a third (39%) reported members withholding contributions to the congregation. "In the United States conflict is a synonym for congregation" (Dudley 2001). Conflict, as a mixture of cooperation and competitiveness between interdependent people (Deutsch and Coleman 2000), is endemic to congregational life. Consequently, Christian faith communities should improve their ability to dealing openly with conflict in order to avoid, reduce, or redirect conflict.

Penny Edgell (Becker), professor of Sociology at the University of Minnesota, presented an organizational approach to congregational conflict from a new institutionalism perspective in her *Congregations in Conflict*. It is an interesting and valuable theoretical and empirical contribution to the issue of congregational conflict. However, our perspective on conflicts in faith communities should not be restricted to new institutionalism theory within the discipline of sociology. In order to interpret the multidimensional phenomenon of an internal religious group conflict, reductionism should be avoided. Understanding this phenomenon requires multiple disciplinary approaches and empirical methods (McGrath 2006, 209-226; Osmer 2008, 118-121). That warrants relating Becker's institutional approach to congregational conflict with the work of church consultant Speed Leas, as well as with the ethical approach developed by the Hungarian American family-therapist Ivan Boszormenyi-Nagy (1920-2007).

First, I will map Becker's disciplinary perspective, the root metaphor of her theory and the conceptual field that is implied. After the analysis of Becker's conflict theory, I will elaborate on a systems approach to congregational conflict in order to broaden Becker's argumentation. Beyond systemic theory, I will advance a contextual-ethical approach, by identifying with a contextual working pastor consulting a congregation in conflict. The different theoretical and practical approaches to congregational conflict will be compared and interpreted and their interconnectedness discerned against the background of Richard Osmer's "communicative model of rationality" within a "transversal model of cross-disciplinary dialogue" (Osmer 2008, 100-103,114-128, 170-172). I will present the three approaches or perspectives on congregational conflict as complementary, although I am slightly inclined to the contextual approach, because the root metaphor of "balance of trust" resonates in a remarkable way with the theological discourse in Scripture and tradition.

Power struggle
Building on a research review, Becker (1999) stated that the dimensions of congregational size, polity and culture do not qualify as causes for conflicts, as previous literature presumed. These dimensions do have some effect on conflict, but they fall short in predicting and explaining the overall pattern of conflict. Becker found a more adequate explanation in the culture of the congregation as a group, and in congregational models that define the particular congregations. This is part of the organizational approach of new institutionalism, developed by Paul J. DiMaggio and Walter Powell. Organizational cultures consist of local interpretations of identity and mission that are presented as bundles of core tasks (Becker 1998; DiMaggio 1998). Becker identified four dominant patterns or congregational models in nearly all of the twenty-three congregations she researched: a house of worship, a family, a community, and a leader congregational model. Only four of the congregations, characterized as "congregations in transition," deviated from the identified models. Becker deduced a selective affinity between these cases and the intractability of

conflict. In all the researched congregations she discovered conflicts, but only in the congregations in transition were conflicts "intractable, acrimonious, uncontainable, protracted, escalated," and part of a "destructive and escalatory cycle of conflict." Becker wondered how these cases could fit in the interpretation of conflict and decided to combine them into a category of their own: mixed congregations. Mixed congregations fight over identity and opposite expectations. Not so much a "culture war," in the sense of liberals and conservatives fighting each other over same sex marriages or the creation-evolution controversy, this could be considered more a "between frames" argument over the identity of the congregation and differing identity assumptions.

By using concepts like "transition," "mixed" and "between frames" related to the intractability of conflict, Becker reveals a bellicose root metaphor in her congregational conflict discourse. As a sociologist, Becker is at ease with perceiving conflict as a "battle" of incompatible interests, a "struggle for power," people that "vie for control" and two tribes "going to war."

In one of the four mixed congregations, the conflict comprised a series of collisions (Becker 1999, 149-157). There were three main points of discord in this Unitarian Universalist church in the Chicago area, all related to the pastor. An "anti-pastor group" came into existence that brought mostly long-time members together, who experienced the congregation as a family. They stood against the pro-pastor faction composed of newcomers who favored social action and outreach. At the end, the pastor resigned and people on both sides left the congregation. There was "a great consciousness of winners and losers." The newcomers reproached the older members with feeling disproportionate ownership, while the older members in return accused the others of trying to take over. The collisions became "opportunities for two different groups with two different visions of congregational identity to vie for control. This conflict centered on the pastor, who symbolized which direction the congregation should take. As the president of the congregation put it, it was between a group of people who wanted the congregation to stay more intimate, more "face-to-face," and those who wanted the congregation to grow and to become centered around outreach" (Becker 1999, 156).

Becker perceived this conflict case with hindsight. She met the congregation in the aftermath, when the factions were already formed. Becker's root metaphor, the power struggle, is one way of discerning the essence of congregational conflict. However, it raises the question whether it is possible to retrace in the case description indicators that leave space for a different outlook.

Systemic fear
In Becker's work, we do not find other, less martial models for analyzing and dealing with congregational conflict, like the "levels-of-conflict" framework developed by Speed Leas. Leas (2002) identified five levels of conflict in ascending difficulty:

problems to solve, disagreement, contest, fight/flight, and intractable situation. The essential presumption of Leas' level framework is that conflicts develop over time and relate to the quality of congregational decision-making. When congregations end up in intractable conflict, it is possible to trace, with hindsight, the absence or lack of a series of variables: 1) problem definition and acknowledgment, 2) adequate sharing of information, 3) a willingness to address the real issues, 4) strategies to reduce fear, 5) communication skills, 6) conflict norms and structures, 7) the ability to negotiate, and 8) trust. Incorporating Leas' framework for conflict management implies taking a different perspective on the connection between intractable conflicts and identity collision within congregations. According to Leas, the escalation of conflict inevitably leads to the positioning of two opposing groups. Congregations enter a win-lose dynamics. Factions emerge and cluster around specific causes. Perceptual distortions (magnification, dichotomization, over-generalization, deluded assumptions) become a problem. Personal attacks become endemic. Emotional appeals increase the level of conflict. The subgroup cohesiveness becomes the central concern. Being right becomes the dominant theme. Primitive survival responses cause detachment, unawareness of the other's pain, and self-righteousness. At the highest, or lowest, level of conflict, outside help is necessary to prevent all-out war. To sum it up, the ultimate division does not seem to be the outcome of an identity struggle, as Becker states. Leas shows that conflicts tend to escalate and because of that, the parties involved cluster around ideologically charged themes. Intractability appears to be more the result of conflict running amok, than the consequence of "between frames" conflict.

In order to ground Leas' framework, I will read anew Becker's above-mentioned case. The first thing to be mentioned is that there were several conflicts. We could even say a sequence of conflicts. Secondly, because of the tolerant, liberal religious tradition, it is possible that the competence of coming to grips with a serious difference of opinion was not an asset of the congregation. It might be assumed that the congregation as a group was not well versed in dealing with conflict on a collective scale. Thirdly, Becker's case description shows that the conflict progressed (or regressed) from one level to the next. This might indicate that congregational conflicts have origins that predate the venting of disagreements. Becker starts the series of events with the pastor's announcement that he does not want to live in the parsonage. According to Leas (2002, 13-16), this might have been a warning sign. The congregation disagreed on what to do with the emptied house, but voted for restructuring the parsonage. The pastor publicly voiced his opinion on this topic. He favored the very option that the longer-term members rejected. That is when the anti-pastor faction took off.

A second incident, transpiring one year later, was rather complicated. The church building is a national landmark, administrated by a restoration board that consists of church members and outsiders. Apparently, the church board and the restoration board had some misunderstanding about their agreement. The congregational board attempted to negotiate the misunderstanding to no avail. Then the pastor urged the board to severe the ties with the restoration board, which they did. "This caused a huge and emotional conflict" (Becker 1999, 155). People were upset that this decision was made without a congregational vote and reacted with the circulation of petitions. At a specially convened congregational meeting, the relationship with the restoration board was reinstated, and it improved steadily over time. However, the congregational discourse was "rancorous and personal." A large segment of the congregation had reached a win-lose situation. "The pastor was not above the fray" (Becker 1999, 155). From the pulpit, he called the people who circulated the petitions "dissidents." His opponents reproached him with being egomaniacal and paranoid. A third incident involved the pastor announcing an ultimatum from the pulpit, in order to force his idea on some issue. The majority did not like his ultimatum and the pastor had to resign.

By employing Leas' levels of conflict to reread the above case, I conclude that opposing factions originated because of poor conflict management. Intractable conflicts develop over time because of insufficient decision-making and of conflict management coming up short, at different stages of the process. That seems to be a more likely reading than any suggestion of congregational division preceding the intractability of conflict. Congregations split up because of the inability to deal with conflict in a constructive and healthy way. The other three cases of "mixed congregation" conflict in Becker's research (Becker 1999, 1-3, 161-163) seem to point in the same direction.

Leas is a long-time consultant to religious organizations working with the Alban Institute. For some time now, an important segment of the Alban consulting work has been done from a systems approach, for instance through the work of Peter Steinke (1993; 1996). Steinke's approach, similar to Edwin Friedman's groundbreaking book on congregational systems (Friedman 1985), is based on the theory of family therapist Murray Bowen (2002). According to David Brubaker (2009, 4), the introduction of family systems theory to congregational studies has revolutionized the understanding of congregational systems. A church functions as an inherently anxious emotional system. Healthy congregations have learned to address actively and responsibly its disturbances. A non-anxious presence of leaders and members in the midst of dependencies, changes and conflicts is a sign of a healthy differentiated system. Briefly, this is the congregational systems theory. A healthy homeostasis in the emotional system must be considered as the root metaphor of this theory. This explains why Leas (2001) presumes that fear is the biggest problem to overcome in conflict management. Our bodies are survival systems that make us respond powerfully and decisively to any perceived threat to our existence (Leas 2002, 8). Leas wants to confront this very primitive "survival theology" with a decent Christian theology: "If one believes that there is hope for the next world, if one believes that death is not ultimate, if one believes that out of failure can come new life, new opportunity, new growth and hope, then one is not so prone to move into the body's program of flight or fight responses" (Leas 2002, 8).

This functional perspective on theology might be rather unsophisticated, but at least it points beyond our biological drives and neurological reactions towards a more ethical system based on justice and trust. Theologically speaking, reconciliation is not something we produce; it is a gift from God. What we can do, and that is the aim of conflict management, is to create an environment in which the possibilities of reconciliation increase in order to help people to be faithful to themselves and to one another. Therefore, a more profound existential theory is required, with another root metaphor, to do justice to the multi-layered complexity of conflict reality. Congregational conflict is not only about a cultural war or about an unbalanced and fear-induced emotional system. Conflict within faith communities is also about a lack of trust and recognition.

Balance of trust
The systems approach appears to be a meaningful addition to perceiving conflict as predominately a power struggle between competing identity models. However, we need to reconsider two systemic aspects. First, from a systemic perspective individuals are only portrayed as far as they are part of the system process. Individual motives are subservient to group interests and to the homeostatic forces of the system. Secondly, systems rotate around the presence of differentiation, at least according to Edwin Friedman. The health of the system improves through a higher level of differentiation. Consequently, the main assignment seems to be cutting through the ties of dependency. The worst that could happen is being stuck in an "undifferentiated ego mass" (M. Bowen), a system characterized by fusion and enmeshment. In order to prevent this from happening, one should be aware of triangulation and other people's claims. Therefore, in the case Becker described, a systems consultant could have advised the pastor to be careful about interfering with the tension between the old-timers and the newcomers. In addition, the consultant could have advised the church board to respect the accountability of the restoration board and to be clear about the responsibility issue. Behind all this, however, a somewhat negative concept of "the other" might be assumed. People are driven by fear, trying to contain their insecurity by freezing the status quo, and unloading their emotional strains by trapping other people in their destructive triangles.

These two critical factors—the under-appreciation of the role of individual agents and the reduction of man's motives to anxiety—prompt me to propose a third perspective on congregational conflict: the "contextual" approach, developed by family therapist Ivan Boszormenyi-Nagy. Nagy's family-therapeutic approach was processed for practical theology by the Dutch pastoral theologians Hanneke Meulink-Korf and the late Aat van Rhijn (d. 2002). They developed a contextual-pastoral care practice and theory based upon Nagy's work and inspired by Emmanuel Levinas (e.g., Mos and Meulink-Korf 2009). The contextual-pastoral perspective implies another root metaphor and a different anthropology. Here, the adjective 'contextual' refers to the fabric or textile of relationships between, for instance, the members of a congregation. Nagy's concept of a person is highly influenced by the work of Martin Buber (Boszormenyi-Nagy and Krasner 1986, 28). Nagy interprets Buber's dialogical philosophy within a family therapy framework. Justice and trustworthiness are crucial requirements for viable relationships. All relations need to embody some degree of trust. Nagy emphasizes the importance of earning entitlement or meriting trust for relational reality; this is in diametric opposition to power-based expediency, superiority, and the intention to defeat the other. Merit is earned by being reliable, responsible and accountable, by taking the other's interest to heart, by being concerned and duly considerate, and by acting carefully. Conflicts of interest cannot be avoided, but acknowledging each person's entitlement to pursue his own interest and autonomy is healing in itself. Facing conflict and exploring how they can be addressed and reworked in a constructive way is a major improvement over acting out frustration and general discontent.

This dialogical and relational stance implies a concept of personhood in which the individual finds meaning in just and fair relations with others. That people are more alive to other people's hurt than their own is an experiential fact. We may not explain that away by reducing it to some individual psychological factor (e.g., fear) or to a transactional game move (e.g., power). Human relations are effected by life events, feelings and emotions, and systemic transactions, but there is also an *ethical* dimension that cannot and should not be reduced to the foregoing aspects (Krasner and Joyce 1995, 55). The ethical character of the relational context indicates the anthropological importance of trust and trustworthiness for human sociality. Trustworthiness is earned over the long-term by balancing the consequences of give-and-take between two relatively reliable partners. "Since fair relating is anchored in trustworthy attitudes which then warrant trusting, trust building has subsequently become a primary goal of contextual therapy" (Boszormenyi-Nagy and Krasner 1986, 37). "Rejunction," the process of restoring responsible concern for the balances of justice among people who are related, is a primary methodology. In this respect, the contextual-ethical approach that looks for residual trust is more effective than a pathological approach that looks for dysfunctional behavior. Thus, contextual theory and practice is a promising venue for an alternative perspective on congregational conflict.

Obviously, inviting people who are caught in an intractable conflict to trust each other does not make much sense. The contextual approach is predominately important for preventing escalating conflicts. That is why I commend a third reading of Becker's case, one that starts before the conflict outbreak. The first thing Becker noticed when she visited the Unitarian Universalist congregation, and the first thing she writes about, is the church building. She reports that the longer-term members have a strong sense of the congregation's heritage. They proudly perceive their sanctuary as the spiritual and philosophical centre of the congregation and they also appreciate their tradition of doctrinal openness and spiritual seeking and discovery. Respect for their heritage and tradition is what they expect from newcomers. The "hard-core old-timers," as Becker calls them, invested a lot of energy, time and money in the congregation. They became the core group and directed the congregational identity. Becker mentions that they talked about "the pastor as peripheral to the ongoing congregational community." According to Becker, they exhibited a 'mistrust of the pastor as a newcomer and outsider," and were, in general, "hostile to any manifestation of pastoral authority" (Becker 1999, 153).

From a contextual perspective, these observations suggest that there seemed to be some sort of order in the congregation, even before a series of events ignited the conflict. The character of this order is related to terms of membership and levels of investment, but apparently not to ecclesial authority or the ability to regenerate the congregation. The reasons the long-term members honored and privileged the congregation deserve acknowledgement: they took care of the building and guaranteed a save haven for people to explore their own spiritual path. Along with the giving and caring, however, comes a sense of ownership that could be considered an earned merit. Members that gave so much and for so long seem entitled to have a dominant stake in deciding on the future of the congregation. Only to his detriment could a pastor ignore this and pursue his own agenda. Obviously, the pastor disregarded the order and the long-term member's entitlement, and withheld from them his affirmation of their perceived privilege.

Another mode of conduct, one that could establish the trust needed to deal with conflict, might have been considered. In that vein, the contextual consultant might have posed some questions to the long-term members. Could they remember how, in the old days when they were the outsiders, the patriarchs and matriarchs then received them and what leeway they were giving to find their own place in the congregation? Have they given due credit to their predecessors? What stories could they tell about how they were initiated into the spiritual meaning of the sanctuary? Could they explain the source of their loyalty to the building? What made them fall in love with the building? Who taught them the value of the architecture and the national landmark status? Could they clearly articulate the importance of the congregation as a social center, as a gathering of friends, for their daily existence? What sort of experiences would they want to share with the new members, aside from respect for tradition, e.g., the importance of friendship, the willingness to embrace new thoughts and creativity, welcoming the stranger, faith in future generations? Could they credit the new members for prioritizing a social action agenda and for keeping a close eye on the finances? These and similar, inviting questions might have been addressed in an ongoing congregational dialog in which all the different groups were present, with the intention of rejoining everyone in the responsible sharing of views and opinions. Rejunction means choosing to earn entitlement through relational integrity rather than defensiveness or mistrust.

When the conflict is already inflamed and escalating, the situation becomes different. The chief contextual attitude and method best deployed in the midst of conflict are "direct address" and "multidirected partiality." Direct address is "that catalytic claim for connectedness that will to test the possibility that in one's own voice is the voice of a relating partner's suppressed longing" (Krasner and Joyce 1995, xix). Multidirected partiality is a principle of inclusiveness, linked to the determination to discover the humanity of every participant (e.g., the pastor is not egomaniacal and paranoid and members who circulate petitions are not dissidents). The contextual consultant sequentially sides with (and even against) the parties involved. She tries to empathize with and credit everyone on a basis that actually merits crediting. When the consultant cannot credit a person for present behavior or attitude, she can at least credit a person by acknowledging the biography that preceded the destructive course of events.

In the conflict case we discussed so far, the contextual consultant could start by asking the pastor, as part of a mutual dialog, how he experienced being on the receiving end of mistrust and hostility with regard to his authority and leadership. Did he ever experience something like this before, in previous tenures or in his family of origin and, if so, how did he learn to cope with it? Is seems that he reacted in a confrontational manner on the one hand, but on the other hand he also showed signs of withdrawal and detachedness. His interpersonal shyness and the refusal to live in the parsonage might be interpreted in this manner. What did the support of the newcomers meant to him? Was it the support he needed? Did it remind him of situations in his previous life where someone did see him when he was in need of care and attention? What did he experience the moment someone really saw him? How has this been a resource later on in life, in times of adversity?

The consultant could proceed with siding with the senior members, searching for residual trust. Maybe they could tell about the previous pastors. Whatever gave them the idea that Unitarian ministers tend to have extraordinary egos? Were all their ministers alike, and appreciated in the same way? What was the justification for their allergic reaction to authority and leadership? Might there have been a connection between the pastor's urge to make unwisely public statements and the professional authority that they did not grant him? Considering that they were reproached by the newcomers for "disproportionate ownership" of the congregation, could it be that the senior members felt the responsibility to parent the congregation; were they "parentified" (Boszormenyi-Nagy and Krasner 1986, 419) because of the absence of parent-pastors, who were peripheral to the ongoing congregational community? How did they inform the pastor about their expectations, and was there some clearance for him to present and implement his own agenda? Could they recall what his attraction was when they invited him to pastor their congregation? Has there ever been a moment that they did see the pastor's hurt and solitude? If so, did they reach out? Could it be that his public demeanor hid his longing for fairness and trust? The pastor could be asked the same question. What about his parentification? What part of his drive to draw in new members with social action goals, coinciding with a somewhat aggressive conduct, could be traced back to "the little boy that would make everything right"? Why did he not trust the elderly members to reach a mutually satisfying solution, together with the new members and himself?

People might not be aware of their inner needs or, if they are, they might lack the verbal skills to express them. Another possibility is that they do not feel safe to reveal what is going on inside. They might not trust the other person to understand or be respectful, or not even trust the relationship to survive the sharing. At the end, trust—or the lack of it—is always the final problem.

Conclusion

The root metaphor of the pastoral and ethical contextual approach to (potential) conflict is a dynamic balance of fairness, justice and trust. It is not difficult to understand justice and trust within a theological discourse. The contextual perception of responsible human beings able to keep a dynamic relational balance of fairness is remarkably close to the anthropology of the Jewish-Christian tradition. That prompts me to propose that the contextual approach is a practical-theologically sound alternative and addition to conflict management based on perceiving conflict as a power struggle, or as the reaction of a fear-induced emotional system. "The Lord loves righteousness and justice; the earth is full of his unfailing love" (Psalm 33:5, New International Version).

References:

Becker, Penny Edgell. 1998. Congregational Models and Conflict: A Study of How Institutions Shape Organizational Process. In *Sacred Companies. Organizational Aspects of Religion and Religious Aspects of Organizations*, ed. N.J. Demerath, 231-255. New York: Oxford University Press.

_____. 1999. *Congregations in Conflict: Cultural Models of Local Religious Life*. Cambridge: Cambridge University Press.

Becker, Penny Edgell et al. 1993. Straining at the Tie that Binds. Congregational Conflict in the 1980s. In *Review of Religious Research* 34, no. 3:193-209.

Boszormenyi-Nagy, Ivan and Barbara R. Krasner. 1986. *Between Give and Take. A Clinical Guide to Contextual Therapy*. New York: Brunner/Mazel.

Bowen, Murray. 2002. *Family Therapy in Clinical Practice*. Northvale, NJ: Jason Aronson Publishers.

Brubaker, David R. 2009. *Promise and Peril: Understanding and Managing Change and Conflict in Congregations*. Herndon: Alban Institute.

Deutsch, Morton and Peter T. Coleman, eds. 2000. *The Handbook of Conflict Resolution: Theory and Practice*. San Francisco: Jossey-Bass Publishers.

DiMaggio, Paul. 1998. The Relevance of Organization Theory to the Study of Religion. In *Sacred Companies: Organizational Aspects of Religion and Religious Aspects of Organizations*. ed. N.J. Demerath, 7-23. New York: Oxford University Press.

Dudley, Carl S. 2001. *FACTs on Fighting. Data from the Fact2000 study* [Faith Communities Today], Hartford; http://hirr.hartsem.edu (accessed 29 June 2009).

Edgell, Penny. 2003. In Rhetoric and Practice: Defining "The Good Family" in Local Congregations. In *Handbook of the Sociology of Religion*, ed. Michele Dillon, 164-178. Cambridge: Cambridge University Press.

Friedman, Edwin H. 1985. *Generation to Generation: Family Process in Church and Synagogue*, New York: The Guilford Press.

Krasner, Barbara R. and Austin J. Joyce. 1995. *Truth, Trust, and Relationships. Healing Interventions in Contextual Therapy*. New York: Brunner-Mazel.

Leas, Speed B. 2001. The Basics of Conflict Management in Congregations. In *Conflict Management in Congregations*, ed. David B. Lott, 20-44. Bethesda: Alban Institute.

Leas, Speed B. 2002. *Moving Your Church through Conflict*. Bethesda: Alban Institute.

McGrath, Alister E. 2006. *A Scientific Theology: Reality, Volume 2*. London: T & T Clark Ltd.

Mos, Kees and Hanneke Meulink-Korf. 2009. Justice in Waiting—Violence against Older Parents and Old People: A Biblical-Theological and Contextual Approach. In *When 'Love' strikes: Social Sciences, Ethics and Theology on Family Violence*, ed. Annemie Dillen, 235-255. Leuven: Peeters Publishers.

Osmer, Richard R. 2008. *Practical Theology: An Introduction*. Grand Rapids: Wm. B. Eerdmans Publishing Co.

Roozen, David A. 2007. *American Congregations 2005* [Faith Communities Today], Hartford; http://hirr.hartsem.edu (accessed 29 June 2009).

Steinke, Peter L. 1993. *How your Church Family Works: Understanding Congregations as Emotional Systems*. Herndon: Alban Institute.

Steinke, Peter L. 1996. *Healthy Congregations: A Systems Approach*. Herndon: Alban Institute.

World Council of Churches (WCC). 2005. *The Nature and the Mission of the Church: A stage on the way to a common statement* (Faith and Order paper 198). WCC: Geneva.

Between Remembrance and Restitution:
A Practical Theological exploration of the impact of the Truth and Reconciliation Commission within the South African Context

Johan Cilliers

Abstract: *The role of the Truth and Reconciliation Commission (TRC) in post-apartheid South Africa is well known and generally appreciated throughout the world. The TRC had a clear political agenda and operated within set legal structures. But it also reflected a deep theological and ethical concern for the future and wellbeing of South Africans on all sides of the deep divide that apartheid created. In recent times the impact of the TRC has come under scrutiny and it has even been criticized as acting prematurely. In this essay we consider some of these evaluations and pose the question whether certain key concerns of the TRC need to be adapted or expanded in the light of renewed signs of alienation between South Africans in terms of religion, diversity and conflict.*

Truth and Reconciliation: End of the Road?

The South African Truth and Reconciliation Commission (TRC) has, from its very inception, evoked diverse reactions, ranging from extreme skepticism and even hostility, to deep-felt appreciation and international applause. Although a commission of this kind was not something new, the TRC was hailed and criticized as unique *inter alia* because of its "overriding focus on reconciliation as a primary goal of its work," and not just judicial outcomes (Hayner 2000, 36), as well as the strong religious (even explicitly Christian) undertones that inevitably colored concepts such as truth, reconciliation, remembrance, justice, restitution, etc. (Mouton and Smit 2008, 50-1). The charismatic figure and presence of Archbishop Desmond Tutu, who chaired the proceedings, seemed to have been pivotal in steering the Commission on a route that opened up *therapeutic and narrative spaces* for many South Africans, victims and perpetrators alike, to articulate their experiences during apartheid.

According to Meiring (1999, 370), 21400 victims related their stories before the Commission within a span of 140 hearings; 7124 people applied for amnesty. This was a daunting task, bringing victims and perpetrators to the same table, facing one another across a chasm of fear and bitterness. The task was especially challenging because it is not easy to define who was a perpetrator in the context of apartheid, because of divergent perspectives from and within both sides of the divide. Broadly speaking, perpetrators (including bystanders and those profiting from the system) were people who violated the basic human rights of others (Thesnaar 2001, 26-28). It is also not that easy to define victims in the apartheid context, because of the phenomenon of so-called "black-on-black" violence. Speaking broadly, victims are those people who suffered human rights violations under apartheid, but who were also affected negatively politically, economically, socially and in terms of religious persecution (Thesnaar 2001, 28-31).

In spite of the unique character of the TRC and the constraints and conditions put on its activities by the historic political compromise that preceded it, it has been pointed out by many that the TRC was not an end in itself. Rather it was a point of departure, an initiation into a new South Africa that would hopefully operate with a new ethos and spirit of reconciliation between its citizens (cf., Du Toit 2006, 199; Villa-Vicencio 2006, 2-8; Maluleke 2006, 103). This would be in keeping with an understanding of human dignity and appreciation of the other that embodies the African spirit of *ubuntu,* which basically means: a person is a person through other persons (Van Binsbergen 2003, 428; also Wüstenberg 2003, 130). Archbishop Desmond Tutu himself declared:

> The TRC was an important turning point for South Africans—but it was only a starting point. We need to keep working at reconciliation... We are in many ways still strangers to one another. We have got to get to know and to trust one another. We need to tell one another about our hurts and our fears. We need to heal one another's wounds. We need to listen to one another's stories. This can open a space within which to address the economic and other woes that our people face. If reconciliation does not lead to people contributing in some way to transformation and the improvement of the lives of all South Africans it will, with some justification, be dismissed as a factitious thing to be ignored (quoted in Villa-Vicencio and Du Toit 2006, i).

Because it was only a starting point, it seems inevitable that the TRC's handling of key concepts such as truth and reconciliation has not only been applauded, but also criticized. For many, the TRC's intention to tell the "truth, the whole truth, and nothing but the truth" (De Gruchy, Cochrane and Martin 1999, 3) fell short. Many perpetrators did not accept the invitation to receive amnesty after giving their version of what happened under apartheid, their stories consequently never being told. Furthermore, many victims did not appear before the Commission simply because they did not suffer explicit gross human rights violations, although living under apartheid conditions (Holiday 1998, 47-48). Others have pointed out that the TRC never had a forensic understanding of "truth" but operated with a nuanced interpretation that included the forensic as well as narrative, social and healing dimensions of truth (Mouton and Smit 2008, 55; also Thesnaar 2001, 109-111). The same could be said about the Commission's understanding of reconciliation. Some are of the opinion that we have underestimated the devastating impact of apartheid on South African society, even up to now, not realizing that three hundred years of racism cannot be eliminated within the span of a mere fifteen years. Could it be true that we have misused the notion of reconciliation (embodied in *ubuntu*), as a *premature pacifier*, which has had the ultimate effect of creating a spirit of denial among us, as Van Binsbergen claims (2003, 451)? Did we go too far with our belief in "reconciliation"?

Ironically, others feel strongly that reconciliation has in fact *not* gone far enough, in the sense that it has not come to fruition in restorative justice and tangible restitution, and that the pursuit of reconciliation—the leitmotif of South Africa's transition—can in fact imperil the achievement of justice (Du Bois and Du Bois-Pedain 2008, 291). For many, it is too soon to "close the books" and to "move on" (cf. Thesnaar 2001, 7). According to them, forgiveness and reconciliation should not lead to forgetfulness, resulting in the suspension of restitution (Lapsley 1996, 22-3). They stress that we cannot simply "forgive and forget." In short, *for some people the TRC's version of truth went too far, and for others it fell too short*. It would seem that truth and reconciliation have been difficult to square with one another in post-TRC South Africa. The divide between them remains, and might even be growing. Does this mean the end of the road?

Of course this is not the only picture that could be drawn of the impact of the TRC on South African society. There are many instances where the revealing of truth and acts of reconciliation could be linked to the ethos that was created by the TRC. For instance, the former Minister of Law and Order, Adriaan Vlok, stunned South Africans by literally washing the feet of Rev. Frank Chikane, spokesperson in the office of former President Thabo Mbeki. This symbolic act of repentance was expressed towards someone whom he had planned to assassinate by means of poisoning during the apartheid years. In another incident a Dutch Reformed congregation in the town of Paarl voluntarily gave back a church building and surrounding land to a congregation of the Anglican Church (St. Stephens) which had previously been evicted under the apartheid laws enabling forced removals. One would also like to believe that the iconic image of Nelson Mandela wearing a Springbok rugby jersey (bearing number 6, the same as that of captain Francois Pienaar), sharing in the triumph of the rugby world cup in 1995, was at least partially the result of the groundbreaking reconciliatory work being done by the TRC. For many, this event symbolized the unification of a nation previously torn apart along ethnic lines: a prominent black leader, who spent 27 years in prison, shaking hands with a white man playing rugby—a sport often equated exclusively with Afrikaners.

Examples and symbols of reconciliation like these could be multiplied, as could those that demonstrate the contrary. An alarming number of recent incidents in post-apartheid society exemplify the apparent breakdown of reconciliation: a young (white) man, barely 18 years of age, walked into a squatter camp called *Skierlik* and started shooting indiscriminately, killing scores of (black) people, including a 3-month-old baby and her mother; a so-called "colored" (brown) South African was refused entrance to his house in Khayelitsha (a predominantly black township); a shocking video was made and unashamedly screened by students in a previously all-white hostel at the University of the Free State, showing black workers being humiliated in the worst possible way.

In 2008 South Africa was plagued by unprecedented and widespread incidents of xenophobia. More than 50 people were murdered, 25000 people (some with refugee status, many illegal aliens, but also legal immigrants) were forced to flee their homes and abandon their livelihoods, and 47000 people subsequently decided to return to their home countries. Many reasons for this extreme form of social ostracism have been offered, but the most probable cause was underdevelopment and unemployment, leading to a harsh struggle for economic survival. Perhaps it would be closest to the truth to say that this frenzy of xenophobia was an *expression of extreme, systemic anger*. People were trapped in institutionalized poverty for centuries; they were promised a new life by the present government—but this seems frustratingly slow in coming. Although Africans are renowned for their resilience and patience, the seemingly uncontrolled influx of people from other countries into areas that were already straining under poverty, crime and HIV and AIDS burst the walls of endurance. The ongoing state of poverty in which a majority of South Africans still find themselves seems to place our hard-won reconciliation under strain. The lack of concrete restitution, after so many years of struggling for freedom, in fact challenges our understanding of "reconciliation." It would seem as if diversity has once again become a source of conflict, rather than of reciprocal enrichment.

How are we to face these challenges? Can religion play a role? Of specific interest here, how can (practical) theology make a contribution? I am of the opinion that this can be done on at least two levels: *first, by revisiting the notion of truth, and second, by re-visioning the goal of reconciliation (understood as restitution).*

Truth: Remembering the Past

Remembrance forms a characteristic part of all religions; religion has always had a memorial aspect (Landres and Stier 2006, 1). The Christian religion could also rightly be called a religion of remembrance. The root word for remembrance in Greek (*anamnesis*; the mnē group) covers a concept which is fundamental to the Bible and encompasses the whole of divine and human life (Bartels 1978, 246).

On the one hand, the past is indeed *past*. It lies behind us and cannot be repeated. It cannot and should not be resuscitated. On the other hand, this does not mean that we should forget the past. The past is of the utmost significance for the present. The reason why people are interested in the past is because the past reveals certain patterns. To find and honor historical patterns remains an important task of theology, especially liturgy (Vos 1999, 101). In this sense, we need to continuously cele-brate the past, or celebrate the acts of God in the past. In remembering our transition the "miracle" of 1994 should never be forgotten—we should constantly remind ourselves of our "divine salvation from exile" (Lapsley 1996, 19-20).

We also have reason to lament the past. *Lament faces the truth, in view of reconcili-ation and restitution.* The art of lament needs to be recaptured. In fact, we need to rediscover the (liturgical) tension between celebration and lament. The two-pronged liturgical question in this regard would be: do contemporary worship services in South Africa create spaces where we can indeed celebrate the gifts of God's interventions in the past; but do they also create spaces where we can lament over experiences of conflict and suffering, as painfully experienced under apartheid and in its aftermath? Do we celebrate and lament in such a way that the atrocities of apartheid may never, never happen again? Those who cannot remember the sins of the past are condemned to repeat them (George Santayana, as quoted by Mouton and Smit 2008, 62).

In the light of our history and in the wake of the TRC, this much is clear: we need a responsible, hermeneutical dialogue with the past, as we so often tend to apply a reduced form of remembrance, a selective memory, if not lapse in total amnesia. We underestimate and overestimate the past, often in keeping with our current agendas. The ever changing and accelerating culture of consumption furthermore tempts us to move forward so fast that we forget to look backward; the past becomes "like a landscape viewed from a fast-moving train—a blur that quickly fades to black" (Volf 2006, 39). There is a real danger, especially for the younger generation, that the painful past as well as the miracle of our transition can become nothing more than a blur and, in the end, a meaningless void.

Ricoeur has written extensively on both the vulnerability and weakness of our acts of memory, but he also indicates the potential of memory to interpret the past in a hermeneutically responsible manner. Memory is all that we have to link us to the past (Ricoeur 2004, 21). But memory can also be abused in a variety of ways, for instance, on a pathological and therapeutic level, on a practical level (especially in terms of finding and defending our identity), and on an ethical-political level (cf. Vosloo 2007, 279f).

The liturgy of the church seems to offer a unique space for remembrance—both in terms of celebration and lament. For this to be effective, however, we need an acute and active hermeneutics of remembrance, as we so often tend to forget not only where we have come from, but also block out our past wrongdoings and find no need to lament them in the present. *In this sense the past is often strangely absent from our liturgies.* We seem not to understand that our past wrongdoings, especially those with grave social consequences, are not issues that can be settled and "buried in the past" with official denominational declarations. Rather, these must be worked through in continuous discussions in a process of questioning and listening, and especially of liturgical remembrance and reflection (cf. Lapsley 1996, 22). Indeed, we should "grasp the past for the sake of letting it go" (Shriver 2005, 125).

In this regard Vosloo pleads for a responsible historical hermeneutics that neither romanticizes nor demonize the past, but rather stresses the continuity and discontinuity between past and present. Such a hermeneutic guards against our tendency to remember exclusively and overlook the inter-connectedness of our stories; it evokes the possibilities of a dynamic understanding of tradition in our efforts to remember and not to forget (2009, 282-288).

A striking case in point would be the argument that the very existence of apartheid could be traced back to the fact that Afrikaners were never allowed after the Anglo-Boer war to articulate or lament their suffering in something like a TRC. Consequently they formed an enclave, an exclusive identity, ultimately institutionalized in apartheid. According to Mouton and Smit, "The stories of a painful past contributed to the making of a future that, in turn, became a painful past for new generations. The continuing struggle between Boer and Brit for economic power and social and political control contributed to the later policies and practices of apartheid" (2008, 41). The past, not faced in a responsible way, came back to haunt the Afrikaner. The question is: *will our present handling of our (inclusive South African) past become another ghost in our future?*

Restitution: Re-visioning the Future
Remembering the past should re-vision the future. It should help shape our agenda. But what should this agenda then be? How should the (religious) community in South Africa respond to the challenges of a degenerating state of reconciliation? I mention but two options.

Creating "spaces for interfacing"?
The "dream" of the new South Africa was translated into reality in the 1990s when leaders started to face and talk to one another. Spaces were created for "inter-facing" and for dialogue (cf. De Gruchy 2002, 148f). I am of the opinion that the concepts of *space and inter-facing* remain of paramount importance if we hope to move forward in South African society. Facing is the opposite of fear, of phobia, of xenophobia. It is also the opposite of denial. The latter seems to be a useful technique, implemented especially by politicians (cf. Cilliers 2007, 158f).

These spaces can be created, as noted already, within liturgy, but other innovative ways should also be found to bring South Africans and specifically South African leaders, together again. This calls for an understanding of ecclesiology that is open to ecumenicity, bridge-building, and linking of shared interests; in other words an ecclesiology that does not only serve its own interests.

In order to achieve this, the notion of creative and respectful space for inter-facing must be revisited (Cilliers 2009, 267-268; cf. also Du Toit 2003, 212-217). "Space for inter-facing" does not indicate neutrality or inactivity, or a type of new enclave or *securocracy*. On the contrary, it is intended to denote a space of reciprocal enrichment. In my opinion, what is needed in South Africa at present is exactly such a reciprocal space for revisiting and redefining our identity. Furthermore, I believe that the church as faith community can operate as a definitive and formative space-creator and space-setter within South African society.

The fostering of such an ecclesiology that is open to ecumenicity, bridge-building and linking of shared interests within safe spaces was in fact envisioned and strongly advocated by the TRC. In its report (Volume 5, Chapter 8) the TRC postulated that "religious communities will establish institutional forums to promote reconciliation. They will establish theologies that are designed to promote reconciliation and a true sense of community in the nation" (cf. Finca 2007, 3). This brings us to our second option.

A "theology of reconstruction and restitution"?
The creation of such spaces for inter-facing in South Africa could also be instrumental in the formation of new and meaningful theological paradigms that will indeed promote reconciliation and community, as the TRC foresaw. The fact that glaring economic inequalities lie at the root of many of South Africa's societal problems, and the view that the church should urgently take part in this debate, have been acknowledged many times before (cf. Smit 1984, 71). In essence, what is needed is a theological paradigm that does not shrink from this debate, but rather helps to set the agenda and provide relevant content. According to Finca (2007, 4), "Restitution is not a political issue. It is moral and ethical. It lies at the centre of moral theology."

It is, however, not easy to describe this paradigm. It has, for instance, been called a *theology of reconstruction,* as opposed to the paradigm of liberation theology (Villa-Vicencio 1998, 2f.). According to Mugambi (2003, 61), the period of political liberation, with its concomitant liberation theologies, should now be complemented by a theology of reconstruction, in which the issue of systemic poverty is tackled head-on. According to him, liberation and reconstruction represent different socio-political processes within specific cultural contexts, requiring different theological paradigms (2003, 61).

This theology of reconstruction, however, is not an elitist enterprise – it encompasses, and is nurtured within, the community (Mugambi 2003, 74). The *pedagogy of reconstruction* is aimed at harnessing the energies and resources of the communities in a collaborative effort to rebuild society. It takes a hard look at the root causes of injustice, especially in its economic and systemic modes of appearance (Elliot 1987, 181-182). The challenge is not to return to old modes of doing theology, but to work with all relevant partners in constructing an innovative theology that builds on the humanity and dignity of life (Villa-Vicencio 1998, 2). In short, a theology of reconstruction demands a new form of discourse, which is in principle open to other disciplines and strives to address the issue of poverty within a different paradigm than just alleviation through "compassionate hand-outs" (Swart 2004, 9).

Other authors, such as Muleleki, prefer to talk about a *theology of restitution*, especially in the light of the fact that the notion of reconciliation can be misunderstood, misappropriated and softened (2008, 684). It is furthermore important to understand that a theology of restitution should not be confused with charitable acts (Muleleki 2008, 687).

Swart takes this further and states that the South African churches, like their NGO counterparts in post-apartheid South Africa, are faced with the challenge to move beyond conventional welfarist and local project-centered modes of intervention in poverty, towards more sophisticated modes of development intervention, in other words to "look beyond the individual community and seek changes in specific policies and institutions at local and national levels" (Swart 2008, 123 & 126). In this regard churches as faith communities can play an important role because of their "politics of ideas," i.e., to contribute towards "change to be brought about by the power of ideas, values, transformed relationships and communication" (Swart 2008, 128). In this way restitution can become a truly people-orientated movement, not only towards "poor people," but also as a double movement "in which the imperative of renewal, conversion, and change should as much be directed to the life-worlds of the economically rich and privileged" (Swart 2008, 134).

It is impossible to talk about restorative justice in South Africa without also touching upon the issue of *land restitution*. This remains a sensitive and complex challenge. There are many theories underlying the *modus operandi* of land restitution, for instance, the so-called special-right-based (SR-based) argument for private property, which justifies private property as being necessary for the protection of property rights that have been legitimately acquired by, or transferred to, the holder. The general-right-based approach, in contrast, justifies private property as essential to the development of individual freedom (Roux 2008, 147). The South African endeavor to restore land ownership leans strongly towards the principle of rectification of injustice, which permits state interference to re-legitimize the property rights order. Roux suggests that we revisit the notion of land restitution by removing the artificial time limit imposed on the finalization of the land restitution process; by brokering deeper and more meaningful settlements; by involving current landowners in the search for settlement solutions (in other words: by bringing people together in safe spaces for negotiation and collaboration); by investing more resources in monuments and museums (thus rekindling remembrance); and by calling for an apology from white South Africans for apartheid forced removals, therefore re-inviting re-conciliation into the process (Roux 2008, 168-171).

Whatever route we choose to follow, it should indeed be all about "reconciliation restoring justice," or in the words of De Cruchy, "… to recover the full meaning and rich texture of reconciliation, and to demonstrate its inseparable connection with the restoration of justice" (2002, 2). The impetus for this recovery of reconciliation that restores justice lies *inter alia* in the way that South Africans will, in the future, remember their past.

In whatever way the religious communities respond to the challenges facing South Africa at present, whether through mediatory space-creation or new theological paradigms, the time for making a difference is running out.

References:

Bartels, Karl-Heinz. 1978. Remember, Remembrance. *The New International Dictionary of New Testament Theology,* ed. Colin Brown, 3:230-47. Exeter: The Paternoster Press.

Cilliers, Johan. 2007. Preaching as language of hope in a context of HIV and AIDS. In *Preaching as a Language of Hope.* Studia Homiletica 6, ed. Cas Vos, Lucy L Hogan and Johan H Cilliers, 155-176. Pretoria: Protea Book House.

Cilliers, Johan. 2009. Creating Space within the Dynamics of Interculturality: The Impact of Religious and Cultural Transformations in Post-Apartheid South Africa. In *Secularization Theories, Religious Identity and Practical Theology,* ed. Wilhelm Gräb and Lars Charbonnier, 260-270. Münster: Lit Verlag.

Cochrane, James; John De Gruchy, Stephen Martin. 1999. Faith, Struggle and Reconciliation. In *Facing the Truth. South African Faith Communities and the Truth and Reconciliation Commission,* ed. James Cochrane, John De Gruchy, Stephen Martin, 1-11. Cape Town: David Philip Publishers - Athens: Ohio University Press.

De Gruchy, John. 2002. *Reconciliation Restoring Justice.* Minneapolis: Fortress Press.

Du Bois, Francois and Antje Du Bois-Pedain. 2008. Post-conflict justice and the reconciliatory paradigm: the South African experience. In *Justice and Reconciliation in Post-Apartheid South Africa,* ed. Francois Du Bois and Antje Du Bois-Pedain, 289-311. Cambridge: University Press.

Du Toit, Fanie. 2003. *Learning to live together. Practices of social reconciliation.* Cape Town: Institute for Justice and Reconciliation.

Du Toit, Fanie. 2006. Beyond the TRC. In *Truth and Reconciliation in South Africa: 10 Years On,* ed. Charles Villa-Vicencio and Fanie Du Toit, 199-204. Claremont: New Africa Books (Pty) Ltd.

Elliot Charles. 1987. *Comfortable Compassion? Poverty, Power and the Church.* London: Hodder and Stoughton.

Finca, Bongani. 2007. Restitution Imperative in a Fragile Democracy. Paper delivered at the annual meeting of the Foundation for Church-led Restitution. Cape Town: Unpublished Document.

Flanagan, James. 1999. Ancient Perceptions of Space—Perceptions of Ancient Space. *SEMEIA* 87:15-43.

Hayner, Priscilla. 2000. Same species, different animal: how South Africa compares to truth commissions worldwide. In *Looking Back Reaching Forward. Reflections on the Truth and Reconciliation Commission of South Africa,* ed. Charles Villa-

Vicencio and Wilhelm Verwoerd, 32-41. Cape Town: University of Cape Town Press - London: Zed Books Ltd.

Holiday, Anthony. 1998. Forgiving and forgetting. In *Negotiating the Past. The making of Memory in South Africa,* ed. Sarah Nuttall and Carli Coetzee, 43-56. Cape Town: Oxford University Press.

Landres, Shawn and Stier, Oren. 2006. Introduction. In *Religion, Violence, Memory, and Place,* ed. Shawn Landres and Oren Stier, 1-12. Bloomington and Indianapolis: Indiana University Press.

Lapsley, Michael. 1996. Bearing the Pain in our Bodies. In *To Remember and to Heal. Theological and Psychological Reflections on Truth and Reconciliation,* ed. Russel Botman and Robin M. Petersen, 17-23. Cape Town: Human and Rousseau.

Maluleke, Tiniyiko. 1999. The Truth and Reconciliation Discourse: A Black Theological Evaluation. In *Facing the Truth. South African Faith Communities and the Truth and Reconciliation Commission,* ed. James Cochrane, John De Gruchy, Stephen Martin, 101-113. Cape Town: David Philip Publishers - Athens: Ohio University Press.

Maluleke, Tiniyiko. 2008. Justice in post-apartheid South Africa: Towards a Theology of Restitution. *Verbum et Ecclesia* 29, no. 3:681-696.

Meiring, Piet. 1999. *Chronicle of the Truth Commission.* Vanderbijlpark: Carpe Diem.

Mouton, Elna, Dirkie Smit. 2008. Shared Stories for the Future? Theological Reflections on Truth and Reconciliation in South Africa. *Journal of Reformed Theology* 2, no. 1:40-62.

Mugambi Jesse. 2003. *Christian Theology and Social Reconstruction.* Nairobi, Kenya: Acton Publishers.

Ricoeur, Paul. 2004. *Memory, history, forgetting.* Chicago: University of Chicago Press.

Roux, Theunis. 2008. Land restitution and reconciliation in South Africa. In *Justice and Reconciliation in Post-Apartheid South Africa,* ed. Francois Du Bois and Antje Du Bois-Pedain, 144-171. Cambridge: University Press.

Shriver, Donald. 2005. *Honest Patriots. Loving a Country Enough to Remember its Misdeeds.* Oxford: University Press.

Smit, Dirkie. 1984. Wat beteken status confessionis? In '*n Oomblik van waarheid.*
Opstelle rondom die NG Sendingkerk se afkondiging van 'n status confessionis en
die opstel van 'n konsepbelydenis, ed. Daan Cloete and Dirkie Smit, 14-38.
Kaapstad: Tafelberg Uitgewers.

Swart, Ignatius. 2004. Community-centred congregational ministry in South Africa:
a plea for renewal. *Nederduitse Gereformeerde Teologiese Tydskrif, Supplementum*
45, no. 2:328-339.

Swart, Ignatius. 2008. Meeting the Challenge of Poverty and Exclusion: The
Emerging Field of Developmental Research in South African Practical Theology.
International Journal of Practical Theology 12, no. 1:104-149.

Thesnaar, Christo. 2001. Die Proses van Heling en Versoening: 'n Pastoraal-Herme-
neutiese Ondersoek van die Dinamika tussen Slagoffer en Oortreder binne 'n Post-
WVK Periode. DTh. thesis, University of Stellenbosch.

Van Binsbergen, Wim. 2003. *Intercultural Encounters. African and anthropological*
lessons towards a philosophy of interculturality. Münster: Lit Verlag.

Villa-Vicencio Charles. 1998. *A Theology of Reconstruction. Nation-Building and*
Human Rights. Cape Town: David Philip Publishers.

Villa-Vicencio, Charles. 2006. What a truth commission can and cannot achieve. In
Truth and Reconciliation in South Africa: 10 Years On, ed. Charles Villa-Vicencio
and Fanie Du Toit, 2-8. Claremont: New Africa Books (Pty) Ltd.

Volf, Miroslav. 2006. *The End of Memory: Remembering Rightly in a Violent*
World. Grand Rapids: Eerdmans.

Vos, Cas. 1999. Die Towertyd van Liturgie. *Praktiese Teologie in Suid-Afrika* 14,
no. 1:99-126.

Vosloo, Robert. 2007. Reconfiguring ecclesial identity: In conversation with Paul
Ricoeur. *Studia Historiae Ecclesiasticae. Journal of the Church History Society of*
Southern Africa 32, no. 1:273-293.

Vosloo, Robert. 2009. Herinnering, tradisie, teologie: Op weg na 'n
verantwoordelike historiese hermeneutiek. *Nederduitse Gereformeerde Teologiese*
Tydskrif 50, nos. 1 & 3:280-288.

Wüstenberg, Ralf. 2003. *Die politische Dimension der Versöhnung. Eine theologi-*
sche Studie zum Umgang mit Schuld nach den Systemumbrüchen in Südafrika und
Deutschland. Chr. Kaiser: Gütersloher Verlagshaus.

National Identity, Ethnicity and Affirmative Actions: Challenges for Pastoral Practices

Valburga Schmiedt Streck

Abstract: *In spite of Brazil's rich cultural background, the dominant culture of the country is White European. Although we cannot speak of ethnic conflicts as in other countries, the "racial democracy" which makes us so proud is an illusion and ethnic problems go hand in hand with social class inequality, be it in Church, in law, in education, in political institutions and so forth. The White elite always set the tone for Christianity, for justice, for beauty, for culture, for civilization and for democracy since the times of colonization until today. It is well known that the Roman Catholic Church has tolerated the African religion among their members and the Theology of Liberation movement introduced ecumenical services with African and Indian elements. From this movement emerged different pastoral practices, which helped to open the discussions around affirmative policies. Many of the ethnic groups organized today have their roots in church settings. This study brings some perspectives on the issue of racial and national identity and the role of practical theology, mainly from the perspective of the Lutheran Church, which is gradually integrating into its membership people from other ethnic groups.*

Introduction

The migratory movements in Brazil in the last decades displaced a large number of people from south to north and vice versa, bringing together different cultures. We experienced technological revolutions and evolved from a rural country into an urban one. The industrial revolution that caused the urbanization contributed to ethnic groups living in isolation to become more open and integrate themselves into the broader society. We cannot speak of ethnic conflicts as in other countries in the world where there are armed conflicts. However, when we lift the veil of silence that covers the "other" marginalized by their color which also keeps them far away from the financial success of this large country then we come to some troubling questions. We are ranked the seventh country in world consumption, but 70% of our population is excluded from consuming. The neoliberal economical system deepens the social exclusion in our country. Increasingly color and poverty are associated with social exclusion. To tolerate people of different colors does not mean that the "other" is accepted as equal according to some assimilation ideal. We have to admit that the "racial democracy" which makes us so proud is an illusion and that the ethnic problem goes hand in hand with social inequality. It is important to recognize that in Brazil this happens in a different way than in countries such as the US, which had a segregationist policy for Whites and Blacks, or in India where there is a caste system. In Brazil social class and ethnicity are interconnected in such a way that it is almost unnoticed. When we look at the faces of the people that are included in the system, the European type is evident, and when we read the newspapers we will not be surprised that the burglars and criminals that appear in the crime pages have dark skin and curly hair.

In order to understand this complex dynamic in Brazil I will begin with a brief reflection about the formation of the Brazilian people showing how we came to a White imaginary in spite of being a "colorful" nation. I will then comment on initiatives directed toward integration in pastoral practices of the Lutheran Church.

Eradicating and enslaving the "other": scars in the Brazilian history
In our first years in school we learned about the "discovery" of our country, Brazil, as in a fairy tale. These history lessons would begin that in the year 1500 the Portuguese on an adventurous journey to find a route to India (from where they got spices and other goods for their commerce) accidently landed on a great island. There they found a paradise with exuberant flora and fauna. The "savages" that lived here were considered "primitive" because they behaved completely different from Europeans, were naked, lived in the forest and were not Christians; they were also recognized as cannibals. First the land was called the Island of Santa Cruz, or Ilha de Vera Cruz. Finally it was baptized Brazil because of the special wood found there called *pau brazil*, which yields a red ink used for dying clothes. The Portuguese who arrived to colonize Brazil were mercenaries, political prisoners and criminals without any necessary commitment or ability to work in the newly discovered land. The Catholic Church was there from the beginning. The colony was exploited and its wealth was taken to Europe. The Indians, so named because this was first thought to be India, were forced to work as slaves; this, however, would fail. The Indians, accustomed to living free in nature, would flee to the forest and were unwilling to submit to the dictates of the farmers. Many Indians were taken to Europe and displayed in European courts, amusing royalty and displayed as typifying savage behavior in comparison to polite and moral European behavior. This is how the idea of the "other" was used to educate the White European!

During the colonial period the wealth of our natural resources was exploited and taken to Europe. The massacre of natives happened in part because of the diseases brought by Europeans such as syphilis and small pocks. More fundamental was a belief that these people had no soul and were to be treated like animals. This gave the colonizers the right to kill the Indians and in 500 years native Brazilians have been almost eradicated from our land. Today few are left and many live in very precarious conditions. The fate of the Black African slaves was not much different.

The seven settlement missions of the Jesuits were a 17th century experiment in colonizing Indians in Brazil, Argentina, Paraguay and Uruguay by allowing them to live in free communities. This was a singular experience of educating the Indian population, contradicting the belief that Indigenous people were human beings and had the same capacity for learning as the White person. Thus far the Portuguese had tried to force the natives to work the land but the experience turned out to be a failure because the Indigenous people fled to the forest. Thus it was believed that they were too sensitive and unable for any work required at the colony.

Frustrated by the efforts to enslave the Indians, the Portuguese crown, already active in the slave trading business, introduced Black Africans to the colony. Slavery brought 4 million Africans to Brazil between the years 1534 to 1850, which means that 40% of the Black slaves kidnapped from the African continent came to Brazil. Due to the proximity of the African continent slaves were cheap. As the Catholic Church was closely allied with the colonial system it little questioned this practice. Before slavery, the colonies did not produce much and were not economically attractive. However, with sugar plantations becoming profitable, the slavery business was of great importance in the whole of the Americas. Brazil had 350 years of slavery. During these years Black people did all the manual labor, while the White master commanded (Nascimento 2002; Ribeiro 1995). When slaves came from Africa to Brazil they were separated from their kin so that family members had virtually no contact with each other. It is also recognized that the Portuguese were some of the most violent slave masters. As White masters preferred Black woman as their mistresses, this has been a significant and sad contribution to our colorful society. In 1818 50.6% of the Brazilian population was of African descendants, which meant that to maintain order the White man had to oppress and repress (DaMatta 1985). Black slaves were ordinarily forced to work for eight to ten years and then were discarded. Many Black resistance communities were formed. Some of these still survive today, though not as resistance communities but as isolated Black communities in very poor living conditions.

With society turning darker, the idea of whitening the population became stronger and gained acceptance among the dominant White population. This was accomplished by having children with Black women and later, when slavery was not longer needed, by bringing in cheap labor from Europe. In the beginning of the eighteenth century, industrialization required new labor forces. When the abolition of slavery finally occurred in 1888, a total of 700,000 people were thrown into the streets. This very large population generally did not have work, food or shelter. Poverty and unemployment have their roots in these times (Santos 2002, 30).

There has always been a tendency in Brazil to deny the existence of racism. An example is a study conducted in São Paulo in 1988 in which 98% of the interviewed persons said that they did not have racial prejudice while 99% said they knew people among their close relationship that have racial prejudice. It seems that Brazilians live on islands of democracy surrounded by people who are racists (Wade 1997; Fonseca 2000; Adesk, 2001). Today we have 192 million inhabitants with more than 76 million of Black or African descent. This makes us the second largest Black population in the world, only behind Nigeria. Of the 76 million, 10.4 million are

Black and 66 millions are Mulatto. A closer look at these statistics reveals that 18% of Blacks above 15 years of age are illiterate

The role of Practical Theology and Ethnicity at the IECLB

With the expansion of capitalism and the demand for free labor in the 19th century, a large White immigration to the Southern part of Brazil occurred between 1824 and 1930. Loads of ships arrived with peasants from Germany, Austria, Switzerland, Italy, Poland, Japan and other places. If it was a relief for these countries to send away their poor population, these new immigrants were welcome in Brazil because they had more education than the Black or remaining Indian population. Accustomed to hard work and because they were free citizens, they were able to develop a new type of agriculture in the country, contrasting with the large landowners and the plantations. Willing to forget their past, they started a new beginning in this country. European immigrants made their settlements building a church and a school, and for decades gathered in closed communities.

The Evangelical Church of Lutheran Confession in Brazil (IECLB) has its root in this immigration movement and its members came mainly from Germany, Austria or Switzerland. The Church functioned as a *Volkskirche* (Church of the People) in the sense that people belonged to this Church for generations. Closely identifying with the IECLB was an important way for immigrants to hold together during many decades of hostility in the Brazilian territory, especially during the period around World War II. An important contributing factor was that for centuries the official religion in Brazil was Roman Catholicism; in many places non-Catholics were still discriminated against as heretics until the1950s. Today the IECLB has 720,000 members. In spite of the rapid urbanization in the 1960s, resulting in more than 70% of the population livings in cities, the IECLB can still be considered a rural Church.

The 1960s were a turning point for the Church because during this time many debated what it meant to be an Evangelical Church of Lutheran Confession in Brazil. Furthermore, at this time the Lutheran Theological Seminary (Escola Superior de Teologia, or EST) created in 1946 stopped offering classes in German as there were now teachers able to teach in Portuguese. Parochial ministers, trained in Brazil were able to speak Portuguese which helped to insert our Church into the Brazilian context. With this movement a theological discussion emerge rooted in our context. In the 1970s pastors and theology students of the EST were moved by the ideas of Liberation Theology and tried new pastoral practices called *Pastoral Practices of Living Together* and *Pastoral Practices of the Hoes* (*Pastoral de Convivência* and *Pastoral da Enxada*). These practices mean that pastors inserted themselves in the suffering and oppression of our people. Some of them lived for many years in the Amazon forest with Indigenous peoples; others lived in slums while others settled with landless farmers. It was a time for redefining what it meant to be a missionary and what it meant to insert oneself in others' world and suffering. This was seen as a missionary reeducation

The stance of the IECLB on several ethical issues related to citizenship, according to the official documents of the Church, reveals a basic consistency throughout the last few decades. The concept of citizenship refers "to the rights and duties of inhabitants born or naturalized in a State and who have their rights foreseen and guaranteed in the Constitution or law" (Sinner and Majewski 2005, 34). It is understood that the Churches have the responsibility to address a "critical constructive position vis-à-vis the State and can with their privileged position in relation to the larger population make a significant difference in constructing citizenship" (Sinner and Majewski 2005, 34). Regarding the subject of race, this issue has been a constant concern for the IECLB. Members and leaders of the Church have discussed ways of integrating people coming from other backgrounds besides White German descendants.

The first experiences of integrating Black students and pastors at EST and in the wider church in the 1970s and 1980s resulted in a failure, largely due to the predominance of White German descendants in our parishes. However, the 1990s were a turning point; this coincided with the Black movement in the country and the work of the Black professor Dr. Peter Nash at the theological school. In this decade at the national level Black NGOs tried to fill the gap of social practices such as the health-care of Black women, education and the development of the youth. The main goal of these groups committed to Black consciousness is to combat racism by rescuing the contribution of Black culture for the national patrimony as well as by denouncing the continuing genocide suffered by this ethnic group. Policies of pragmatic action are being developed by the national government allowing the registration of the remaining territories of the *quilombos* (land of Blacks) where the descendants of slaves have lived until today. An inter-ministerial work group focused on the appreciation of the Black population has been created at the national government level to formulate compensatory policies that provide new opportunities. The goal is to correct longstanding social inequalities (Adão 2003; Oliveira and Silva 2003; Boff, 2000). Anti-racist policies and affirmative actions are addressing the socially marginalized as in the cases of the Indigenous and Black populations. The main goal is to protect the cultural diversity of Brazil and rescue the aspects of the Black culture as well as to "encourage interethnic contacts and to create a definition for the national collectivity" (Adesky 2001, 231).

The affirmative policies for Black people received new backing in the present government with the installation of a *Secretaria Especial de Políticas de Promoção da Igualdade Racial* (Secretary of Special Policies and Inter Racial Promotion) with ministry status. The government officially recognized that racism exists and that it has to be eradicated. This discussion is a common subject in the Brazilian press. The implementation of the quota system for Blacks and their descendants in public universities and federal centers of technological education is one action that has been implemented. In the academy there is a movement to open this topic for discussion, and African history is now an obligatory course taught in schools.

In 2000 the Black Lutheran students at the EST founded the Group of Black Students and also started to publish a *Bulletin* with materials aimed at helping people rescue their identity and to feel proud of it. In 2005 the school hired its first Afro-Brazilian teacher, a woman. This year a course on Afro-cultural studies was offered to the theological students and there was intentional outreach to cultural and ethnic movements in the area. From that outreached emerged the research group called *Identity Group*. It is engaged in discussing Black theology and spirituality as well as in publishing material on different subjects related to the Afro-identity. The group participates in local and international events, conducts discussions and forums and also offers consulting to the Church on the issue of Black culture.

As mentioned above, Indigenous people have survived in Brazil. Fortunately among them are groups increasingly empowered to stand up and claim their rights. The Indigenous College in the State Mato Grosso just graduated its first students who hopefully will return to their settlements to teach. The *Council of Mission among Indigenous People* (COMIN) was formed in 1982. This institution is linked to the IECLB and located at EST. Its main purpose is to assess the Church's work with the Indigenous population in Brazil. To accomplish this goal COMIN works with different groups creating partnerships and giving support in areas of education, health, land- and self-sustainability. Its principle is to support the priorities of the Indigenous population and communities and to respect their cultures. Engaged in this work are professionals in areas of agriculture, education, health, social work and pastoral work (http://www.comin.org.br).

Both Afro-Brazilian and Indigenous-Brazilian groups are starting to unite their efforts and to plan common actions. Some of the actions proposed for the IECLB are:

1) *Organizing workshops* together to study how to implement the legislation for both cultures (law 10.639/03 and law 11.465/2008–Afro and Indigenous culture and history classes must be taught in all schools) as well as to consider issues of health, social relations, education and religiosity for teachers, social educators and school boards.

2) *Reflecting on the issue of land.* Both Afro and Indigenous population have a significant problem with this issue. The Indigenous people are constantly harassed by the large land lord system in the country.

3) *Reflecting on issues of Theology and Ethnicity.* There are publications on both sides on the subject and efforts can be made to join publications, and to find and develop new resources related to intercultural issues.

4) *Support the Latin American Council of Churches* on the issue of the *Quilombolas* (Black population settlements).

Conclusions

The discussion of ethnicity in the larger society and mainly from the perspective of ethnic groups seems to have two major dimensions that deserve consideration. One of them relates to the affirmation of the ethnic groups, in our case Indians and Black African descendants, and attempts to value the African and Indian cultures based on models provided by North American affirmation policies. It is necessary to raise the national consciousness that half of the population is of Black descendants, rescue these forgotten culture as well as establish their political, economic and social rights. This will not be a peaceful movement in a White hegemonic culture. A large part of the population recognizes ethnic and social inequalities. However, it also emphasizes that Brazilian people have a national ethnic identity called *Brazilian* that becomes more and more prominent through increased miscegenation in the country. It defends ethnic affirmation policies, but not ethnic separation into groups because our people are already interracially mixed. This dominant perspective also makes a prevision that in the future we will have a homogeneous and racially mixed culture in Brazil. I think both perspectives have important elements and can be combined. Many of the organized ethnic groups have their roots in church settings and in this way the Christian Churches have contributed meaningfully to the integration of Black and Indian people. Of course one has to question if this integration is being done on the condition that Black and Indian people had to accept Christian faith and deny their cultural background. There are sectors in the Catholic Church, for example, that are less tolerant with members worshiping in both Catholic and *Umbanda* services, and this contributes to the fact that many Afro-Brazilians are moving away from the Catholic Church.

Today the majority of Black people are Pentecostals. Like the historical Protestant churches, Pentecostals also prohibit their members from attending *Candomble*, *Umbanda* and spiritual centers. The same is true with the Indigenous population which in the last decades has converted to Pentecostalism and in this way denies their own culture and considers it as something evil. This perspective contradicts those introduced through Liberation Theology allowing ecumenical services with African and Indian elements. The latest national statistics indicate that 11,951,347 of Afro-Brazilians are evangelicals. Of those, 8,676,997 are Pentecostals, while 253000 are *umbanda or candomblé* (Afro religion). Charismatic movements and fundamentalist movements can be found in all historical Churches in Brazil. There are groups in historical Churches that either break away from their Church or demand a delimitation of interaction with other Churches and their religious practices.

The IECLB is constantly being challenged by different groups and movements among its members. As a result, we now have three theological institutions for educating pastors—the two besides EST have an evangelical fundamentalist perspective. Hit by the economic crises, EST had to bow to market pressure and accept students at the undergraduate level from other denominations and religious movements. New adaptations had to be made in order to survive and at the same time to continue being a recognized institution at the national level. Plurality is healthy when it is well managed, but it can become dangerous when it ends in confrontation. The tendency is to exclude the different. To integrate and to empower the different is the ideal but not such an easy task. An *integrated plurality* means that as Christians we can dialogue with the different and have them join with us in community (Brakemeir, 2009). This is the way that communities have to be built. Traditionally the Lutheran Church has been known for having sound reasoning, good theology and an ability to enter in dialogue with others.

In this fluid situation practical theology is in constant dialogue and under constant challenge. We have students from different denominations in our classes. Recently I taught a class on *Pastoral Counseling and Psychological and Social Approaches,* which included two Catholic priests (one of them Black), Presbyterians, students who are Assembly of God and Baptist, members of three new Pentecostal movements, besides a few Lutherans. I see this as a challenge and an opportunity that is unique for pastoral practices and practical theology.

Practical theology is challenged to help improve the dialogue among the different theologies of Christian churches and religious movements. We have to learn from one another and have to value the message of the Gospel as one that can transform life. This does not mean that one has to be obedient and submissive to orders and dogmas. It will require action, such as joining efforts to empower people to assert their right to decent living, education, health care, public transportation, land reform and other things. These efforts at *diakonia,* however, should be integrated with *koinonia*, the building of a responsible caring community.

References:

Adão, Jorge Manoel. 2003. Práxis educativa do movimento negro no Rio Grande do Sul. In *Negro e educação. Identidade Negra*, ed. Iolanda Oliveira and Petronilla Silva, 59-70. Rio de Janeiro-São Paulo: ANPED-Ação Educativa.

Boff, Leonardo. 2000. *A voz do Arco-Íris*. Brasília: Letraviva.

Brakemeir, Gottfried. 2009. "*Somos igreja! Que igreja devemos ser?*" Exigências eclesiológicas luteranas no contexto brasileiro. Unpublished paper.

D'Adesky, Jaques. 2001. *Racismos e anti-racismos no Brasil*. Rio de Janeiro: Pallas.

Damatta, Roberto. 1985. *A casa e a rua: espaço, cidadania, mulher e morte no Brasil*. São Paulo: Brasiliense.

Fonseca, Maria Nazareth Soares. 2000. Visibilidade e ocultação da diferença. In *Brasil afro-brasileiro*, ed. Maria Nazareth Soares Fonseca, 87-116. Belo Horizonte: Autentica Press.

Freyre, Gilberto. 1961. *Casa grande e senzala*. 10th ed., no. 1. Rio de Janeiro: José Olympio.

Nascimento, Abdias do. 2002. *O quilombismo*. Brasília-Rio de Janeiro: Fundação Palmares.

Ribeiro, Darcy. 1995. *O povo brasileiro*. A formação e o sentido do Brasil. São Paulo: Companhia da Letras.

Santos, Hélio. 2002. *Os dois Brasís*. Journal Carta Capital 216:30-36.

Sinner, Rudolf von and Majewski, Rodrigo Gonçalves. 2005. A contribuição da IECLB para a cidadania no Brasil. *Journal Estudos Teológicos* 45, no 1:32-61

Wade, Peter. 1997. *Race and Ethnicity in Latin América*. London: Pluto.

Wetteranus est: Reconciliation and Re-identification of Jewish and Christian Citizens in Germany 70 years after the 1938 *Reichsprogromnacht*

Constanze Thierfelder

Abstract: *In Germany, once there was a diversity of religions that is not to be found anymore. The small town of Wetter in Hessen, Germany was a place where Jewish and Christian families formerly lived together and shared everyday life; that changed with the growth of anti-Semitism and finally the terror from 1933 to 1945. Wetter is also an example of the courage to heal, to seek and to extend understanding and reconciliation between Christian and former Jewish residents. Theories of discourse and of ethno-psychoanalysis help to differentiate the various layers of facts and meaning.*

Introduction

Before 1930 in Hessen, situated at the centre of Germany, some or several Jewish families were part of the community in almost every small town or village. Now there are none. Only in larger cities like Marburg, Frankfurt and Cologne can you find Jewish communities, populated mostly by immigrants from Russia. In these small towns and villages before 1933, Christian and Jewish families lived together for centuries. They were neighbours, colleagues and friends. What happened when the Nazi-regime took over? How can one describe the emergence of suppression, persecution and Holocaust amidst the routine of everyday life? We will consider such changes by examening the small town of Wetter, located 15 kilometres north of Marburg and 100 kilometres north of Frankfurt.

Picture 1: Stiftskirche in Wetter

In medieval times the city of Wetter was famous for its outstanding scientists and scholars, whereas Marburg was nothing but a small village. In that period to say of someone *Wetteranus est* ("he is a Wetteran") was a title of honour and respect. In November 1938 in Wetter—like in most German towns—Jewish families were persecuted and the synagogue was destroyed. Most Jewish citizens left Germany; 26

Jewish citizens of Wetter were deported and killed. I will use two methods to explore and to analyze what happened during and after the Nazi-regime: Irigaray's concept of difference and the ethno-psychoanalytical understanding of the dynamics of difference.

Living together in Wetter
Until 1933 the small city of Wetter had Christian and Jewish inhabitants. Of about 2000 inhabitants approximately 5% of the population (87 people in 17 families) was Jewish. Wetter had a *Stiftskirche* dating from 1260 for Christian worship, and a Synagogue built in 1897 for the Jewish community. There was a Christian cemetery beyond the town wall and a Jewish cemetery in the Wollenberg, a forest boarding other villages whose Jewish families also used this cemetery.

Christians and Jews living in close proximity to each other in German cities, small towns and villages was a delicate balancing act. Sometimes everyday life was undermined by prejudice, by transferences and projections especially from the Christians. Most of the time, however, everyday life worked as a matter of mutual interests. One person from a small village close to Marburg describes this living together this way:

> *Somehow they belonged to the community, blemishes and all. On Good Friday out of the blue some "good" Christians may remember that it was Jews who nailed Jesus to the cross and they let their Jewish neighbours feel their anger. But the next day it was all over. It was an impulsive action.* (Händler-Lachmann 1995, 33)

In Wetter Jewish and Christian children went to school together, Christian and Jewish women baked bread together, and Christian and Jewish families took part in the town and villages activities. At the *Grenzegang*, a several day long celebration every seventh year, the whole community walked along the town's borders to check on the boundary stones. One part of the celebration was and still is a procession of all associations, clubs and societies of the town and the surrounding villages. In front of each wagon children carry signs indicating where the wagon comes from. Jewish as well as Christian groups carried such signs.

Jewish and Christian children were friends. They tasted each other's sandwiches; the beef sausages of the Jewish children were of special interest to their Christian friends. They visited each other at their homes and saw nothing fundamentally different from what they knew from their own home. Sometimes Jewish children were criticized by their parents because they ate non-kosher foods like bacon at their friend's home. Christian children commented about Jewish children neither going to school on Saturday nor being allowed to carrying their schoolbags on that day. It was common knowledge that you could not buy anything at a Jewish shop on Satur-day but you could go there on Sunday if you needed something. Many young Christian girls were employed by Jewish families to help with the housekeeping especially on the Sabbath. Interreligious marriages were rare but not impossible.

Jewish men were respected in cattle and horse trades. They were butchers and sold beef to Christian and Jewish customers. In Wetter in 1930 there were nine Jewish men in the cattle trade, and two others in the horse trade. Cattle and horse trading was conducted in Yiddish; thus, Christian traders had to learn some Yiddish to do their job. From 1933 on the Nazis directed the public to boycott Jewish shops and traders. This did not have much of an effect on horse and cattle trading because farmers were accustomed to trading with Jewish partners and trusted them. Several Christian farmers who continued trading with Jews were bullied by a special force of the Nazi regime the SA (special agents). The Nazis asked people to report such farmers to the regime.

In 1935 the Nazi-regime began auditing the book-keeping of Jewish tradesman looking for even the smallest of irregularities and subsequently confiscating registries of trade. In 1936 the trading of cattle and horses by Jews, like most other Jewish business, came to a stop. As most Jewish families lived through trade, they lost their livelihood; many sold their shops for almost nothing and emigrated (Händler-Lachmann 1995, 83-93).

Picture 2: Helmut with his Jewish grandparents and his father seated in front of their house, courtesy of Harry Weichsel, Bridgeport CT

The David Hess family in Wetter worked in the cattle trade. David and his wife Frieda had seven children. Flora was the sixth child, born in 1913. She married Fritz Kutsch from Wetter who was not Jewish. Their son Helmut Kutsch was born in 1933. The Nurnberg Laws were passed in 1935. Hitler's racial ideology held that the (Christian) Germans belonged to a "superior Aryan race," whereas the Slavs in the East as well as the Jews were an inferior race. Nurnberg Laws included anti-Jewish racial laws. Jews were no longer considered German citizens; Jews could not marry Aryans or have relations to them. Existing marriages between Jews and Christians were declared invalid. In 1935 Fritz Kutsch separated from his Jewish wife Flora Hess. In 1936 Flora moved to Frankfurt to find employment. Helmut stayed with his Jewish grandparents in Wetter.

On November 9 and 10, 1938 many synagogues in Germany were destroyed; the synagogue in Wetter, symbol of presence and pride of the Jewish Community, was destroyed on November 10th. One day after synagogues all over Germany were burned to the ground, 20 members of different Nazi organizations gathered in a cowshed next to the Wetter synagogue waiting for the darkness to come. When the streetlights were switched of—with official permission of the mayor—they started to devastate this Jewish place of worship. They smashed the windows and the furnishings, they took down the Star of David from the tower and they threw the Torah scrolls on the street and into the gardens around. They did not set fire on the synagogue, though, since fire would have spread easily to the other houses in old town Wetter. The fire brigadier Reinhard Gausmann refused to take any responsibility if they set fire to the synagogue and promised to take no measures to prevent the fire from spreading. The noise of the destruction attracted other people who gathered in the street by the synagogues until they were sent home by the police who eventually arrived. Two hours later, everything was calm again (Boerma 2004, 32f).

The next day in Wetter, like in the neighbouring towns and cities, the media reported—under pressure from the regime—that public rage against the Jews was to blame for the destruction of the Synagogues. On November 11, 1938 an article in the *Oberhessische Zeitung* reported: "Penalty for the worldwide Jewry: Wetter, November 10th. Spontaneous protest and flaming outrage of the inhabitants expressed themselves by attacks on Jewish property, especially on the synagogue. Its windows were destroyed and its furnishings were affected." Even in 1938, demolishing and torching of Jewish property without reason was still not allowed by the law. The fabrication of a spontaneous outburst of an anonymous crowd was necessary to legitimize these planned devastations.

These actions together with random imprisonments made it obvious that there was no place whatsoever for Jews in Germany. One example of the latter happened to Julius Dannenberg from Wetter. He was imprisoned after the pogroms in November 1938. He was not released from prison until December 1938 when he agreed to sell his farm and his property and to emigrate from Germany. In 1940 he moved from Wetter to the city of Marburg and applied for emigration, but in 1941 he was deported to the Ghetto of Riga and was probably murdered there.

After the November pogrom Flora Hess took Helmut to an all-Jewish boarding school in Frankfurt, because he could not attend school in Wetter or Marburg and because she thought he would be safe in Frankfurt. Her brother Oskar had been arrested in the November pogrom. In 1941 with the help of her brother Herbert, already in the US, and new friend Ernest Weichsel from Frankfurt, Flora was able to get a visa for herself and Helmut. After a long journey through France, Spain and Portugal they departed on the ship *Mouzino* from Lisbon and arrived at New York's Staten Island in September 1941 as one of the last groups of fugitives that were accepted in the US before the war. Flora Hess married Ernest Weichsel and they moved to Bridgeport, Connecticut. Helmut Kutsch changed his name to Harry Weichsel.

In 1942 Flora's parents, Frieda and David Hess were deported to Theresienstadt; their son Oskar was deported to Majdanek. They never returned. The last Jewish inhabitants of Wetter, Fanny and Moses Lehrberger, were deported first to the Ghetto Theresienstadt and finally were murdered in Maly Trostinec. Wetter was *judenfrei* (free of Jews). The otherness had ceased to exist. There was only *Ein Volk—ein Führer—ein Vaterland* ("one people—one leader—one Fatherland"). Twenty-six members of Jewish families had been killed in concentration and elimination camps; 43 Jewish inhabitants emigrated to Palestine or the US. The synagogue was put up for compulsory auction and sold to the Wagner family. After the war the Stöhr family bought the former Synagogue and used it for agricultural purposes. A few former inhabitants did return. Fred Buchheim, imprisoned in 1938, escaped from the prison camp and went first to the Netherlands then to the UK. He joined the British army to fight Nazi Germany. After the war in 1947, he returned to live in Wetter where he died in 1968 (Händler-Lachmann 1992, 215f).

Steps toward Reconciliation and Re-identification
In 1988, 50 years after the demolition of the synagogue, through the impetus of Hans-Uffe Boerma, school director in Wetter, some inhabitants met to prepare a brochure and to organize an exhibition about "Jews in Wetter." Through the initiative of Mayor Dieter Rincke, in 1992 the City of Wetter invited former Jewish citizens to remember the deportation of the last Jewish inhabitants in 1942. Twenty former residents with their families accepted the invitation, though others did not accept the invitation as it was too fraught with emotion. The gathering took place from September 3-10, 1992. Former Jewish inhabitants and people of Wetter met in a reception in the community centre, participated in a Sabbath service in the synagogue of Marburg, visited the Jewish cemetery and went on excursions and sightseeing tours around in the country. Highlights were the ecumenical service in the Stiftskirche of Wetter and the unveiling of a memorial plate on the wall of the town hall:

The city of Wetter remembers the people who were persecuted, tortured, deported and murdered under the people-despising national-socialistic regime because of their ethnicity, their faith, their conviction or because of their resistance. The victims remind us: Stop it before it begins.

On this occasion Harry Weichsel, the former Helmut Kutsch from the Gänseberg, made these remarks:

Since I left Wetter at seven years of age, I have returned many times to my earliest memories: to what was, to what I heard of it and to what I remember only in a blurred way. I was always eager to reconcile the past and the present—and to confirm my faith in the Truth and in human goodness.... My first memory [of Wetter]: we were at the Gänseberg. I sat on grandpa's knee, while he was playing cards—and today I still enjoy a good game of cards... I remember a friendly house, a warm oven, I remember my grandma always baking cakes and always a small cake for little Helmut. I remember my grandma preparing for the Sabbath, the clean smell and the freshly baked cakes. I remember walking the cobble stone paved Gänseberg to the Synagogue with Grandpa and Grandma... I remember Wetter and my Grandma and Grandpa Kutsch. Watching the huge Christmas tree at their home at Christmas... These are wonderful, loving and caring memories of Wetter.

But there are also the dark memories: I remember one November night in Wetter, Kristallnacht, when my Grandma and my Grandpa tore me out of bed and put me between them under a large featherbed. I could hardly breathe, when the stones flew into the upper bedroom on the bed. I remember when they came and kicked down the front door; my grandfather wanted to go down the steps and somebody threatened him: "Mr. Hess, don't come down or we will kill you." I remember that night—upstairs we cowered together full of fear—they searched the house, stole the radio and heavens know what else.

It has to be over, so that the coming generations are not] burdened with accusations. You, the ones here in front of me, you are not guilty of the death of my grandparents, nor am I guilty of the death of Jesus Christ. But we, as sons and daughters, have the responsibility make sure that we learn from the past and that what happened in the past will never happen again (Boerma 1997, 42).

Picture 3: The Former Synagogue in Wetter rebuilt as a memorial and cultural center in 2004, picture courtesy of Gerhard Lenz

In 2000, at the initiative of Mayor Rincke, the City of Wetter bought the former synagogue. Several people of Wetter founded a support group to renovate the synagogue and to use it as a centre for cultural and memorial purposes. Then in November 2008, the city of Wetter invited the former Jewish residents to open the newly renovated former synagogue and to commemorate the 70th anniversary of *Kristallnacht,* when the synagogue had been demolish and many Jewish citizens had been threatened and deported. In preparation for this event the new mayor of Wetter, Mayor Spanka, arranged an ecumenical service at the Protestant church with the Jewish community from Marburg. The support group for the synagogue prepared a memorial event at the former Synagogue.

The invited Jewish families also prepared for their visit. Eva Hausmann, sister of Harry Weichsel and daughter of Flora who was born in the US, wrote to her family in October 2008:

As we embark on our journey to revisit Wetter, Germany, I am compelled to share both some personal reflections and some historical perspective regarding our past. As the child of Holocaust survivors and the only one in the immediate family that was fortune enough to be born here, I was haunted by the past both emotionally and intellectually for much of my youth.

> *The Emotional Part:*
> *Oma Frieda, Opa David, Uncle Oscar and Oma Dora were names that I repeatedly heard throughout my childhood. They were the grandparents and Uncle I never knew but those names were mentioned frequently and most often GG Oma (Flora) as you all know her would cry as she considered her past. As I matured I realized that she had "choiceless choices." She could have stayed and perished alongside her loved ones or leave, save Harry and begin new life in America while suffering from guilt and sorrow for the rest of her days. Choiceless choices for sure.*
>
> *The intellectual part:*
> *I wanted to understand how such horror could possibly exist. I researched Hitler's life looking for answers that did not come. How could one person have done such horror to so many, I queried? Well, that took maturity to understand. He didn't do it alone. Most people were participants in the crimes against humanity. Whether they were Perpetrators or Bystanders, who stood by and did nothing, there was guilt to go around. There simply weren't enough allies— people who would take a stand against evil. And it didn't happen quickly. It was a slow degenerative process of morals, ethics and ultimately genocide.*
>
> *"Let us remember what hurts the victim most is not the cruelty of the oppressor but the silence of the bystander" (Elie Wiesel).*
>
> *So, I thought it would be helpful if I tried to give you some background both historically and specific to our family. Hope it helps, Love Eva* (Hausmann 2008).

In 2008, the visit in Wetter began with a gathering in the community hall. People of Wetter met with former inhabitants of Wetter and their families. Harry Weichsel arrived with his sister and several children, nieces and nephews. The deported and murdered Jewish citizens were commemorated, speeches were given and the male choir of Wetter sang, as they always do at official celebrations. It was during this visit that Harry Weichsel said that since his emigration, when he was asked to name his hometown, he said he was from Bridgeport, Connecticut. But from now on he will say: *"Wetteranus sum"* (Latin, "I am from Wetter").

During the next days former Jewish citizens walked through the streets they knew from their childhood and commented on the changes that had taken place. Some had old pictures and looked for their former homes. Christians and Jews went together to the synagogue in Marburg and participated in a conservative Jewish service. A Sunday Christian service in the Wetter Stiftskirche commemorated what had happened and tried to find words for the past terror and the hope of new beginnings. On Monday evening in the newly renovated former synagogue of Wetter the presence of Jewish residents in Wetter from the Middle Ages as well as their stigmatization were remembered. Students of the local high school recalled Jewish inhabitants of Wetter who were deported and killed.

On the last evening Harry Weichsel invited his Jewish family members from the US and his Christian family members named Kutsch to have dinner together. They shared old photos and shared their respective family histories. Finally, Harry Weichsel asked everyone to share their thoughts with the others at the table. While very emotional, all were grateful for this open invitation.

Two ways of Interpretation the Dealings with Diversity and Religion in Past and Presence

Irigaray's Analysis of Difference and Discourse
According to Luce Irigaray the most common instrument to turn the notion of difference into suppression of the other is to deny difference. If you deny difference you will establish the idea that there is only one gender, one colour, one ethnic, one religion. Irigaray refers to the dominance and terror of the norm and the normal over the abnormal and the deviant other. This idea is resonant with the theoretical framework of Michel Foucault and his theories of discourse (Dryfus-Rabinow 1994, 274f). Unlike both of them, however, Irigaray recognizes that the rhetoric of discourse can not only include or exclude their subjects, but can also erase those who deviate from the norm, which was exactly what the Nazi-regime did.

An analysis of discourses helps to identify a way of impersonal, collective knowing and understanding of the world. Discourses give moral and ethical guidelines in a non-reflective way that is seen as "natural" or "self-evident." Discourses are the glue that connects individuals and that forms groups. Most often discourses are shaped by common knowledge which is neither questioned nor reflected upon: *Das tut man und denkt man* (This is thought and done); *Das tut man und denkt man nicht* (This is not thought and not done).

Important characteristics of discourses are:

- No one really feels responsible for it.

- They cannot be changed easily, whether by individuals, governments or churches. Yet they change over time, especially through the force of propaganda and mass media.

- Discourses tend to struggle for omnipotence. The ones in power try to erase the others.

- Discourses not only exist in people's minds but tend to materialize in actions.

In Wetter, as is true throughout Germany, one can observe how various discourses were and are at work, whether that be a discourse of exclusion and oppression or one of reconciliation.

Ethno-psychoanalytic Understanding
Ethno-psychoanalysis is concerned with how to understand the other who is strange, exotic and in some way threatening. Maya Nadig suggests that in order to understand another culture, it is important not only to gather knowledge, but to let yourself be touched by the other. It is only then that you understand: "Every human person is in certain respects (a) like all others (b) like some others (c) and like no other" (Lartey 2003, 34).

In Wetter in the 1980's several people embarked on this journey into the unknown that had existed right in front of their doorsteps. The city of Wetter and its mayors had some experience of welcoming foreigners, such as the refugees after WW II from Hungary; this may have contributed to their ability to invite former Jewish citizens. Yet, it was also the former Jewish residents and their families who were interested in returning to Wetter. People like Flora Hess stayed connected to Wetter after emigrating, although she had not only lost her parents but had been forced by the Nazis to divorce her Christian husband. Nevertheless, she tried hard not to let the terrors of the past completely prevail over her cherished memories of her childhood in Wetter. Similarly, Harry Weichsel kept alive the religious heritage of his mother, was eventually capable of integrating his Jewish and Christian roots, and was finally able to re-identify himself as a citizen of Wetter.

Conclusion
This process of reconciliation that occurred in Wetter can be considered, on the one hand, as a change of discourse and, on the other hand, as an effort of special people to reconnect. Both of the methods briefly explored above are necessary to understand these multilayered phenomena. The method of understanding the discourses neglects the activity of people, of their motives and shortcomings. Ethno-psychoanalysis tends to leave blind spots about "the unspoken rules," which cannot be explained at the

personal level. Both methods in concert show the damage and terror that conformity and hidden anti-Semitism can produce without being intentionally "evil" as well as the opportunity and promise of confronting hidden fears and the shadows of the past.

References:

Boerma, Hans Uffe. 2004. *Jüdische Bewohner in Wetter*. Schriften zur Stadtgeschichte. 15. Wetter: Private publication.

Dreyfus, Hubert L., Paul Rabinow. 1994. *Michel Foucault. Jenseits von Strukturalismus und Hermeneutik*. Weinheim: Beltz.

Händler-Lachmann, Barbara, Harald Händler, Ulrich Schütt. 2005. *Purim, Purim, ihr liebe Leut, wisst ihr was Purim bedeut? Jüdisches Leben im Landkreis Marburg im 20. Jahrhundert*. Marburg: Hitzeroth.

Händler-Lachmann, Barbara, Ulrich Schütt. 1992. *"Unbekannt verzogen" oder "weggemacht" Schicksale der Juden im alten Landkreis Marburg 1933-1945*. Marburg: Hitzeroth.

Hausmann, Eva. 2008. "Personal reflections and historical perspective on our visit to Wetter." Unpublished manuscript.

Irigaray, Luce. 1980 (1974). *Speculum – Spiegel des anderen Geschlechts*. Frankfurt: Suhrkamp.

Keller, Reiner et al., ed. 2001. *Handbuch sozialwissenschaftlicher Diskursanalyse*. Vol.1: *Theorien und Methoden*. Opladen: Leske & Budrich.

Lartey, Emmanuel Y. 2003. *In Living Color. An Intercultural Approach to Pastoral Care and Counseling*. London-New York: Kingsley.

Nadig, Maya. 1997. *Die verborgene Kultur der Frau. Ethnopsychoanalytische Gespräche mit Bäuerinnen in Mexiko*. Frankfurt: Fischer.

Thierfelder, Constanze. 2009. *Durch den Spiegel der Anderen. Wahrnehmung von Fremdheit und Differenz in Seelsorge und Beratung*. Göttingen: Vandenhoek & Ruprecht.

Wetteraner Geschichtsfreunde—Verein für Wettersche Geschichte e.V. 1997. *Spaziergang durch Wetter ... Stichwort: 100 Jahre Synagoge in Wetter. 10. September 1897–1997*, Wetter: Private publication.

Preaching, Ritual and Worship

Religious Communication and the Challenge of Diversity: Between Disruption and Discernment

Peter Meyer

Abstract: *The shift from secularization theories to the diagnosis of religious trans-formation increasingly challenges practical theology in Europe. While diversity of lived religion rather than deviance from institutional religion comes into view, it becomes vital to formulate consequences for organized Christian practice. The concern is not with proper academic conceptualization alone: rather, it responds to the widely spread awareness of crises in Christian congregations. Focusing on the practice of preaching in German Protestantism, this contribution analyzes the most common interpretation of this crisis as being a crisis of communication. Taking a closer look through a theory of religion, quite different approaches to such a "crisis of communication" are to be distinguished. As a result, a comprehensive under-standing of this crisis as discernment within diverse and sometimes conflicting reli-gious ways of communication is achieved. Accordingly, the consequences for a professional Christian practice within a religiously diverse, intersubjective field are explored, highlighting possible connections to both contemporary theories of lan-guage as well as classical theological notions. Subsequently, homiletic tasks are outlined. Exploring the diversity of speaking and hearing as well as sharpening one's own awareness for others' experiences and practices, one arrives at a theo-logically sound as well as diversity-oriented practice in Christian religion.*

Introduction: Diversity and the tasks of Practical Theology

Religious life no less than academic theology is quick to embrace diversity, yet significantly more reluctant when dealing with substantial irritations met along this path. By human intuition, but even more so by hard institutional logic, the first actual sighting of diversity tends to be named "deviance." Hence, self-critically and realistically, (practical) theology as positional, "positive science" (*positive Wissen-schaft*)—as Schleiermacher introduced it (cf. Schleiermacher 1830)—must not underestimate the theological discernment necessary to appreciate diversity in itself. For Western European theologies, this challenge has only just begun: boosted by general scholarly insight into the analytical failure of the secularization paradigm, religious diversification rather than deviance from religion must be identified as the core of empirically undeniable transformation processes (cf. Knoblauch 2009, 15-42).

Practical theology, teleologically related to a morphologically distinct yet not once and for all times solidified religious practice, faces challenges imposed by this trans-formation in Western Europe, certainly in Germany. Lead symptoms still are: 1) individualization and high fluidity of religiosity, 2) pluralization of institutionalized religion, 3) re- and new-institutionalization, 4) a changing perception of what con-stitutes religious communities, dwindling of explicitly religious legitimizations in the public sphere, 5) societal conflicts about legal privileges of old and legal rights of publicly emerging religious groups, and 6) diminishing visibility of unambiguously identifiable "religious" practices. Increasingly, analytical attention is paid to competition between religious bodies, political and juridical fights about traditional or emerging symbols of religion in public space, and fluid new conceptions of religious identities. In public discourse, the perception of these developments as possible roots of conflict and disorientation prevails. Christian congregations—and pastors as well— not only take sides but also feel alarmed by these phenomena. After an era of joining the sometimes anxious, sometimes fatalistic analyses of deterioration or after remaining in a state of denial, the scene is presently changing: one need not possess a heightened sensitivity in order to discover religious diversity even within one's actual congregation. Faced with (and sometimes simply frustrated by) anything from complication to disruption of religious communication, pastors and congregations feel that their religious practice, religious institutions and faith are in *crisis*.

In an attempt to contribute some clarity to such morphologically identifiable *religious practice*, this essay focuses on preaching as an exemplary issue for practical theology. It attempts two main reflective moves. First, to deepen insight into communicative practice, substantial analysis is necessary: on the one hand based on theory of religion, on the other hand inspired by empirical inquiries into human practices and praxis. Second, to challenge the intuitive equivocation of religious diversity and the jeopardy to the continuance of (Christian) religion, practical theology has ample conceptual resources that allow for accessing and appreciating religious diversity.

Why describe the crisis of German Protestantism as a crisis of religious communication?

As a matter of course, crisis is no entity "out there." Nor does crisis talk point at instability or change as such. By definition, crisis is a concept reflecting a state of discrepancy: between customs and factual practices, between expectation and experience, between wish and reality. Regarding the perceived crisis in German Protestantism—and, one may well say, in main line Christianity—the following visible symptoms are frequently noted: 1) financial resources are drying up, 2) literacy in the Christian tradition is close to vanishing, 3) church affiliation and bonds to faith practice cease to be established by socializing processes, 4) different milieus are exhibiting increasingly different preferences regarding ecclesial activities, and 5) involvement in religious communities necessitates complex individual lifestyle decisions (cf. Hermelink 2006b et al.).

Each of these wide ranging symptoms is related to sociologically complex and multifactorial processes within late modern Western European cultures. However, straining to hear the *cantus firmus* at the root disruption as well as the most probable solutions in church and (practical) theology, one inevitably arrives at one term:

communication. There is much talk about communication being in crisis, communication as a dogmatically central function of the church and communication of the Gospel, culminating in the new key theological term: "religious communication."

Methodologically, this term allows for superimposing a powerful diagnostic description (i.e., disruption of communication) on a dogmatically central feature of Protestantism (i.e., the communication of the Gospel) and hence for envisioning a viable conception of responding (i.e., reinforcing, restoring and revitalizing religious communication). Admitting the disruption of communication aligns with the perspective that recognizes the essence of Christian practice as by and large linguistically framed. At the same time, it allows for including interdisciplinary perspectives. Sociology of religion in Europe, for example, following trends in the sociology of knowledge, particularly focuses on linguistic interaction in religion.

As premature as much enthusiasm connected to the common use of the term communication may be, and despite possible critique concerning reductive advances, a deeper look into the matter is worthwhile. This is especially true to the extent that it informs an empirical-theological perspective interested in the *potentials* of disruption and crisis. Methodologically, fundamental decisions affect the way of depicting the issue at stake. In order to treat this decision-making explicitly, I here outline three dimensions of analysis that match three characteristic empirical approaches to religion:

1. Attendance of the central "agency" of Christian religious communication—worship—has decreased to a 4% average of the likewise radically decreasing Protestant church membership (Pollack and Pickel 2003; EKD 2008). On an average Sunday in 2008 less than 2% of the German population opted to take part in this main event of Protestant religious communication. One may call this a crisis in the *social environment of positively religious communication*. It concerns the socially patterned as well as biographically formed preference to join regularly a distinct form of public religious practice. The saturated forms of religious semantics in a ritually distinct setting constitute the meaning of this practice for long time participants, proselytes and ex-participants only, albeit not for "real outsiders." In terms of sociology of knowledge, semantic fields or zones of meaning of this kind by and large constitute social knowledge (Berger and Luckmann 1966, 41).

2. Qualitative studies prove the precarious situation of religious communication "from within." Language that is semantically impregnated by religious traditions or that refers to materially religious entities is hardly ever actively employed, except for people acting in institutionalized, religious roles. This is equally true for those identifying themselves as being Protestants or religious as well as for those identifying themselves as not being Protestant or religious (Sammet 2006, 397; Nassehi 2007). One may call this a crisis of *individual participation in ordinary religious communication*. It concerns personal competence, preference and performance in using religious articulation. With regard to this classical realm of "positional reli-

gious communication" (cf. Kähler 2006, 405), crisis phenomena are shared by insiders and outsiders when measured against the institutionally provided positively religious communication. A qualitative-empirical approach holds much potential for analyzing this dimension of communication, as does competent Christian hermeneutics. Thus, it is perhaps closest to traditional inner perspectives of Christian religion and theology.

3. In the light of empirical work on the experience of preaching in congregations in urban areas in Germany (and in the US), one can observe that people who come to worship services in Germany perceive this kind of communication as the official property of experts. Worshippers may or may not enjoy its fruits. Most of them feel competent to judge the plausibility of the arguments or the acceptability of its pragmatic, mostly ethical implications. However, their own attempts to use fractions of religious semantics are frequently marked by linguistic means as deviant, distanced or odd: Their active usage of religious language is "bracketed" by comments or constructed in indirect and excusatory ways. Strong convictions and underlying values are in most cases neither actively connected to nor immanently linked with religious talk in a formal sense. One may call this a crisis illuminated by *lived practices in the horizon of religious semantics*. It highlights the tension between forms of lived religion and ordinary religious language on practical but also on theoretical grounds. This article argues in favor of the benefits emerging from taking this perspective seriously.

In sum, there is no such thing as "religious communication in crisis," but there are *several dimensions* of disrupted continuities in communication. The crisis aspect *therein* is dependent on the theory of religion *thereof*—and hence on the anchor point of theological evaluation: Is it about participation, communicative competence, or religious practice? As a reflection on religious practice will substantiate, it is by no means superfluous to raise this question.

What can be dysfunctional about a communicative core practice?
Only recently has theology as a whole discovered the significance of the communication crisis on a broader scale, readjusting from a deviance- to a diversification-paradigm of analysis. Practical theology may have been among the first to incorporate this changing point of view. As interesting as it would be to outline implications for various sub-disciplines, here we will pursue a more limited and concrete focus on preaching in the light of diversity. Aside from any dogmatic arguments that might be brought forward in support of this choice, we hope to provide powerful explanations that may be helpful for the construction of theological education and practice in Germany around this most widely described and visible communicative practice.

As both common opinion and sociological theories maintain, "interaction between persons" is the hallmark that unites practitioners in the societal subsystems of healthcare, jurisdiction and religion: a perspective notably introduced to practical theological discourse by Isolde Karle (Karle 2001). For the religious and pastoral profession, the "mediation of a significant tradition, a subject matter" constitutes the *core practice* (Karle 1999, 6; also Lange 1972, 157f; Kronast et al. 2005). Indeed, as empirical research has shown, next to pastoral care, no other practice is as central to defining ministry for German pastors as preaching (cf. Kronast et al. 2005, 525). Obviously, they feel especially well equipped for communicating in typical ecclesial settings such as worship, both in terms of training and motivation. Consequently, it is no surprise that in interviews, pastors in Germany express their appreciation of preaching 1) as a truly *practical* location for *theology*, 2) as a verbal conveyance of theology parallel to what they enjoyed in university classes, and 3) as a source of delight for communicating the Gospel.

At first sight, this is fully in line with the Protestant ideal of Christian ministry. Isolde Karle states, "It is the task of professions to mediate here and to achieve a *bridging of distance* related to the relevant subject matter" (Karle 1999, 5f). In this view, communication is at least partly understood as a reduction of diversity insofar as it is an effort to share information, stances, and positions, and in the process to integrate others into this sub-systemic realm.

In what way does this relate to the diversity-induced crisis in communication as outlined above? Helpful provocations come from a theory of praxis developed by empirical research into the work of social and caring professions. In these fields, life patterns different from those of the professionals under study, socially defined or pre-scripted differences, quasi-hierarchical roles, etc., are central issues in doing such practice, e.g., in social-worker/client or nurse/patient relations (cf. Heimbrock and Wyller 2010). The approach might seem awkward at first, because it highlights such deviant practices as belittling parishioners and making people means and not ends, mirroring marginalization. Yet, as extreme forms, these difficulties underscore precisely what generally is at stake.

In nearly all these professions, there is a gap between two types of activity. First, "technical practice" makes up the core of the *caring activity*, such as providing counsel, restoring health, helping someone readjust to everyday-life, etc. Such professional core activities are under strict control by social institutions. Features of this control include: a high degree of theoretical reflection (e.g., secured by academic training), an exact description and monitoring of its functionality (e.g., through procedures of quality management), and a concern with ethical soundness in the core practice itself (insured both by reflection and training).

Second, empirical studies point to spheres of practice *beyond* the "officially" scripted core activities to spheres of practice which inevitably are part of any practitioner-client encounter. These include a myriad of other activities such as small talk, organization of personal space, etc. These spheres, however diverse, significantly exhibit one trait of the practitioner-client relation: the "I-do-to-you"-model is expanded. Notably concerning linguistic practice, the technical setup of the core activity is copied and applied. As a consequence, it tends to circumvent diversity.

Communication is, in this regard, a constant problem for intersubjective spheres that are constituted by participants from diverse backgrounds, orientations, convictions, etc. Language use is likely to be organized in accordance with this technical model: the trajectory of professional action targets a deficit by means of the state of the art practice. This trajectory tends to be mirrored in the trajectory of professional language use. Consequently, the main concern is to get rid of possible disruptions in the communicative act. In terms of Aristotelian theory of action, the instrumental, *poietic* aspect of a practice becomes the object of quite intense (ethical) reflection, whereas the linguistic aspect is automatically modeled in accordance with the *poiesis* pattern of "bringing a point across."

This produces side-effects: it mirrors the practitioners' social preferences, theoretical dominances, hierarchical position etc., while neglecting the other subjects' "otherness," their preferences, concerns, spheres of relevance, etc. Perhaps the best known and most intensively scrutinized example of such an amalgamation between core activity and language practice can be found in physician-patient communication.

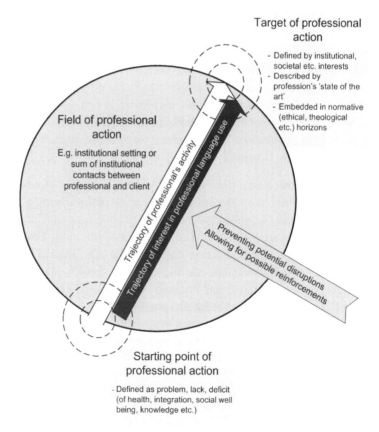

Characteristics of practice in social professions

The conceptual frame achieved through this kind of research provides a framework for considering the crises of communication in the context of religious diversity. Academic training and societal prescriptions provide the technical competences (e.g., organizing theological semantics and exhibiting highly theorized practice) for the informational core activity. Only with regard to the first dimension of communicative crisis described above can this practice model be seen as both adequate and beneficial: as an attempt to target integration-deficits, and as an attempt to overcome the disruption of positively religious communication. The second dimension, however, focuses on circumstances beyond this alleged core activity. Concerned with individual competences of speaking religiously, it asks: What are the conditions of using religious semantics? Additionally, in the third dimension, speaking in the horizon of religious semantics, one comes to ask what may be eminently religious about communication. Thus, the crisis as *disruption* becomes a crisis as *discernment* concerning communicative practice. As such, it highlights relevant issues deriving from the second and third dimension of crisis analysis.

Crisis as discernment: issues about language and praxis
This analysis of (communicative) practices needs closer scrutiny in the horizon of diversified religious life and professional practice, both from empirical perspectives. In doing so, one can turn to a conceptual frame of quite inhomogeneous origins, namely from various language-related perspectives of research and from Protestant theologies of preaching.

Some insights concerning language and language use
The crisis of religious communication urges to rethink common understandings of language. Language—as it first seems and is often simply presumed—is the perfect tool to cross the abyss of otherness by "sending a communicative package across." Of course, such an understanding would allow for a short circuit between theological reflection, *theologia practica* and the task of proclamation, similar to a dominant focus on the "core activity" of religious practitioners. However, it does not fit current insights into the conditions of human language use. Significant parts of 20th century philosophy (e.g., Merleau-Ponty; Wittgenstein; Blumenberg), linguistic inquiries into the evolutionary roots of language (e.g., Pinker; Kenneally), linguist ventures into meaning-making (Lakoff/Johnson), discoveries in sociolinguistics and ethnomethodology, as well as cognitive and developmental psychologists (Pinker; Tomasello) are united by surprisingly similar observations. Their interesting insights point to at least the following corresponding traits:

Language insinuates itself as a realm in its own right. Yet, this notion, expressed in metaphors such as "tool," "resource" or "structure," is nothing but a secondary phenomenon in terms of theoretical categorization. Other perspectives on phylo- and ontogenetic processes, social behavior, symbolic interaction, action theory, etc., suggest that at no point is a substantial understanding of language as separate entity necessary, and in some cases is quite misleading.

As Bourdieu (Bourdieu 1991) and others have pointed out repeatedly, even within linguistic communities linguistic practice functions as a subtle but influential defining force of social, cultural groups. Discourse analysis has yielded impressive examples of absolutely well meant as well as completely dysfunctional attempts to bridge those gaps via spoken interaction. Language is designed to stabilize existing social communities. It does not *per se* solve conflictive challenges of intersubjective behavior, but rests upon the existence of social intuitions and is subjected to social formations.

Language is rooted within bodily behavior, inscribing intentionality into a situated subject just as movements do. There simply is no possibility to gain deliberate distance from how we speak or what we say.

Last but not least, pragmatic aspects about language connect to complex dimensions of lived life. Semiotic and semantic theories, inquiries into truth or felicity conditions point to this complexity rather than offering unequivocal once-for-all solutions.

Practical theological reflection, then, should critically introduce the range of linguistic (im-) possibilities to both theological reasoning and professional consciousness.

Remarks on language and the practice of preaching on theological grounds
Already in Schleiermacher's practical theology, one finds this warning addressed to preachers: "The more logical correctness dominates, the more uniformity will emerge" (Schleiermacher 1850, 258). The real task is "to handle one's topic in a way that the *listener* would expect exactly this and nothing else.... from this maxim, it will be possible to develop an infinite diversity in disposition" (ibid. 258f, emphasis added).

Thus, the ruling principle of religious communication is to be found within the field of listening, structured by the plurality of personal expectation. Resting on his qualitative understanding of religion as feeling and immediate self-consciousness, Schleiermacher envisions openness for mutual religious stimulation as the professional task. Paying attention to diversity for Schleiermacher is not close to *crisis as disruption*, but points to diversity in its productivity for ambitious religious speech. Sharing religious truth decidedly aims at including the other's otherness in practice, as a potential advancement of religious life.

Self-critically, the Reformation tradition has to acknowledge certain forgetfulness about the difference between the mechanics of theological speech *about* religion and the religious practice *of* speaking. Yet, in light of the old scholastic question, Martin Luther opted for another model of theology. In his view, it should be understood as *theologia practica*, both faith and praxis together "because the practical meant to him the life itself that needs to be coped with" (Ebeling 1971, 33). According to Luther, the religious actor is determined theologically by the determining sphere of his or her activity itself, the utter passivity preceding any action, namely the relationship with God.

Praxis then refers to both determining personhood as absolute passivity and the subsequent activity sphere. This resists the temptation to reconstruct the task of religious communication as a work accomplished through words. "At first, any type of homiletics will have to focus on the fact that the well known phenomenon of preaching is but a particular type of religious mediation, an utterance particular to the religious life of Christianity" (Jetter 1982, 387). The point of this quasi-behavioral re-opening of religious communication is an awareness of the dysfunctionality resulting from separating thinking and ritualistic behavior, faith life and everyday life, words and experience.

Doing Practical Theology in the horizon of diverse ways of (religious) language use
Of all the options for dealing with diversity in the horizon of religion, the most ambitious is not only the ethically favorable, but also the most fruitful for aspiring to a new understanding of practice: expecting the other's strangeness to be of potentially unconditioned relevance for one's own convictions. For preaching, the practical theological concern could then be the overlooked and somewhat surprising religious diversity of people engaged in worship services. This means taking seriously diverse habits of dealing with "religious communication" on different levels. It is a virtue of the empirical study of religion to override the dominating institutional hard facts of "religiosity," and it is the task of present practical theology to actively participate in this endeavor because of its interest in one "positive" form of religious life. Yet, there is no shortcut from the direct subject of practical theological research to the practice itself. Practical theology is rather obliged to work on the phenomena of lived religion in its diversity, including the practice in communication. Practical theological contributions to preaching, for example, are not to result in a canon of what is to be preached, but to serve as an impulse for the perception of one's own practice as embedded in spheres of religious interests and expressions. At the same time, it maintains an institutionally interested and not arbitrary perspective.

Some concluding remarks on what this might look like. Religious practice in preaching is understood as constituted by the *perceiving intentions* involved, i.e., contemporaneous ways of making religious sense are present with churchgoers. These need to be perceived and explored. This means neither reducing the problem to a "preference" for a certain way of speaking, such as traditionally Christian, nor denying the value of particular forms of speaking, such as narratives, structured fields, and semantic conventions as powerful parts of lived Christian religion. Both must and, more importantly, can travel together.

What empirical research can strive for, then, is a *perception shift in practitioners*: taking crisis as discernment and unfamiliar forms or patterns of living as impulses for possible changes in one's own perspective is not dismissing existing praxis, but pointing to its potential growing edges. The idea is to empower practitioners to reflect more critically the language use within the contemporary societal situation of identity struggles, diversity and conflict—even within seemingly homogenous religious groups—as elements inherent in the process of finding words.

The modes of speaking religiously, also speaking from the strands of Christian tradition, cannot be detached from working on what already works among speakers and listeners. Due to the non-isolation of language, true understanding of the other-spheres involved rests upon the explorations of the experiential horizon of the other (cf. Schütz 1967). As result of socialization, subjects are not easily able to acquire distance from their personal semantic patterns. Language and forms of life are amalgamated: life provides semantics with meaning. Common forms of "explaining" religious language as symbolic or indirect are but preliminary attempts that tend to ignore the problem of pervasive diversity. Any hermeneutics has to recognize that the praxis of speaking does not "transcend," but instead names, structures, draws close to and distances itself from life, bearing all marks of human behavior.

A first concern for practical empirical theology then is with *rehabilitating the possible thickness of religious language*. Revisiting the three communicative dimensions discussed above, "other" experiences and behaviors are to be taken seriously as religiously relevant in dealing with institutionalized religious communication rather than "fixing" their disruption. Of course, there is no theoretical way of reconstructing meaning giving and orienting forms of language that at the same time guarantees the survival of their power (cf. Blumenberg 1998). However, there are interesting phenomena such as the enjoyment of fiction and story that may inspire thoughts about the ambiguity of present day reality perception, or the preference for stories when dealing with the most important aspects of personal life, or the eminent reluctance to speak through religious language.

At a time when identity building for faith communities in the midst of religious diversification is ranging high on the agenda of religious institutions in Europe, this practice model might sound like a reluctant stance, like reluctance to proclaim the Word that needs to be heard. However, it demonstrates a trusting attitude towards diversity: other ways of life are neither naively taken as "the same as mine" nor categorically localized beyond empathetic understanding. Empirical approaches in theology model an understanding that reckons with constitutive strangeness and futile familiarity as one possible outcome, instead of feeling forced to fixate both from the beginning (cf. Waldenfels 1999). Exposing Christian key practices to their factual position among religious diversity yields two major consequences: 1) the demand to work on differentiated models of (religious) praxis, since this is decisive for defining academic theology in its role as venture which is not symbiotic with lived religion; and, 2) the respective necessity to broaden theoretical understanding of the different practices relevant to religious practitioners: theology works *on* practice, without ever getting *ahead* of it.

References:

Berger, Peter L. and Thomas Luckmann. 1966. *The Social Construction of Reality.* New York: Anchor Books.

Blumenberg, Hans. 1998. *Paradigmen zu einer Metaphorologie.* Frankfurt am Main: Suhrkamp.

Bourdieu, Pierre. 1991. *Language and Symbolic Power.* Trans. Gino Raymond and Matthew Adamson, ed. John B. Thomson. Cambridge MA: Harvard University Press.

Ebeling, Gerhard. 1971. *Einführung in die theologische Sprachlehre.* Tübingen: Mohr Siebeck.

EKD (ed.). 2008. *Statistik über die Äußerungen des kirchlichen Lebens in den Gliedkirchen der EKD im Jahr 2006.* Hannover: EKD.

Heimbrock, Hans-Günter and Trygve Wyller. 2010. *Perceiving the Other: Case Studies and Theories of Respectful Action.* Göttingen: Vandenhoeck & Ruprecht.

Hermelink, Jan. 2006a. Einführung: Die IV. Mitgliedschaftsuntersuchung der EKD im Blickfeld kirchlicher und wissenschaftlicher Interessen. In *Kirche in der Vielfalt der Lebensbezüge: Die vierte Erhebung über Kirchenmitgliedschaft*, ed. Wolfgang Huber et al., 15-39. Gütersloh: Gütersloher Verlagshaus.

_____. 2006b. Die Vielfalt der Mitgliedschaftsverhältnisse und die prekären Chancen der kirchlichen Organisation. Ein praktisch-theologischer Ausblick. In *Kirche in der Vielfalt der Lebensbezüge: Die vierte Erhebung über Kirchenmitglied-schaft*, ed. Wolfgang Huber et al., 417-435. Gütersloh: Gütersloher Verlagshaus.

Jetter, Werner. 1982. Redliche Rede von Gott—über den Zusammenhang zwischen Predigt und Gebet: Eine Erinnerung an Gerhard Ebelings Beitrag zur Predigtlehre. In *Verifikationen. FS Gerhard Ebeling*, ed. Eberhard Jüngel et al., 385-424. Tübingen: Mohr.

Kähler, Reinhard. 2006. Kommentar. Religiöse Kommunikation zwischen Bedürf-nislosigkeit und Bedürfnissen, Anmut und Zumutungen. Von kommunikativen Prozessen, in denen religiöse Bezüge plausibel werden. In *Kirche in der Vielfalt der Lebensbezüge: Die vierte Erhebung über Kirchenmitgliedschaft*, ed. Wolfgang Huber et al., 405-413. Gütersloh: Gütersloher Verlagshaus.

Karle, Isolde. 1999. Was heißt Professionalität im Pfarrberuf? *Deutsches Pfarrerblatt* 99:5-9.

_____, ed. 2001. *Der Pfarrberuf als Profession. Eine Berufstheorie im Kontext der modernen Gesellschaft.* 2nd ed. Gütersloh: Gütersloher Verlagshaus.

Knoblauch, Hubert. 2009. *Populäre Religion. Auf dem Weg in eine spirituelle Gesellschaft.* Berlin-New York: Campus.

Kenneally, Christine. 2007. *The First Word. The Search for the Origin of Language.* New York: Viking Press.

Kronast, Manuel et al. 2005. Pfarrberuf zwischen Selbststeuerung und Organisation. Die Daten der Pastorinnen- und Pastorenbefragung in der Evangelisch-lutherischen Landeskirche Hannovers erlauben einen detaillierten und neu geschärften Blick auf das pastorale Selbstverständnis. *Deutsches Pfarrerblatt* 105:525-530.

Lakoff, George and Mark Johnson. 1980. *Metaphors we live by.* Chicago-London: University of Chicago Press.

Lange, Ernst. 1982. Die Schwierigkeit, Pfarrer zu sein. In *Predigen und Beruf. Aufsätze zur Homiletik, Liturgie und Pfarramt,* 142-166. München: Chr. Kaiser.

Latzel, Thorsten. 2008. Mitgliedschaft in der Kirche. In *Kirche empirisch. Ein Werkbuch,* ed. Jan Hermelink, 13-33. Gütersloh: Gütersloher Verlagshaus.

Merleau-Ponty, Maurice. 1973. *The Prose of the World.* Trans. John O'Neill. Evanston IL: Northwestern University Press.

Nassehi, Armin. 2007. Erstaunliche religiöse Kompetenz. Qualitative Ergebnisse des Religionsmonitors. In *Religionsmonitor 2008*, ed. Bertelsmann Stiftung, 113-132. Gütersloh: Gütersloher Verlagshaus.

Pinker, Steven. 2007. The Stuff of Thought. Language as a Window into Human Nature. New York: Viking Press.

Pollack, Detlef and Gert Pickel. 2003. Deinstitutionalisierung des Religiösen und Religiöse Individualisierung in Ost- und Westdeutschland. In *Kölner Zeitschrift für Soziologie und Sozialpsychologie* 55:447-474.

Sammet, Kornelia. 2006. Religiöse Kommunikation und Kommunikation über Religion. In *Kirche in der Vielfalt der Lebensbezüge: Die vierte Erhebung über Kirchenmitgliedschaft*, ed. Wolfgang Huber et al., 357-399. Gütersloh: Gütersloher Verlagshaus.

Schleiermacher, Friedrich D.E., ed. 1830. *Kurze Darstellung des Theologischen Studiums zum Behuf einleitender Vorlesungen.* 2nd ed. Reprint Darmstadt: Wissenschaftliche Buchgesellschaft (1973).

_____. 1850. *Die Praktische Theologie nach den Grundsäzen der Evangelischen Kirche im Zusammenhange dargestellt. Aus Schleiermachers Handschriftlichem Nachlasse und Nachgeschriebenen Vorlesungen*, ed. Jacob Frerichs, sämmtliche Werke I:13. Berlin: Reimers.

Schütz, Alfred. 1967. *The Phenomenology of the Social World.* Evanston IL: Northwestern University Press.

Tomasello, Michael. 2003. *Constructing a Language. A Usage-Based Theory of Language Acquisition.* Cambridge MA: Harvard University Press.

Waldenfels, Bernhard. 1999. *Vielstimmigkeit der Rede: Studien zur Phänomenologie des Fremden 4.* Frankfurt am Main: Suhrkamp.

Wittgenstein, Ludwig, ed. 1973. *Philosophical Investigations.* 3rd ed. Upper Saddle River NJ: Prentice Hall.

Differences in the Accessibility of Sunday Services in the German Protestant Church

Uta Pohl-Patalong

Abstract: Within the Protestant Church in Germany there are great differences in the accessibility of Sunday worship services, the expectations for such services and aversion to the format of the some of them. What does this mean for the structure and the future of the Sunday worship service from a practical-theological perspective? Empirical research is helpful for a practical-theological perspective.

An Overview of the Contemporary Situation

Attendance at church services of the Protestant Church in Germany has been tracked statistically since the 1950's. On a normal Sunday in 2006, 3.7% of the Church's membership attended worship, which is 941,359 people attending a total of 25,551 Sunday services. Percentage-wise, these numbers have not changed significantly since the 1970s, and they are not a revolutionary change from the 1960s, when the number was about 8%. It is somewhat typical for a member of the German Protestant Church to distinguish between being a Christian and going to church. Nonetheless, this situation ought to give the Church something to think about, especially since people are continuing to go to church less and less often. Considering also that approximately one-quarter of the membership of the Protestant Church has officially withdrawn since the 1970s, the situation appears even more precarious: obviously it is *not* the case, as has long been assumed (and hoped), that everyone who took the Christian faith less seriously would eventually withdraw from the Church, leaving behind a remnant with an intensive, binding commitment to what the Church has to offer.

Even for the majority of the Church's remaining members and—as sociological surveys have shown—for those remaining consciously uncommitted to the Christian faith, regular attendance at Sunday worship is not very attractive and apparently has little relevance for their faith and for their lives. We get a very different picture, however, if we view attendance not only over the course of a week, but also over the course of a year or of a lifetime. Statistics have shown an increasing number of people attending church on religious holidays beginning in the 1980s, and this is an upwards trend. In 2006, for example, 37.8% of the Church membership attended a Christmas Eve service. There is continued demand among Church members for christenings and weddings; more and more non-members desire these as well. Participation in services marking the beginning of children's first year of school has increased enormously in recent years. When events transpire that disturb society, people are requesting and holding Sunday services much more often than even a few years ago, and some of these services have had enormous attendance. It is apparent that people perceive regular Sunday worship in a very different way than services on such special occasions. A monthly rhythm can be discerned as well: increasing numbers of people go to church neither every Sunday, nor exclusively on special occasions, but rather approximately once a month, depending on what their local church offers (e.g., family, thematic, or specially organized worship). Some people are even going to church on an individualized schedule. There obviously need to be plausible reasons for going to church on Sunday morning, as opposed to the many other ways one could spend that time.

It is long been clear that such reasons for or against going to church are not only a question of faith, but also depend to a high degree on independent factors such as age and gender. The perception of these relationships in practical theology in the German-speaking countries has become more clearly differentiated in the last few years. The so-called "milieu theory" has been helpful, particularly regarding church attendance: it shows us that the accessibility of church services depends significantly on people's identifying themselves with certain "lifestyles," and in turn on aesthetic, socio-cultural factors and on people's individual preferences. One's lifestyle has a significant influence on whether one goes to church; if one does go to church, one's lifestyle influences the rhythm of one's attendance as well as the criteria for attending church. Older people who lead more traditionally oriented lives and who are highly educated attend services most regularly; this is also true to a lesser extent for older people with average educations. The reach of the Church extends least into the youth culture and—what is especially alarming from a theological perspective—into marginalized and disadvantaged social groups. Between these extremes are two social groups comprised of the middle-aged. One group, those mainly living in urban contexts, primarily attends church services on special occasions, while the other group attends church primarily on family occasions. Besides their frequency of church attendance, there are also significant differences in what these groups expect from worship. One notable difference can be discerned between those attendees who have what could be considered high cultural expectations (i.e., an orientation toward organ music, cantatas and a sophisticated sermon) and those who expect a friendly and genial atmosphere (i.e., a non-liturgical greeting and a sermon that reflects every-day life). An especially significant difference separates those who expect the traditional liturgical form versus more experimental elements (e.g., skits, dance, etc.). Even musical tastes vary greatly. Whereas one group cannot imagine worship without traditional hymnody and, whenever possible, some Bach cantatas, for others modern songs and alternative instruments are essential.

This variety of preferences regarding church services reflects the fact that the worship landscape in Germany has become highly pluralized in the last few years. Since the 1990s there have been so-called "alternative" forms of worship in more and more parishes, sometimes known as "free-form services" or "Channel Two." These do not seek to replace the traditional, liturgical Sunday morning service, but instead to complement it. They ordinarily take place on Sunday evening. They appeal predomi-nately to people who do not find the traditional forms of worship inviting—either in its aesthetics or content—and they are especially appealing to those who have distanced themselves from the Church or feel little connection to it. These services are mostly designed around the search for orientation and meaning, around the experiencing of religion and of more open forms of community. They try to show the relevance of the Christian faith in the individual's life. Accordingly, they make a particular effort to remain comprehensible and do not assume that people will slowly grow into the worship. These services are usually prepared by a team, and they provide a range of opportunities for participation. Creative elements such as short skits, dance and one-on-one dialogue are typical, as is modern music, often performed by professionals performing contemporary songs. Such services try to appeal to the senses and to the emotions, standing in opposition to what could be considered a culture of more intellectually oriented services. In this way they are suited to today's experience-oriented society. These worship services are challenging the still dominant parochial logic of the German Church, according to which the local parish feels responsible for all the Church members within a specific geographic location. Instead such services presuppose an aesthetic choice made on the basis of a subjective conviction that says: "I'm going to the Church service whose structure appeals to me" instead of "I'm going to Sunday worship at my local parish."

Theological Considerations

From the perspective of theological reflection, the current situation is ambivalent. On the one hand, the diversification of services confronts one problem of traditional worship services, namely that they are so strongly oriented toward a certain social group that they are made inaccessible to the majority of the membership. At least since the advent of these alternative forms of worship, it has become clear that the traditional service is really aimed at a certain target group that does not, in fact, live up to its ideal of being open to all Christians. In light of the Church's mission of communicating the Gospel to all the world and of supporting people in their faith and in their lives regardless of their social status, this is eminently important theo-logically. From this standpoint, the diversification of forms of worship ought to be redoubled, because the alternative forms still reach the youth only in a limited way, and they fail completely to reach disadvantaged social groups.

On the other hand, the diversification of services creates a situation that contributes to various social groups closing themselves off from one another, and it makes the experience of a community of Christians founded in Jesus Christ more elusive than ever. The idea of Sunday worship being the focal point of the congregation is farther beyond reach than ever. The pluralization of society and its thorough orientation toward the subject and toward his or her individual preferences puts church services in a precarious situation. Apparently there is now no form of worship that appeals to all Church members (or even to non-members) across social classes and across the spectrum of members' needs. Can practical theology not only recognize this, but can it instead contribute something positive to the situation as well? Intensive empirical research seems the most sensible way to do this.

Intensified Empirical Research

In recent years, a few sociological studies and a few practical-theological studies of participation in Church services have been carried out in the German-speaking countries. Their methods were either quantitatively oriented, or they surveyed Church members qualitatively about their preferences toward Church services and placed them into various "types," e.g., persons who participated in worship only at Christmas, persons who participated in worship only sporadically, and persons who participated in worship regularly (Roßner 2005, 264ff). Other studies focused on those who rejected worship, who thought positively about worship but personally preferred other activities and associations, and those who thought worship important (Martin 2007). These studies revealed that the preferences differed significantly between the groups.

As I delved deeper into this topic, I was astounded to find that no one has yet questioned church goers in detail about how they experience religious services, what elements are especially important to them and why, and what aspects are critical for people's attendance. I made this the goal of an empirical study currently in progress. My co-workers and I carried out 22 interviews with people from across social groups, age, sex, urban and rural settings, and East and West Germany, who regularly or occasionally attend Protestant Church services. I was explicitly not interested in classifying them or in discerning types, but wanted instead to listen closely and to understand the subjects' experiences, longings, and desires. We asked them about their subjective experience of the various elements of the worship services such as the sermon, readings, prayer, the blessing and music. We also asked them about such things as the importance of the others participating in the services, the role of habit, the importance of being greeted at the door and about what they expected of the minister. Currently I am evaluating the interviews and can only report some preliminary results. Already, we are gaining very interesting insights that could be helpful in addressing the problem I sketched previously.

1. The people we have interviewed have diverse aesthetic preferences. This becomes especially clear regarding music styles: for some the centuries-old, familiar songs in the hymnal are essential, while for others cheerful and contemporary songs are important ("...I especially like modern religious songs...with guitar, piano, [and] drums, because they hold so much vitality," *twenty-five year old male*). Some appreciate the traditional liturgy ("it has its routine, I'm familiar with it, I can own it and ... somehow that gives me security and orientation and clarity," *sixty-six year old male*). Other appreciate new elements ("I also like it when they try new things," *thirty-nine year old female*). However, approximately half of those questioned do not draw clear conclusions on these questions and cannot explicitly comment on the

various styles of worship ("they can go ahead and vary things up," *seventy year old female*). It is interesting that precisely those individuals who express flexibility with regard to the *kind* of church service demand that the service be "real" and "authentic," and that it provide an atmosphere corresponding to the content expressed ("for me style doesn't count as much as the fact that it is done with care. If I can hear the soul coming through, it's all good," *forty-seven year-old male*).

2. We found a similar situation regarding the sermon. For most of those questioned this is a very important part of their church experience. However, we find differences as well. For some the sermon must above all be comprehensible and not too long, while others want a solidly grounded presentation of biblical text ("a sermon is no pre-packaged event, with pretzels and cola. The meal served should be a challenging one," *sixty-six year-old male*). Almost unanimously, subjects say that the sermon must speak to them about their faith and about their lives, and they demand that it be relevant ("that I get something out of it that I can use in my day-to-day life," *twenty-five year-old male*). The great majority explicitly expect the sermon to offer critical reflection on how they lead their lives and not so much be a source of comfort , as is often assumed ("that [the sermon] gives inspiration on how it's possible to become a better person," *twenty-six year-old female*).

3. People reported various expectations as to the role of the minister, but here there is also surprising consensus. One example concerns the authenticity of the minister's presence and of their preaching which, for almost everyone, should exhibit "a really natural charisma. Nothing put on or forced" (*sixty-nine year-old female*). The lack of authenticity is also a point of criticism for some ("...I also have the impression, that they don't even know what they're saying. Because they've developed it from a theory, but aren't living it," *forty-seven year old male*).

4. Almost all those surveyed see the service as a way to connect to the essence of life, to God and to themselves. They seek a departure from the day-to-day and, at the same time, would like to gain strength and orientation for daily living ("somehow, you know, I get really torn away from it all and just get another perspective on my life, ... to be thankful again and again, you forget a lot, you know, how beautiful it all really is," *thirty-nine year old female*; "...that you leave every-day life outside and go into an environment that appeals to what's inside me," *thirty-five year-old female*).

5. Almost all those questioned highlighted the importance of the blessing at the end of the service. Interestingly, people interpret it in very different ways ("People who receive a blessing can pass it on to others," *eighty-two year old female*; "When the minister gives the blessing, you feel yourself to be a member of a community, of Christ's community," *twenty-five year-old male*; "It's such a nice way to round out the whole thing and ... that's what you take with you, you know, for the days to come," *forty year-old female*; "so that you can just come out feeling stronger,"

twenty-seven year-old male). The same element can be understood in very different ways, and yet be very meaningful for everyone.

6. Likewise there is a desire among all social groups and all age groups to find one's own self during the service and to receive something for one's own life ("...I like to be spoken to or touched, *"fifty-nine year-old female*). There are many ways in which this can happen: through the welcome feeling that arises upon being greeted, through contents of the sermon that are relevant to one's life, through the familiarity of the others present, and especially through the music.

What Can Be Learned from This Study
With all due caution, one important result that emerges from this study is that the variety of preferences and orientations toward Church worship services, while certainly present, is in fact quite relative. It is not surprising that Church-goers follow aesthetic criteria similar to those of their every-day lives. It is more surprising that, for many, these are *less important* than other factors that include: 1) an authentic atmosphere and an authentic organization of the service, 2) relevance to their own lives, 3) an experience of being spoken to in a way that touches and respects their authentic self, and 4) being inspired in their own lives and in their own faith. Many Church members apparently can find such content in various forms of worship. As to the reasons why people participate in so-called "alternative services," it is not uncommon to hear them say that the traditional liturgical services often do not meet these criteria. In the practical-theological debate about the Protestant Church in Germany right now, it is possible that the discussion of content of the contemporary worship is revolving too much around questions of formal diversification and plurality of aesthetic preferences. The new forms of church service do not only see themselves as "alternatives" with regard to form, but also claim to provide content that in general is not being offered in traditional Sunday morning services, e.g., they speak to people on a personal level, support them in their faith and in their lives, and be relevant. My study reveals a similar demand, but one expressed especially with reference to the traditional form of worship.

At the same time, the plurality of new styles and forms of worship is in no way meaningless, but can be interpreted as an indication of a movement toward worship that speaks to people beyond traditional worship forms and that shows them the value and provides motivation for going to church. Practical theology in Germany would be well served to support this movement by carefully attending to the participating subjects and their experience and by considering worship services more through the lens of what is important to people rather through a focus on the aesthetic form. Perhaps the whole of a worship service can be informed by the way(s) people have spoken in our interviews about the blessing, i.e., how one element is perceived and interpreted differently, but it is equally important to all.

References:

Martin, Jeannett. 2007. Mensch - Alltag - Gottesdienst. Bedürfnisse, Rituale und Bedeutungszuschreibungen evangelisch Getaufter in Bayern. In *Bayreuther forum TRANSIT Kulturwissenschaftliche Religionsstudien* 7:115-131.

Roßner, Benjamin. 2005. *Das Verhältnis junger Erwachsener zum Gottesdienst. Empirische Studien zur Situation in Ostdeutschland und Konsequenzen für das gottesdienstliche Handeln.* Leipzig: Evangelische Verlagsanstalt.

Re-Claiming Sabbath as Transforming Practice: Critical Reflections in Light of Jewish-Christian Dialogue

Claire E. Wolfteich

Abstract: Dialogue among Jews and Christians has advanced considerably—in the Roman Catholic world, particularly since the Vatican II document Nostra Aetate *(1965). Yet significant areas of conflict persist. While the topic of Sabbath usually is not at the forefront of Jewish-Christian dialogue, Sabbath could be an important entry point into difficult questions about the relationship between Judaism and Christianity and the complexities of practice in pluralistic communities. Sabbath practice represents both a point of shared heritage and a divisive force within and among communities. These issues provide a kind of training ground for practical theology and interreligious dialogue, potentially opening up life-transforming practices.*

The Sabbath is a powerful gift and alternative theological witness in contemporary US culture obsessed with activity and productivity. Sabbath practices witness to a Creator God who is Source of all life and who models the creative rhythm of work and contemplative rest. Sabbath practices should be integral to Christian spirituality and religious leadership. Yet, the culture of theological education and church life often nurture the same kind of frenzied activity prevalent in society at large. It is vital that practical theologians consider how to teach Sabbath practices in life-transforming ways that fully engage the complexities of Jewish-Christian dialogue and open up mutual understanding. This task will sometimes require radical critique of educational and religious institutions.

Introduction

Chanting filled the room as the sky darkened outside the chapel windows. Shadows played on the Charles River below; the Orthodox Hillel students—men and women separated by a white curtain—*davened* and chatted and settled in. A young woman leaned over to tell us, Christian visitors from a neighboring theological school, about the prayers and how they were greeting the Sabbath like a bride. The door was thrown open, the Sabbath welcomed. The joy was palpable—to us, both strange and inviting.

In the Conservative chapel next door, students entered and moved around freely, laughing and greeting one another. The rabbi appeared and began a sermon about Sabbath. He told the story of a Jewish man who took a job during the Great Depression that required working on Saturday. Though he worked to feed his children, he despised the choice he had made and thereafter saw himself as a Sabbath breaker. He would not read the Torah in the synagogue. The students debated with the rabbi: was it permissible for the man to work on the Sabbath under those circumstances? Could he have kept the Sabbath and still kept his family alive?

They intensely debated and the Christian theology students joined the energetic conversations in the hallway after the service.

From a third chapel came the calm sounds of guitars and strains of prayers chanted in English. The Christian theology students entered into this Reformed service more easily, reading prayers along and singing the gentle songs that greeted the evening. When services ended Orthodox, Conservative and Reformed students spilled into a hallway for Kiddush then a shared Shabbat dinner. The Christian students were warmly welcomed at the meal.

In the practice of keeping Sabbath, differences within the Jewish community were plain to see. Three chapels, three services—practices that were the same yet not the same. The divisions did not prevent coming together in the shared Kiddush and meal. Community and diversity coexisted without irreconcilable conflict. Practice held the community together, even a practice about which the Jewish community is deeply divided. Surely, this was an unusual model of shared Shabbat practice.

The Christian visitors welcomed in various ways into Jewish community practices, encountered Shabbat—a powerful practice that ritually narrates a long story of conflicted relationships between Jews and Christians. Might this practice transform Christians? To ask this question opens a range of complex issues. Does the Sabbath command have its origin in a creation ordinance—and hence is binding on all persons—or is it part of a particular covenantal relationship between God and the Jews, given through Mosaic law? How does the celebration of the resurrection of Christ on Sunday, the Lord's Day and eighth day, relate to observance of Sabbath on the seventh day? Where might contemporary Jews and Christians meet in a shared appreciation for the gift of Sabbath, while avoiding supersessionism or misappropriations of Jewish understandings of Shabbat?

Sabbath Practices, Practical Theology and Jewish-Christian Dialogue
Dialogue between Jews and Christians has advanced considerably. In the Roman Catholic world this is particularly true since the publication of Vatican II's "Declaration on the Relation of the Church to Non-Christian Religions" (*Nostra Aetate*, 1965). This document called for a more open and close relationship with Jews, stating: "Since the spiritual patrimony common both to Christians and Jews is of such a magnitude, this Sacred Synod wants to foster and recommend mutual understanding and respect which is, above all, the fruit of biblical and theological studies as well as of fraternal dialogues" (no. 4). Yet significant areas of conflict persist. For example, the 2010 visit of Pope Benedict XVI to the Synagogue of Rome marked an important moment of dialogue and repentance. The pope placed flowers at two memorial tablets—one for victims of the Holocaust and one for a child killed in a 1982 terrorist attack at the synagogue. With the Chief Rabbi of Rome, Benedict called for deepening mutual understanding and solidarity between Christians and Jews. However, the visit also underscored continuing tensions

between Catholic and Jewish leaders on the Vatican's apparent silence during the Holocaust. Benedict's benevolent interpretation of Pius XII's "discreet" actions during the Holocaust contrasted sharply with the critique articulated by Riccardo Pacific, president of the Jewish community of Rome.

Institutions committed to theological education must form Christian leaders with a deep understanding of Judaism and an ability to engage in Jewish-Christian dialogue. Sabbath is ordinarily not at the forefront of Jewish-Christian dialogue—despite the irony that while Benedict was visiting the Roman Synagogue an annual meeting of Italian Roman Catholic bishops and Jewish leaders pondered the Sabbath commandment. Sabbath could be an important entry point for practical theological reflection and interreligious dialogue.

Christian ministers and laity need to learn healthy and faithful ways of structuring and engaging time. Too often cultural fixations on productivity and activity shape our faith communities and schools of theology. Consequently, clergy and laity alike can be lulled into distorted rhythms of work (without rest) and the subsequent tendency to self-identify not according to who they are but what they do. In a research project with US urban pastors, pastors reported being "exhausted in every way," "addicted to busy," "over-functioning" and "workaholic." "We wear our exhaustion as a trophy," said one Virginia pastor (Stone and Wolfteich 2008, 43). Sabbath is a countercultural practice that resists these distortions and carries an alternative vision of time and work within God's good creation. Sabbath re-enacts on a weekly basis the exodus event. As Jewish theologian Abraham Joshua Heschel writes, "The seventh day is the exodus from tension, the liberation of [people] from [their] own muddiness…" (Heschel 1951, 29).

Many Christians today need such liberation but know little of the Sabbath. John Primus of Calvin College asserts, "The Sabbath needs serious reconsideration within Protestantism today" (Primus 1991, 115). In his 1998 encyclical "The Day of the Lord" (*Dies Domini*), Pope John Paul II called Christians to renewed appreciation of the rich heritage of Judaism and the Sabbath, which he considered key to the reinvigoration of Sunday: "In order to grasp the meaning of Sunday … we must re-read the great story of creation and deepen our understanding of the theology of the 'Sabbath'" (*Dies Domini*, no. 8). Theologians such as Jürgen Moltmann and Karl Barth have argued for the importance of Sabbath for Christian theology. Moltmann sees in the Sabbath laws—with their insistence on rest for all people and the earth—a profound principle of ecology and social justice integral to the life of the Christian community (Moltmann 1985). The past decade has seen a spurt of Christian writing on Sabbath (Muller 1999; Bass 2000; Dawn 2006; Wirzba 2006; Buchanan 2007).

While this work provides an important theological foundation, more important is a study of Sabbath and the practices of Sabbath in life-transforming ways, attentive to the interreligious dimensions of this venture. This study of Sabbath practices needs serious attention in both theological education and congregational life. Reflection on Sabbath practices is a significant entry into complex questions about the relationship between Judaism and Christianity, theologies of work, the meaning of Sunday, stewardship and creation. Furthermore, Sabbath practices are deeply formative, shaping community, leadership and spiritual life. Ironically, the cultures of theological education and church life often nurture the same kind of frenzied activity prevalent in the society at large. Those training for ministry too often learn patterns of work that set them up for burnout without the deep spiritual wells from which they can draw. Many congregations unknowingly conspire by overemphasizing programs and meetings, leaving little space for contemplation in community. The invitation to reclaim Sabbath in preparing religious leaders is a powerful theological alternative.

Practical theology has much to contribute here, offering resources for critical reflection on practice, ways of reading the theologies imbedded in practice and constructively shaping practices of faith communities. Practical theology can provide methodologies for studying the intricacies of Sabbath practice and teaching practice in ways that open up both critical reflection and life transformation.

It is not sufficient to study Sabbath in a textbook: practice here is indispensable. Practical theologians have highlighted the epistemological dimension of practice; practice enables us to know things about God and ourselves that we otherwise would not know in the same way. Considering the Sabbath, for example, Craig Dykstra and Dorothy Bass assert that "Christians who keep holy a weekly day of rest and worship acquire through the Christian practice of Sabbath-keeping an embodied knowledge that the world does not depend on our own capacity for ceaseless work.... Observing Sabbath on the Lord's Day, Christian practitioners come to know in their bones that creation is God's gift, that God does not intend that anyone should work without respite, and that God has conquered death in the resurrection of Christ" (Dykstra and Bass 2002, 25).

Concurrently, explorations in Sabbath practices require practical theologians to think about the complexities of practice in pluralistic contexts. While what Dykstra and Bass say is true, it is also the case that Sabbath practices immediately raise complex questions, e.g., 1) what are we doing when we "observe Sabbath on the Lord's Day,"? 2) what does this imply for Christian theologies of Judaism?, and 3) how might Sabbath practices both unite and divide faith communities? Sharing Sabbath practices in their varied forms can be a way into deepened understanding between Jews and Christians.

Religious practice also can be the crux of conflict within and between faith communities. This is certainly true with Sabbath keeping, e.g., the issue of driving on the Sabbath remains a major point of conflict among Orthodox, Conservative and Reformed Jews. Such questions of practice plumb the depths of Jewish identity. To what extent should strict Sabbath observance define Jewish identity? How do we interpret the categories of forbidden work in light of technological developments?

Sabbath also has been a point of conflict among Christians. Seventh-day Adventists, for example, hold Saturday as the Christian day of rest and worship, disagreeing with positions that hold Sunday as the replacement or fulfillment of the Sabbath. Adventist scholar Samuele Bacchiocchi critiques the papal encyclical *Dies Domini*: "The Pope's attempt to make Sunday the legitimate fulfillment of the creative and redemptive meanings of the Sabbath is very ingenious, but unfortunately it lacks Biblical and historical support" (Bacchiocchi 1998, 5). Bacchiocchi argues the Sabbath itself holds creative, redemptive and eschatological meaning—and does not need Sunday to complete it. Rather, he asserts that Christians adopted Sunday following Constantinian legislation that made the Day of Sun a day of rest and worship, in part to avoid anti-Jewish persecution. For centuries, Christians have debated the meaning of Sabbath and Sunday, and the issues have divided parts of the Christian community. Michael Lodahl proposes that it may be possible to hold these different voices in a creative tension within the church. He asserts that Sabbatarian Christians stand as "crucial witnesses pulling the church back to consider its Jewish foundations—as long as they avoid the supersessionist trap....in their own distinctive ways, and certainly without having intended consciously to do so, 'Christians who observe Shabbat' and Christians who worship on Sunday together bear witness to the creative interplay of continuity and discontinuity between Judaism and Christianity" (Lodahl 1991, 268-269).

Sabbath practices also pose interesting and sometimes conflictual datum in pluralistic contexts. The *eruv*, the symbolic fence that permits Orthodox Jews to carry objects within its boundaries on the Sabbath, has ignited conflict in several locations. For example, prompted by residential complaints, the Quebec Superior Court in 2001 considered whether the city of Outrement had the right to dismantle *eruv* wires. The court considered the arguments that permitting the *eruv* wires strung in public space amounted to an unfair favoring or promotion of one religion over another. To the contrary, it decided that dismantling the *eruv* wires constituted a government intrusion on the free exercise of religion (Rosenberg vs. Outrement 2001; see also Stoker 2003).

In the US, Colonial "Blue Laws" instituted by Puritans forbade commercial activity on Sunday. Over time such laws have been modified and challenged, including a protest by Maryland department store workers who argued that the laws unfairly required all to observe Sunday as a day of rest. The 1961 Supreme Court decision McGowan vs. Maryland ruled that while the laws originally were founded for religious reasons, they now could be justified with secular rationales and thus were legal. While blue laws continue to forbid the sale of alcohol on Sunday in many locations, today most stores do open on Sunday. Hence, Bass can propose that a

Christian reclaiming of Sabbath could be a countercultural renunciation of commerce (Bass, 2000, 64). The cultural situation has swung 180 degrees.

Studying Sabbath presents an important entry point for negotiating the complexities of practice within and among diverse faith communities. Entering these issues provides a kind of training ground for practical theology and interreligious dialogue. Sabbath practices should be seen as integral to Christian spirituality and religious leadership. It is vital that practical theologians consider how to teach this practice in ways that open up the gift and fully engage the complexities of the practices in light of Jewish-Christian relations.

Attending to Practice: Explorations in Pastoral Life and Theological Education
Over a period of five years, my colleague Bryan Stone and I co-directed a project entitled "Sustaining Urban Pastoral Excellence" (SUPE), funded by the Lilly Endowment and based at Boston University. Working with 96 urban pastors across the US, we involved them in a program of peer meetings, spiritual renewal, study and a funded sabbatical. Our terminology shifted as we did this work. We began by offering what we called an "enrichment leave." We quickly renamed this "sabbatical" and then framed "sabbatical" more explicitly in theological terms as "Sabbath"—a time of spiritual rest, renewal and re-creation. Pastors described this time of "Sabbath" as incredibly important, sometimes life-changing. To be sure, it gave much-needed rest as well as an invitation to creativity, a reconnection with self and family, space for reflection on one's call, and a new perspective on ministry. One pastor called this a shift from "idolatrous" ministry—overly reliant on his ceaseless work as pastor—to a more balanced and humble ministry that pointed beyond the pastor to what God might be doing in the community." This research underscores the importance of Sabbath practices in the forming and sustaining of excellent pastors (Stone and Wolfteich 2008).

We also found that cultural emphases on productivity distorted even understandings of Sabbath. Pastors too often described Sabbath instrumentally, as a way to recharge their batteries for the work ahead. They often felt pressure from their congregations to rationalize their sabbaticals in productive terms. One pastor preached about his upcoming sabbatical, comparing himself to a lumberjack who takes a break to sharpen his ax (Stone and Wolfteich 2008, 59). Clearly, there is a need for education around and formation in Sabbath, not as a technique for maximizing productivity but as a way of entering into God's creative and life-giving rhythm. Heschel writes, "To the biblical mind ... the Sabbath as a day of rest, as a day of abstaining from toil, is not for the purpose of recovering one's lost strength and becoming fit for the forthcoming labor. The Sabbath is a day for the sake of life" (Heschel 1951, 14). Jewish theologian Aryeh Kaplan describes Sabbath rest as a time for "relinquishing our mastery over the world." In this, we emulate God, who rested on the seventh day not because God was tired but as a way of no longer "asserting ... mastery over the universe" (Kaplan 1974, 19).

At Boston University, we currently are working on a project that hopes to bring the findings from our work with urban pastors into dialogue with programs for the formation, mentorship and teaching of ministry students. This entails curricular and co-curricular initiatives, including 1) the development of partnerships with field education congregations committed to the nurturing of Sabbath practices in student-pastors; 2) dialogue with campus Hillel, area rabbis and Christian groups such as the Lord's Day Alliance; 3) regular spiritual renewal opportunities for students, including retreats and a weekly "Sabbath Space" offering students space and time for rest, fellowship and creative activities in the middle of the busiest day on campus; and 4) a new course entitled "Sabbath: Theology and Practice," conjointly taught by a Jewish Rabbi and Christian practical theologian. It is this last element that we will explicate here more fully.

The Course

In the first year of the course, the instructors were a Roman Catholic practical theologian and an Orthodox rabbi, teaching in a predominantly liberal Protestant university-based school of theology. The students were almost entirely Christian ministry and doctoral students, with one undergraduate Jewish student. We also had the opportunity to dialogue with students from Reform, Conservative and Orthodox traditions at Boston University Hillel. The circles of dialogue included a range of Jewish, Protestant and Roman Catholic voices. Such forms of teaching seem in keeping with what Mary Boys describes as "interreligious learning" or "learning in the presence of the other" (Boys and Lee 2006). Indeed, we found that learning together about Sabbath—studying in pairs, sharing stories, reading texts, debating interpretation, reflecting on experience—opened the potential to discover points of commonality and shared wisdom.

The course was envisioned within a practical theological framework. Historical and theological study of Sabbath in the varied Jewish and Christian traditions was continually brought into contact with contemporary contexts, issues and practices. Furthermore, students designed a practical theological project as a central course requirement. We explored classic texts on Sabbath from the Bible, Talmud the Mishnah, as well as authors such as Heschel, Kaplan, Blu Greenberg, Jacob Staub and Francine Klagsbrun. We also examined historical and contemporary Christian writing on the Sabbath and Lord's Day. Again and again we returned to questions of practice. For many of the Christian students this focus on practice seemed driven by a personal desire and sense that Sabbath might be spiritually renewing in their own busy lives, their congregations and their families.

As a practical theologian whose discipline is spirituality, I understand the incorporation of practice in my teaching to be an important means of coming to understand the subject manner. Scholarship in practical theology and in spirituality points to the important role of practice in pedagogy. Practices are theory-laden; they embody and enact beliefs. Practices also are deeply formative; they shape belief, religious identity and community. As Bonnie Miller-McLemore writes, "Practical theologians teach a practice with the expectation that participation in that practice will cultivate the kind of knowledge, *phronesis*, that deepens students' capacities for further participation in the practice" (Miller-McLemore 2008, 180). Practices also invite us into spiritual wisdom and transformation. Practice is built into ancient Christian traditions of passing on spiritual wisdom. As Burton-Christie demonstrates, encountering the word in early Christian monasticism (whether the word of Scripture or the word of life given by an *abba* or *amma*) had a cost—a response in practice. The "desert hermeneutic" required self-implication and transformed life. To encounter a word implied the question: "What shall I do?" (Burton-Christie 2005, 100). This "desert hermeneutic" carries forward to contemporary contexts of theological education. The study of spirituality is self-implicating and deeply connected to practice. Elizabeth Liebert makes this point when she argues that the study of spirituality requires "doing always what it is that we study (as well as studying what we do)." Here she refers not so much to the importation of spiritual practices into the classroom but more broadly speaks to the practice of communal, self-critical reflection on lived faith (Liebert 2005, 86-87).

Similarly, the best way for students to understand the meaning of Sabbath is by practicing Sabbath in some form or another. They need to be implicated in the practice—open to knowing differently, open to the cost of interpretation, e.g., the call to restructure our time in countercultural ways. Yet, what constitutes "practice" in a religiously diverse teaching context? And do we seek "further participation" when we cross over into another community's practice?

Our class was held on Fridays, and several times during the semester the class moved from our classroom to Hillel for evening Shabbat services and dinner. This was an important "practice" woven into the course. Yet were the students *practicing* Sabbath or were they respectfully *observing* Sabbath practice? These questions can be approached from diverse Jewish and Christian perspectives. From an Orthodox Jewish perspective, for example, Christian visitors to Hillel are not "keeping Sabbath." In fact, the carefully delineated rabbinical categories of what must and must not be done on the Sabbath do not apply to Christians; not only are Christians not obligated to follow these strictures but non-Jews *should not* practice Sabbath as do Jews. Converts to Judaism are encouraged to break the Sabbath until they are fully through the conversion process. From a Christian perspective, one might ask whether the Shabbat experience and subsequent reflection could be understood as a kind of mystagogy. Is there here an entering into a divine mystery that can be lived into and further shaped within the life of the Christian community? John Witvliet writes that "our teaching is, in part, mystagogical. Wise patristic pastors knew that an abstract sacramental theology would mean little to new Christians. One had to experience Eucharist to understand it. After experiencing it, intentional theological reflection offered a source of deeper insight and participation. This ancient post-experience, mystagogical approach to formation provides a helpful model for practice-oriented teaching today" (Witvliet 2008, 129). Can this approach be employed with regard to Christian practices of Sabbath keeping, or is the Friday evening visit better described as a practice of another sort—the practice of being a guest, a deep listener, a respectful conversation partner? Mary Boys argues that "border crossing" practices are critical in religious education and formation: "Were we to consider 'understanding and dialogue' a mandate for those with educational responsibilities in the churches, then it would obligate us to at least two commitments: engagement with the 'other' and employment of pedagogical practices that enable persons to engage in 'border crossing'.... Might we not assert that in a pluralistic world, no Christian can responsibly educate other Christians if he or she has not encountered in some significant way the beliefs and practices of a religious 'other'" (Boys 1997, 87).

The visits to Hillel were powerful and transformative for many of the Christian students. Some longed for what they felt at Hillel—the community, the weekly joy, the rhythm of rest, the gift of Shabbat. They experienced what Boys, following on biblical scholar Krister Stendahl, describes as "holy envy," a key virtue that she believes grounds interreligious learning (Boys 1997, 54-58). At the same time, some students noted a sense of simultaneous inclusion/exclusion. They were welcomed—not as part of the community but as other, as guest. What they were doing was not the same as what the Jewish community was doing. This too is practice-learning to be good guests, being "other" and yet "with." How do we promote "border crossing" while also recognizing and anticipating the boundaries beyond which the other cannot cross with integrity?

For many in the class, integration came while working on practical theological projects. They brought their readings and experiences to bear on constructive work related to their own particular contexts of ministry and life: exploring how to promote Sabbath practices in Korean congregations; rethinking field education in light of Sabbath theology; surveying theology students about their practices of rest and worship; interviewing African American pastors to discern their working theologies of Sabbath and Sunday; exploring Reconstructionist Jewish theology as a resource for liberal Protestant practices of Sabbath; designing Sabbath rituals for Christian families. Ideally such projects could be done jointly by Jews and Christians, addressing interfaith issues at every step of the project, e.g., according to Don Browning's methodology from descriptive to historical to systematic to strategic theology (Browning, 1991).

Conclusion

Practical theologians can foster teaching that opens up the transformative power of practices and cultivates practical wisdom. We also bring critical resources to our study of practices, as we construct a dialogue relationship between historical traditions of practice and contemporary contexts. Sabbath is an excellent focal point. Jewish-Christian dialogue would benefit from further shared reflection on practices of Sabbath keeping and the growing body of Christian literature on the topic. Sabbath offers a rich starting point for discussing the relationship between Judaism and Christianity. Exploration of Sabbath highlights diversity within both Judaism and Christianity, and prompts us to wrestle with the complexities of practice in pluralistic contexts and its power both to unite and to divide communities. Even as Sabbath practice opens possibilities of deepening mutual understanding between faith communities, it also requires careful thinking about hospitality and "border crossing."

The Sabbath remains a powerful gift and alternative theological witness in contemporary culture. Sabbath is a countercultural practice that implicitly critiques a culture obsessively focused on productivity and activity. In the midst of that culture, Sabbath practices witness to a God who is Creator and Source of all life and whose own life models the creative rhythm of work and contemplative rest. While some form of Sabbath keeping practice is critical to the formation of Christian pastoral leaders and laity, cultivating these practices will require some radical critique of educational and religious institutions. Shared dialogue and reflection between Jews and Christians holds great promise as a foundation for such critique and a path to inspiring fresh models of Sabbath practice and Sunday observance in home, congregation and theological education.

References:

Bacchiocchi, Samuele. 1998. *The Sabbath under Crossfire*. Berrien Springs MI: Biblical Perspectives.

Bass, Dorothy C. 2005. "Christian Formation in and for Sabbath Rest." *Interpretation* 59, no. 1:25-37.

_____. 2000. *Receiving the Day: Christian Practices for Opening the Gift of Time*. San Francisco: Jossey Bass.

Boys, Mary C. Boys. 1997. *Jewish-Christian Dialogue: One Woman's Experience*. Mahwah NJ: Paulist Press.

Boys, Mary C. and Sara S. Lee. 2006. *Christians & Jews in Dialogue: Learning in the Presence of the Other*. Woodstock VT: Skylight Paths Publishing.

Browning, Don. 1991. *A Fundamental Practical Theology*. Minneapolis: Fortress Press.

Buchanan, Mark. 2006. *The Rest of God: Restoring Your Soul by Restoring Sabbath*. Nashville: Thomas Nelson.

Burton-Christie. 2005. "The Cost of Interpretation: Sacred Texts and Ascetic Practice in Desert Spirituality." In *Minding the Spirit: The Study of Christian Spirituality,* ed. Elizabeth Dreyer and Mark Burrows, 100-107. Baltimore: Johns Hopkins University Press.

Dawn, Marva. 1989. *Keeping the Sabbath Wholly: Ceasing, Resting, Embracing, Feasting*. Grand Rapids: Eerdmans.

_____. 2006. *The Sense of the Call: A Sabbath Way of Life for Those Who Serve God, the Church, and the World*. Grand Rapids: Eerdmans.

Lodahl, Michael. 1991. "Sabbath Observance as a Theological Issue in Jewish-Christian Conversation." In *The Sabbath in Jewish and Christian Traditions,* ed. Tamara C. Eskanazi, et al., 262-269. New York: Crossroad.

Kaplan, Aryeh. 1974. *Sabbath Day of Eternity*. New York: National Conference of Synagogue Youth.

Kasper, Cardinal Walter. 2007. "Preface." In *The Catholic Church and the Jewish People: Recent Reflections from Rome,* ed. Philip A. Cunningham et al., ix-x. New York: Fordham University Press.

Miller-McLemore. 2008. "Practical Theology and Pedagogy: Embodying Theological Know-How." In *For Life Abundant: Practical Theology, Theological*

Education, and Christian Ministry, ed. Dorothy C. Bass and Craig Dykstra, 170-190. Grand Rapids: Eerdmans.

Moltmann, Jürgen. 1985. *God in Creation: An Ecological Doctrine of Creation.* London and San Francisco: Harper Row.

Muller, Wayne. 1999. *Sabbath: Finding Rest, Renewal, and Delight in Our Busy Lives.* New York: Bantam Books.

Primus, John. 1991. "Sunday: the Lord's Day as a Sabbath—Protestant Perspectives on the Sabbath." In *The Sabbath in Jewish and Christian Traditions,* ed. Tamara C. Eskanazi, et al., 98-121. New York: Crossroad.

Stoker, Valerie. 2003. "Drawing the Line: Hasidic Jews, *Eruvim*, and the Public Space of Outremont, Quebec." *History of Religions* 43, no. 1:18-49.

Stone, Bryan P. and Claire E. Wolfteich. 2008. *Sabbath in the City: Sustaining Urban Pastoral Excellence.* Louisville: Westminster John Knox Press.

Vatican II Council. 1965. *Nostra Aetate* ("Declaration on the Relation of the Church to Non-Christian Religions").

Wirzba, Norman. 2006. *Living the Sabbath: Discovering the Rhythms of Rest and Delight.* Grand Rapids: Brazos Press.

Witvliet, John D. 2008. "Teaching Worship as a Christian Practice." In *For Life Abundant: Practical Theology, Theological Education, and Christian Ministry*, ed. Dorothy C. Bass and Craig Dykstra, 117-149. Grand Rapids: Eerdmans.

Rethinking the Theory
in the Practice

All in the Family:
Recasting Religious Pluralism through African Contextuality

Esther E. Acolatse

Abstract: *The issue of religious plurality and how to accommodate it in an increasingly global situation is debated in the academy. Approaches to the issue range from exclusivism, to inclusivism to pluralism. In the Christian context, the two main sides of the debate argue for seemingly different ways to address the problem. Proponents of religious pluralism such as John Hick argue for a re-evaluation of the main tenets of Christian belief because those beliefs are seen as blocks to inter-religious dialogue; while proponents of Christian exclusivism, especially orthodox theologians like Karl Barth, insist that Christianity is based on revealed tenets and therefore in total discontinuity with any other forms of religion.*

This essay offers a means of healing the bifurcation between Christian exclusivism and pluralism by a "dynamic exclusivism" that seeks to overcome both the triumphalism of current exclusivism and the extreme universalism that attends Christian pluralism. A dynamic exclusivism, based in Barth's understanding of neighbor, allows for authentic dialogic encounters, as well as pastoral formation and ministry in inter-religious veins. Considering the issues within the African context, paying attention to the anthropological rather than ethical underpinnings of religious plurality, and accompanying case studies demonstrate how the pastoral moment provides a theologically sound basis for a Christian response to religious plurality.

Introduction

That we live in a religiously pluralistic world is indisputable, yet schools for religious education and formation for ministry often function in a religiously monolithic mode and even in denial of this plurality. Religious exclusivity in belief and attitude presents difficulties for adherents of various religious traditions in interacting with one another. The fear of compromising one's religious claims and fervor, especially with missional religions, makes the possibility of thinking and framing religious claims in light of a global pluralistic awareness daunting. Debates between religious exclusivists and pluralists on the viability and tenability of distinct religious claims result in patent differences, with the former appearing ultra-conservative, intolerant and self-righteous and the latter appearing liberal, tolerant and also self-righteous. The seemingly proper course of action, both from a philosophical and theological perspective, is to opt for the pluralism agenda as it has been argued by its most ardent proponents, notably John Hick. Appreciative of the depth and riches of other religious traditions vis-á-vis Christianity, Hick believes that it is imperative for Christians to shift the center of their religious understanding from Christ to God, as a theocentric rather than christocentric emphasis augurs well for inter-religious dialogue and existence. At the same time, exclusivists, many of whom inhabit theological institutions and clerical leaders are hesitant to embrace pluralism due to the missional claims that their religious traditions make and the self-identity at stake in losing core creedal statements, despite attendant gains from dialogical interchange with other faiths.

On the other hand, the pluralism project thus far envisaged asks the soteriological question, begins from the ends and often focuses on the means (usually the religious expressions of adherents) to such ends. This approach often places the ethical considerations before the anthropological ones, thus raising and then attempting to answer less relevant questions first. This leads to endless debates about theologies of religion, usually based on comparing promising aspects of one's own religion with the deleterious aspects of other religious traditions. Instead, drawing upon issues and case studies within the African context that have implications for religious co-existence in the twenty-first century, I shall argue that Christian exclusivism is a mutually inclusive means of respecting other religious traditions and embracing one's own.

If we allow for the particularity of the various traditions without conflating them and invite each to ask the larger anthropological question, we are led first to creation (the beginning of our common humanity) rather than salvation (the ends). The reflection on creation, even from diverse religious perspectives (especially the Christian tradition), should enlarge our soteriology to include "all creation which is groaning as in the pains of childbirth for its deliverance" (Rom 8:22). What makes the African context particularly inviting of analysis is that it not only approaches the pluralism question as one of soteriology, a matter of ends and thus of means, but also equally as one of anthropology, of what it means to be human. African Traditional Religions place less emphasis on salvation as an end and location—be it heaven or hell—and more on how the Holy breaks into present life.

African tribal and extended family structures ensure the co-existence of diverse religious practices within the same family but have no illusions about the distinctions of these traditions. In times of individual or familial crises, this separateness is heightened as the rituals of the various religious traditions confront each other. At such crucial moments, attending to the care-seeker should be foregrounded in the rituals that occur. What is needed is a *dynamic exclusivism*, a viable Christian theology that points to the appropriate stance towards other religious traditions and acts in a pastorally responsible way across denominational and religious backgrounds to those in need. Appropriate pastoral formation in divinity schools and seminaries is crucial to disciple Christians for witness and life in a pluralistic world.

In this essay, I first offer a description of the African (particularly West African) context, highlighting examples of its multi-religious existence. Then I consider proposed solutions for accommodating religious plurality (framed primarily within Western cultures), especially the call to pluralism as expounded by John Hick. Next, in critiquing the Hickian position, I present several reasons for its inadequacy in addressing the practical issues of religious believers (especially in West Africa), and propose both a re-evaluation of religious dialogue and the adoption of an exclusivist view as a more viable avenue not only for inter- and intra-religious dialogue, but also for soul-care. Finally, I examine from a Christian perspective examples of how this soul-care works within and across religious traditions.

Religious Existence in Sub-Saharan Africa

The plurality of religious existence is not new in Africa. Its current state wears a post-missionary and postcolonial face that contributes to the conflictual climate surrounding it. The contemporary expression of religious pluralism, especially with regard to the tensions and socially disruptive conflicts it sometimes generates, is largely due to the legacy of colonialism, which decentralized various ethnic states and drove large groups of people—and their accompanying tribal and ethnic identities, as well as religious affiliations—into the large cities.

Most city dwellers in sub-Saharan Africa are familiar with the areas of the inner city, or *Zongo* among Hausa speaking migrants. These are heavily populated Islamic town centers settled by Muslim traders, mainly from the northern territories. Here one is likely to see churches and mosques in close proximity to each other, as well as shrines to local and clan deities. Among the worshippers of these local deities may be found Christians. People of the *Zongo* witness three dominant religious traditions and are affected by each other's religious beliefs and adherences. Additionally, many households encompass these diverse religious traditions, either through inter-religious marriages or conversions.

In Ghana the high holy days of Christianity, Islam and Indigenous Religions are officially observed by the government. However, conflicts arise when one religious tradition is privileged by governments in post-independent Africa. In Nigeria clashes between Muslims and Christians are well documented, especially in the Northern Savannah regions, while in relatively peaceful Ghana the prevailing conflict is between some Christian sects and devotees of local shrines. Amidst these clashes, however, the daily lives of these religiously pluralistic peoples, even during the various high holy days, is interactive and amicable. It is not unusual to exchange greeting cards with one's non-Christian friends at Christmas or join in festivities that end Ramadan with Muslim neighbors. While many Christians and Muslims are overtly syncretistic in practice there is, nevertheless, contention over which practices are cultural and which religious. This is a thorny issue in an environment in which religion subsumes culture. The religious life of the people often bears no resemblance to what their respective religious traditions and tenets require or what various religious governing bodies and clergy advocate in polity and reflect in worship.

There is an obvious acknowledgement of plurality (the co-existence of the various religious groups or religions) but not pluralism. True pluralism goes beyond acknowledging the existence of other religious worldviews or interacting with them as autonomous traditions on equal footing. Religious pluralism does not have as its *telos* the goal of intra-religious unity, nor does not it require metanarratives that can embrace all religious traditions. Unfortunately, familiarity with religious plurality proves, almost paradoxically, a bane to authentic religious pluralism.

The greatest obstacle to moving beyond acknowledgement of religious plurality to real pluralism is the faith claims of the great historic religions. In Ghana and Togo, countries with which I am most familiar, the faith claims of each of the prominent traditional religions are tested when inhabitants concurrently participate in Christian healing services, Muslim fasting during Ramadan and divination practices dependent upon local deities. Within this context the salvific superiority of any one religion is contestable at best. Unfortunately the witness of the Christian church is often pursued as though it were a contest of religious superiority.

The following scenarios vividly illustrate some of the complexities of multi-religious living. They highlight some of the issues that need to be addressed if adequate preparation for pastoral ministry is to be implemented with fidelity and plausibility in African and other contexts. Consider the case of a Moslem man, Ali, married for fifteen years to Laura, a Lutheran. They have established a relatively healthy relationship with the extended families on both sides. At the death of Alice, his mother-in-law, Alice's Pastor, Ashiley, who provided pastoral care during the last stages of Alice's life, both conducts the funeral (which the entire extended family is expected to attend) and provides the family ongoing pastoral care. In another case, identical twins Okoe and Akwete, born into a family practicing a Traditional Religion and whose parents are custodians of the local deity, attend a public school where morning assembly includes Bible reading and hymn singing, resulting in a conversion experience for Okoe. The family's expectation of his engagement in the traditional rites becomes an issue, resulting in estrangement from his family. How does he live both his filial piety and obedience to Christian tenets?

These two vignettes raise similar concerns about religious identity and familial responsibility for the care-seekers, and pastoral sensitivity grounded in a clear theology of religion for the pastors. How may care-seekers and pastors faced with such situations transcend their respective religious practices through faithful Christian pastoral encounters in such a religiously pluriform context? With this question in mind I turn to the debate of the proper Christian stance toward religious diversity and truth, especially as explicated in Western theological debates.

Accommodating Solutions to Religious Plurality: Exclusivism, Inclusivism and Pluralism

In many parts of the world religious plurality goes hand in hand with cultural and ethnic plurality; therefore, multicultural and multiethnic dimensions need to be addressed together with religious plurality. On one side, so it is assumed, are traditionalists and fundamentalists holding for exclusivism, and liberals and progressives on the other who recognize plurality and move towards pluralism. In between are the inclusivists who, observing similar religious sensibilities among adherents of various religions, conclude that there must be a commonality in belief among them, which is merely named differently.

Exclusivism

The dominant position in the church, from its inception through much of its history up to the Enlightenment, has been exclusivist. Major proponents of this position include dialectical theologians such as Karl Barth, Emil Brunner and more recently D. A. Carson. Key to their position is the understanding of general and special revelation, with the former seen through creation and latter through the incarnate son. Insisting that we understand Christian truth claims in terms of encounter with a living God and not a set of axioms, these dialectic theologians claim that God does not reveal or convey truths about Godself, but rather God reveals Godself in the dynamic encounter between God and humankind. Since this encounter finds its ultimate expression in the incarnation where God and humankind are reconciled in Christ, Christ is the ultimate revelation and truth about God. It is this ultimate encounter founded on the Christ event that makes Christianity the true religion. Its dictum is that there is no salvation outside Christ.

Often when exclusivism has been held as the properly religious stance toward religious aliens, conflict ensues, at worst Crusades and Jihads. The disparaging cries against exclusivism, then, are not without bearing or history, and ensuing conflicts in both the past and present are well documented. However, in Africa—especially Nigeria and Sudan, two countries currently witnessing significant bloodshed—while religious diversity might be a factor in these conflicts, post-colonial issues are also implicated. The resistance to Western intrusions through Christian mission and education rather than religious differences per se contributes to the conflict.

Inclusivism

Inclusivism is the blanket term used to describe those who occupy the "middle way" between exclusivism and pluralism. Inclusivists acknowledge the possibility of salvation outside Christ, and believe that the faith of non-Christians can lead to salvation. Here again, salvation is based in Jesus Christ but, unlike the exclusivist position, no declarative faith is necessary for such salvation. The most notable example of this view is that expressed through Hans Kueng's phrase "anonymous Christians," which is based on observable Christ-like behavior among adherents of other faiths (Neuner 1967). Variations within inclusivism exist; Paul J. Griffiths recognizes not only open and closed variations but further proposes a "modalized open inclusivism" as the properly Christian stance towards people of other religions or "religious aliens" (2001, 63). The critique of this view is well known. At the least, such critics argue, all truths are on a par and religions may learn about the way of salvation from one another. While this position might imply some parity as to truth across religious traditions, it also betrays a subtle religious superiority and imperialism. In this vein, it is also akin to pluralism—

which has gained ascendancy as the most viable way for inter-religious dialogue and conflict-free living—in tacitly ignoring the rock-bottom belief systems of the religious that can admit no contradiction, a point to which we shall return below.

Pluralism

The pluralism position appears to have the most potential for conflict-free religious and social life. Its notable proponents—John Hick, Paul Knitter and to a lesser degree Wilfred Cantwell Smith—argue that due to the "ineffability of religious experience," no religion can claim a title-hold on truth. In particular, Christianity is challenged to desist from declaring that Christ is the definitive and normative revelation in whom all truth and ultimate salvation resides, and to shift from a christocentric to a theocentric mode, which allows all religions to be equidistant to God. For Hick and Knitter, this is the only ethical way to promote justice in a religiously intolerant world (1987, vii-xii). There are many critiques leveled against Hick's foundational reasons for enjoining pluralism. In the case of Christianity for instance, Hick's argument for a shift from christocentricity to theocentricity is based on New Testament scholarship primarily from its liberal wing that questions the incarnation and Lordship of Jesus as evidenced in the scriptural witness (Hick 1993, 103-6). Hick had previously submitted that if "Jesus was . . . the eternal creator God become man, then it becomes very difficult indeed to treat Jesus, the New Testament, and Christian faith as being on the same level as phenomena from other religious traditions" (1977, 172). Yet this is the overwhelming belief of Christians whose faith is rooted in the New Testament. To move towards pluralism one must negate this statement, in which case one cannot share the belief of the apostolic and early church. Moreover, Hick's position is itself built on a form of exclusivism with a latent metanarrative, the very metanarrative he faults exclusivists for holding. As D. A. Carson points out, "as soon as it makes an absolute claim that all truth claims are relative, it has forged its own metanarrative" (Carson 1996, 147).

The shortfall that results from removing the foundational belief of a religious tradition, which is then offered back to the believer as a basis for faith and life, has serious implications for a pastoral theology of ministry. It is impossible to be a believing member of a religion and not assume its veracity. With this assumption comes a certain built-in exclusivity, for such belief cannot hold contradictory rock-bottom statements together as such fundamental tenets are essential for religious flourishing on both an individual and corporate level. In real life situations, pluralism seems anemic for soul-care since it tacitly conveys to people of faith that what they believe to be final revelatory truth about the *Real,* as well as their religious experiences and practices, is not reliable. From the Christian perspective, when one removes the incarnation and atonement as well as resurrection, reliance on a providential God also collapses. Even if the primary case for pluralism (peaceful human existence) were considered, it is my experience that in inter-religious encounters, uncertainty about what one believes provides more opportunities for inter-religious conflict than an unshakeable knowledge tinged with personal and communal experience of the *Real*. This surety produces peace in the religious believer and allows for the possibility of peaceful co-existence with religious aliens. Religious plurality is more a boost to dialogic engagement than a bane. In many ways our common humanity is underscored by our distinctiveness rather than our similarity, and an overemphasis on similarity results in a false irenicism that glosses over the critical issues in need of attention. Moreover, as previously stated, the problem with religious conflict in Africa has more to do with residual colonial intrusions than religious plurality *per se*. That being the case, the push for pluralism in such a region may easily be read as itself an imperialist policing of truth claims that demands the parity of all other truth claims but its own (i.e., that all religions are true to some extent) in order to keep all others in their place.

Revisiting Christian Exclusivism: A Barthian Perspective

The pluralist position—as an invitation to live in harmony with religious difference as people on a quest, who only know partially the One Truth—obviously holds much promise for conflict-free living, and hence many want to embrace it. Yet, such promise is illusory and can only be accommodated among the irreligious, i.e., among those who do not take their "faithing" seriously. It is notable that in cultures more or less free of secularism, where biblical skepticism born of higher critical methods is minimal, the case for Christian pluralism is rather slim. Plurality of faiths and truths can be embraced without adherence to religious pluralism as currently framed and envisaged. Key is how one can affirm and maintain one's religious identity without being an exclusivist in a narrow sense and without allowing pluralism to undercut the significant faith claims of various religious traditions. How may religion (particularly Christian exclusivity) be a catalyst for change and conflict-free inter-religious living and a basis for a pastoral theology of ministry for Christians as well as others?

Considering this question within the African context, I turn to Barth for formulating a response that allows for a faithful articulation of Christian exclusivism and soul-care across religious traditions. In his chapter on "The Revelation of God as the Abolition of Religion," he states that since "grace is the revelation of God, no religion can stand before it as true religion" (Barth 1975-, I/II: 326). In this way revelation abolishes religion, but this need not be viewed negatively: "It can be upheld by it and concealed in it. It can be justified by it, and—we must at once add—sanctified." Barth finds this justification attained in the Christian religion because of the Christ event. So he can say without hesitation "that the Christian religion is the true religion" (326). The emphasis on Jesus as the revelation of God, rather than some statements about or from God, undercuts the attempt to view Christianity as one more religion consisting of a set of tenets or propositional truths that do not admit of any internal contradictions. Barth, like other dialectic theologians, insists that we understand Christian truth claims in terms of encounter with a living God and not a set of axioms. God, they say, does not reveal or convey truths about Godself but rather God reveals Godself in the dynamic meeting between God and humankind. Since this encounter finds its ultimate expression in the incarnation, where God and humankind are reconciled, Christ is the ultimate revelation and truth about God and thus makes Christianity the true religion. Therefore all religions not linked with Christ are not true (326). Barth is also quick to point out that all religion is unbelief as it is based inside human effort to do what only God can do. In this regard, when Christianity fails to live up to its identity as God's religion, that is as what God has done for us rather than what we try to do to attain favor with God, it comes under the same judgment.

Barth goes on to demonstrate the relation of other religious traditions or truths to Jesus, who is the Truth. In his account of "words" and "lights" he elaborates, noting that while "Jesus is attested in the scriptures as the one Word of God whom we must hear" (1975-IV/3: 86), this exclusivity does not eliminate but delimits what is to be said of all other words from all others who witness to the truth. More importantly, the one Word of God "can make use of certain men, making them His witnesses and confessing their witness in such a way that to hear them is to hear Him" (1975- IV/3 101). Using the analogy of the circle with its center and periphery, Barth states that the relation between the Word and other words is not that of the center to the periphery for the Word is both the center and the periphery: "for the one truth Jesus Christ is indivisible" (123), and "the capacity of Jesus to create these human witnesses" is not limited to the Church alone but "transcends the limits of this sphere" (1975- IV/I: 118). More could be said about Jesus as the Light among lights, but suffice it to say that Barth's thesis points not to the one Truth—God, seen and expressed in multiple ways—but Jesus as the One Truth encountered in all truths. So there can be human words that are good because they are spoken with the commission and in the service of God (1975- IV/3: 97 ff and 125 ff), and "the more seriously and joyfully we believe in Him the more we shall see such signs in the worldly sphere, and the more we shall be able to receive true words from it" (1975- IV/3: 122).

Barth's insistence on Christianity as the true religion among others in the same genus, as well as his understanding of "neighbor" as one who helps us in praise of God but also who speaks truth to us and who is included in the children of God —"for there is not Abraham without Melchizedek" (1975- I/2: 426)—offers an opportunity to reframe Christian exclusivism. I propose *dynamic exclusivism* as the properly Christian relation to other religious traditions. Dynamic exclusivism allows one to hold the truth of the ultimate revelation of God in Christ via the Church or Christianity, as explicated in Barth's *Church Dogmatics* (17, 18 & 69) which demonstrate the importance of the "neighbor" as our evangelist and as one who offers assistance to the body of Christ, in tensive unity with conceptual priority to the real "neighbor" who is Jesus in whom God and people become eternal "neighbors."

At first blush, Barth's concept of Jesus as Light among lights and Word among words, pointing to the Truth encountered in all truths, seems similar to Griffiths' "modalized open inclusiveness" (a position that in many respects is akin to mine). However, I believe there is a distinction between encounters of truth as axiomatic statements (which allow for internal contradictions to negate the veracity of what is encountered) and the encounter with Truth as a person—the God-man. "Modalized open inclusivism," which suggests the possibility that religious aliens may teach other faiths something that aids in their salvation, still leaves us in the realm of noetic rather than experiential knowledge with Truth as encounter.

Dynamic Exclusivism as a Basis for Soul-care

How may dynamic exclusivism aid in Christian dialogue with other religious traditions, and more importantly allow for soul-care in a context such as Africa, where inter- and intra-religious coexistence occurs within both nuclear and extended families? How may such an approach to soul-care provide optimum attention to presenting problems in pastoral encounters in a manner that allows the religious beliefs of each care-seeker to provide needed succor in crises and at the same time be a Christian witness in "praise of God" (Barth1975-, I/2: 419ff)?

In practice one must avoid the sentimentalism which a forced irenicism born of religious pluralism may produce. A proper understanding of neighbor and neighbor-love allows for agape that tells truth and holds to absolutes with the humility that allows grace to appear in places hitherto unimagined. While there is not space here to demonstrate how dynamic exclusivism will work in the earlier scenarios, I offer a few tentative suggestions that the promise of Christian dynamic exclusivism holds for soul-care in a multi- and inter-religious situation. Dynamic exclusivism allows each religious tradition to maintain its truth claim. What transpires, if the Christian claim is true, is that the epistemological pitting of truth against truth is undercut by the encounter with Truth as a person, who is then invited into the space of our common need and embraces us. If the scriptural attestation is true, and Barth's explication is on target—which I believe to be the case—the pastors in the scenarios do not need to require the care-seekers to exit their religious beliefscapes to be encountered by the Truth. Nor do they need to adjust their own Christian belief to accommodate disparate belief, for in this Truth as a person (co-creator and redeemer) invited into the care-seekers' situation, both seeker and carer are at once judged, found guilty, redeemed and set free for joyful living. This is because in confessing that the Word became flesh, we must state that in Jesus Christ God is for God's creatures, takes up creatures gone astray and elects creatures to participation in God's glory. In electing Abraham down through to Christians via Christ, "what takes place in this election is always that God is for us; for us, and therefore for the world which was created by Him, which is distinct from Him, but which is yet maintained by Him. The election is made with a view to the sending of His Son. And this means always that in Him and through Him God moves towards the world" (Barth, *CD* II/2, 25–6). In this way the anthropological considerations focused on creation rather than soteriology, rightly turns our attention to re-creation via the second Adam (Jesus of Nazareth) who recapitulates the life of all humanity and brings us back to the creator. Soteriological considerations of ends (which which most religious concflicts emanate) become a secondary focus of life with God.

In the above scenarios, then, the pastors could provide soul-care to the Muslim Ali, and to Okoe who may at best be straddling Christian faith and primal religions, with a christocentric stance that brings the finished work of Christ to bear on their particular situations without assent to Christianity, or exiting their religious beliefscapes. Both care-receiver and care-provider are invited to transcend their various religious tenets in the face of the claim of God made through the neighbor, the God-man, on their lives.

References:

Barth, Karl. 1975- . *Church Dogmatics*. Edinburgh: T & T Clark.

_____. 1973. *God and the Universe of Faiths: Essays in the Philosophy of Religion*. London: Macmillan.

Carson, D. A. 1996. *The Gagging of God*. Grand Rapids: Zondervan.

Cook, Robert. 1994. Postmodernism, Pluralism, and John Hick. *Themelios* 19, no. 1:10-12.

_____. 1994. Readers' Response. *Themelios* 19, no. 3:20-21.

_____. 1993. *The Metaphor of God Incarnate: Christology in a Pluralistic Age*. Louisville: Westminster/John Knox Press.

Dickson, Kwesi A., and Paul Ellingworth. 1969. *Biblical Revelation and African Beliefs*. London: Lutherworth Press.

Ecumenical News International, http://www.eni.ch (20 September 2008).

Griffiths, Paul J. 2001. *Problems of Religious Diversity*. Maldon, MA: Blackwell Publishing.

Hick, John, ed. 1977. *The Myth of God Incarnate*. London: SCM Press.

Hick, John, and Paul F. Knitter, eds. 1987. *Myth of Christian Uniqueness: Toward a Pluralistic Theology of Religions*. Maryknoll, NY: Orbis Books.

Knitter, Paul F. 1985. *No Other Name? A Critical Survey of Christian Attitudes Toward the World Religions*. American Society of Missiology Series, no. 7. Maryknoll, NY: Orbis Books.

Neuner, Josef, ed. 1967. *Christian Revelation and World Religions*. London: Burns & Oates.

Thomson, Norman H. 1988. *Religious Pluralism and Religious Education*. Birmingham, AL: REP.

Charles Taylor on Violence and Social Structure

Terence Kennedy

Abstract: *This contribution examines Charles Taylor's analysis of violence and how it impinges and interacts with social structure. It draws on two sources: a 2004 essay on the origin of violence and the section of* A Secular Age *(2007) that takes up violence as an objection to religion. In his vision "categorical violence" has three characteristics: excess, purification and ritual. Taylor pays close attention to the mechanism of sacrifice, especially Girard's theory which he wants to supplement and broaden. The distinction between pre-axial and axial periods is crucial for him. He raises a series of key questions: What is the hermeneutic framework in which we can make sense of violence? Who becomes a target or a victim? What is the relationship of the numinous or the religious dimension to violence and how should it be interpreted? What is the link between "categorical violence" and modernity? He discusses democracy in relation to hatred, exclusion and the craze to cleanse society of the enemies of the state. He finishes with a critique of a therapy based culture and of the mystique of the victim that is typical of contemporary culture. While Taylor has not proposed a comprehensive theory of violence his reflections are truly thought provoking and retrieve forgotten dimensions of this subject.*

Introduction

Charles Tayor has a well merited reputation as a leading exponent of the meaning of modernity. His "The Politics of Recognition" (1992) exposes two sources of conflict in modern political systems, depending on whether Locke's individual rights or Rousseau's social contract are taken as foundational. In this essay he limits his concern to pressing modern problems. When examining violence and its genesis he was compelled to penetrate more deeply into history and from a longer perspective. He has left us two principal sources for reflection on violence. The first, "Notes on the Sources of Violence: Perennial and Modern" (2004), is a series of jottings that trace the contours of its physiognomy. The second is from his monumental *A Secular Age* (2007) where he ponders how violence became a reason for rejecting religion. If violence is rooted in religion then it must be among the principal causes of secularization, whether it is understood as the decline of religious practice, of faith or of the influence of the Churches on society. These two sources should be studied together because their arguments overlap and are closely intertwined. Taylor is a rather maddening author to read since he has a dispersed style that yields rich insights that have to be gleaned patiently from the text.

The core issue for him is "categorical violence," that is, violence directed against whole social classes or categories, be they nations, a genus or sex, or religion, etc. It has three characteristics that appear constantly 1) excess, i.e., it overspills the boundaries of control and social prohibitions, 2) purification, i.e., it is used to destroy or do away with some evil, and 3) ritual, i.e., it is incorporated into a framework that gives it meaning, e.g., in sacrifice. Taken together these would lead one to think—as people often do after witnessing scenes of massacre, rape, or pillage—that violence has a primitive origin, arising before civilization took possession of the human psyche. What therefore is its meaning for us?

Hermeneutical Frameworks

Science explains violence though sociobiology, that is as a constant "wired-in" mechanism that is part of humanity's biological make-up acquired by learning how to repulse enemies or invaders, something necessary for sheer survival and the defense of life and limb, home and kinship group. However, little reflection is required to realize that violence fluctuates throughout history, and differs from situation to situation and nation to nation. In group violence there has to be an enemy and a common action aimed at harming him. It follows that violence has acquired meaning from culture, from the mental and imaginative social framework in which it is inserted.

Yet, is it a throwback to primitive, usually religious practices as people spontaneously presume? It is more truly a case of a new rendition of an ancient tale, or the transferring of an old tune to a new key. It has qualities of both continuity and discontinuity. Therefore, in Taylor's terms, it must have a metaphysical meaning or higher significance. As far as we can go back in history religion has always involved some form of sacrifice which can convey many meanings, such as handing something over into a god's power in order to placate him, feed him or win his goodwill. Unworthiness, fear and guilt play an overwhelming role here. It can also embody a response to threats from destructive forces like hurricanes, fires or earthquakes. Of course, primitive cultures tended to assume these under the category of blind fate. In modernity Nietzsche held that the suffering involved in sacrifice was made bearable not by discovering its meaning but by inventing it. Or reversely, a sense of inadequacy might be the primitive factor needing to be shaped by religion. So suffering was significant when it was seen as punishment that made up for or paid the price for our short comings. Nonetheless, suffering was often first perceived as punishment before being molded by religion.

Religion helps humans to identify with the demands of fate so that destruction itself could be divinized as in Kali-Shiva. Devotees identified with the divinity and were thereby purified by renouncing everything that got destroyed. Wild indomitable forces had to be tamed down to the dimensions of everyday life by depriving them of their terrifying potency.

This was achieved by submission to a superior and exterior will. One way of coping with violence and destruction is to make this superior will the source of vital energy in personal or communal life, thus controlling it symbolically. Hence we have the warrior ethic or battalions under the sign of the skull and crossbones, the mentality of "dead men on leave." Taylor describes it this way: "Then we live in the element of violence, but like kings unafraid, as agents of pure action, dealing death: we are the rulers of death" (2004, 18). Terror is transmuted into exhilaration, the excitement that confirms that one is still alive. The audacity to risk life lays the foundation for an honor code as in dueling, pay-back or vendettas. The turbulence accompanying violence can be stilled by identifying it with an external and benign power. By reversing the poles in the field of fear one no longer cowers before this power but instead identifies with it and so can transcend normal human limits.

The practice of human sacrifice combines and fuses these two responses. "On the one hand, we submit to the god to whom we offer our blood: but the sacrificers also become agents of violence" (Taylor 2004, 18). They wade in gore with sacred intent so that nothing in past times gave so much satisfaction as a sacred massacre.

René Girard has explored the link that fused violence with religion. Sacred violence welds a people together into a social unity; people reestablish harmony by sacrificing one of their own as a victim for all. This provides healing and resolves the problem of mimetic rivalry that would blow a community apart. Taylor adds these three points to Girard's considerations: 1) by offering some goods to god we get to preserve the rest, as with Aztec sacrifices to the god of the corn. We are nourished by the divinity to which we are obliged and have to keep on his right side. 2) Elevation of violence to the level of the sacred makes us partakers in God's power. This requires that we be purified from the evil that divides us from God, and become agents in the destruction of the world's evil. Here Girard's mechanism of the expulsion of the scapegoat is of prime importance. 3) The process of purification concentrates all evil in the victim who is expelled and so put at a safe distance from us.

Who becomes a Target?
There are two explanations, both with their foundation in Girard's theory. First, mimetic rivalry is overcome when the unity and peace of society is restored through the sacrifice of a victim. Second, the scapegoat mechanism vents sacred rage and so is cathartic by embodying all evil in the victim. This shores up the community against corruption from within, breakdown and loss of solidarity. Solidarity can also be achieved by concentrating on an external enemy. This makes war into such a persistent historical phenomenon whose destructiveness is limited only by its being ritualized. The technological rationalization of warfare has rendered it more extensive and more destructive than ever before. Nationalism too functions according to the principle of mimetic rivalry as the rush to carve up Africa in the nineteenth century made glaringly obvious.

The scapegoat mechanism poses the questions of why expel evil at all, and who is to be made the outsider? This is answered on the basis of our beliefs about an ethical order and a worthwhile way of life. Most people cannot tolerate chaos, meaninglessness, wrongness and destruction and can cope only by being separate from them. Instead of perceiving ourselves as morally bad and perpetrators of evil we seek to reverse the field and place evil outside ourselves by transcending it as in Nietzsche's "beyond good and evil."

This putting evil outside means turning it into a contrast case, e.g., as in the roles played by barbarians or savages, or criminals, child abusers, i.e., people with whom we have no contact. Such an outsider is harmless until our actually touching him releases a frenzy of aggression, as in the slave trade or the Crusades. The outsider may be viewed as a threat to one's very existence, as in homophobic myths or stories of the sexual prowess of invaders. When the social order is menaced with fragmentation the temptation is, according to the working of the Girardian scapegoat mechanism, to define the outsider as a polluter operating within the walls, e.g., anti-Semitism in history. Taylor notes that this mentality was typical of an enchanted worldview and that the craze for hunting down witches marked the transition to a rationalized world. The more boundaries are eroded the more people are emancipated so that, for instance, the idea of Christendom can no longer be held tenably. All the above mentioned forces were concentrated in one event, the Nazi persecution of the Jews.

A Grid for Numinous Violence

The scapegoat mechanism can be understood as the conjunction of two vectors. The first affirms our goodness by setting up a contrast with external evil by dividing the pure from the polluted. The second is identified with the destructive power of the numinous and so brings on a sacred massacre. These two vectors combine in human sacrifice, but can be separated as in the Indian caste system. The scapegoat mechanism comes in two forms. First, it leads us to turn on, kill or expel an outsider from the community. The victim represents the contrast case. Second, aggression is turned on an outsider to the community as in a crusade. Here numinous violence couples with purity to form a transcendent unity. A warrior is consequently justified as vindicating God's justice against the wicked by using this "centrifugal violence" (Taylor 2004, 22).

We arrive at the turning-point in Taylor's argument when he asks just what exactly is involved in numinous violence. He goes outside the usual schemas to retrieve the fact that the numinous does not necessarily imply identification with the good. That presupposition is applicable and true only after the axial revolution. In the pre-axial period gods were both benign and malign, usually both together and not clearly distinguished. Benignity here refers to human flourishing in terms of life, fertility, health and wealth. The axial revolution inclined toward identifying the divine with the highest or ultimate good as something beyond ordinary human flourishing, i.e., eternal life or nirvana.

Our conception of morality really starts in the axial period when Old Testament prophets can exhort the chosen people in the name of the living God to put sacrifice away and to succor the widow and the orphan. A secular world goes even further in this direction by developing the idea of responsibility and proportional punishment. Christianity was wont to identify sacred violence with the wrath of God as seen in the persecution of heretics. However, the modern, rationalized moral order has removed such ancient ambiguities so that there is no room left for a wrathful, angry God, with the consequent "decline of hell" even among believers.

Taylor then introduces the fascinating query whether enlightenment thought has succeeded in exorcising violence fully or "whether we do not invent new murderous fantasies in the enlightened, disenchanted world" (Taylor 2004, 23). In his analysis the transition to modernity yielded two new sorts of violence: the entirely evil scapegoat as in witchcraft or anti-Semitism, and the purely righteous sacrifice of youth fallen in battle, a Christian inspired ideal. What are some of the types that emerge in this transition?

Categorical Violence and Modernity

This brings us to the issue of revolution and the institution of a democratic republic. Revolutions are seen as throwing off tyranny and oppression by emancipating a people to follow its own lights and way of life. Violence exercised in a revolution is justified by the freedom gained so that everything appears to be in right order morally.

Taylor focuses on the tradition initiated by the French Revolution and handed on by both Jacobins and Bolsheviks in this formula, i.e., "the link between democracy and violence: the Terror" (2004, 23). He argues that the Terror is not simply like just war, violence against enemies. In fact it satisfies the three conditions specified at the beginning of this essay: 1) Excess came though fabricating enemies, whole categories of persons whose only crime was to have convictions that clashed with the regime's ideology. 2) Purification was justified by a rhetoric that painted these enemies as poisoning and corrupting the republic. 3) The ritual concentrated the extirpation of the evil menacing the republic into the rite of public execution. The guillotine was presented as new, clean, civilized and scientific in contrast with the past. Tayor explains how the revolutionary leaders managed public opinion by harnessing mob fury against those arbitrarily condemned as enemies of the state. Violence entered into the democratic process when the revolutionary regimes formed an alliance with the mob that it was in fact manipulating.

Taylor registers an intriguing paradox: why should the ideal of a republic of perfect equality, of justice and peace end up treating humanity as an impurity to be purged? Democracy is here conceived as a process for creating a new humanity and building a unified nation by purging it of its enemies within. Napoleon, of course, recognized that this program of attacking the state's internal enemies could be extended externally by exporting the revolution to the rest of Europe. The American Civil War is another example that verifies this pattern. The abolitionist plan to extirpate the evil of slavery was transferred from an inner purge to an external one. The contrary theme of atoning for sin was crystallized eloquently in Lincoln's second inaugural address. In both cases we may say that the temptation for nations to tear themselves apart internally was sublimated into a campaign of glorification that reinforced the national identity. That is why patriotism infuses a nation's history and self-consciousness with a glow of sacredness.

The Problem of Cleansing and Democracy

The core of the problem is that a republic in the modern sense presupposes a new agency, the people or the nation. This differs from religious communities or civilizations which previously had been taken as the basic units. Although each nation is unique with its own destiny to fulfill, at the same time it has to be considered an equal with every other nation. It thus underwrites the ideal of universalism as equality among all nations but with the differentiating feature that its unique way of being a nation calls for recognition from others.

The nation is founded on the "will" of the people. Instead of the fixed horizons within which pre-moderns moved, national identity has now to be created by the "will" of the people. Taylor asserts that this conception flows from an ethic of authenticity, another one of his favorite ideas. Each nation has to have its moment and needs to redefine itself as history changes. Identity comes from recognition as the way of being human in the modern world. The idea of "our way" has become increasingly important in contemporary society with demands for greater tolerance and the recognition of otherness.

Democracy has exacerbated the tensions surrounding the search for sovereign identity based on popular will. Although the modern idea of a national identity can be creatively redefined as history progresses it is usually linked to a language, a territory, tradition and frequently religion. From time immemorial those who do not share these values are classified as outsiders and so become a threat. Often those in power guaranteed security to minorities without conceding them rights in our sense, e.g., Jews and Christians had an assigned place under the Caliphate. We now live in an unprecedented context, for the principle of popular sovereignty stipulates that the people must ultimately determine identity. But how is a minority with its cultural differences to be included in a people? Are they to be denied citizenship—a basic right of modernity—simply because they are different? By being excluded and denied such rights they are seen as aggressors, the reason why a benign context turns malignant.

In a benign context all peoples are treated as equal with an identical right to identity. Yet, when a group, usually a minority, claiming distinctive rights threatens this balance it can be considered as hostile to the others by depriving them of their rights.

Relationships between groups may then rapidly precipitate into chaos and turn sour. The scene is set for ethnic cleansing when a group believes that it is impossible to live out its identity within its own territory and with its unique culture, as happened tragically in the Balkans.

The victim scenario is typical of modernity and develops within a framework of equality. If a people feels frustrated and cannot express itself freely it must be because it is being put down or suppressed, i.e., it is an underdog. The modern moral order intensifies this feeling by moralizing the issue with its strict standards of rationality and equality. Previously Christians and Muslims in the Balkans thought of each other as traditional enemies and so they became habituated to violence as somehow strangely normal. The modern universalist understanding, however, has invalidated that stance by introducing the idea that all participate in the same moral order: the others have violated it while we are innocent. This moralization assumes a double form. First, rights are violated. Second, popular sovereignty is highly moralized by demanding self-responsible action that condemns every action that contradicts its standards. This only raises the level of violence by giving group hatred a new charge of holy rage. Hence, Communists could annihilate kulaks in the Ukraine in the 1930s, or the way the Bharatiya Janata Party stereotypes Muslims as invaders in India. Such violence grows out of a sense of grievance. The logic here is: we have been unfairly treated, so we can lash out. An identity threat becomes a mortal threat. The original threat is interpreted as an act of aggression and all that is needed to spark the final conflagration are some vivid atrocity stories. This begins a spiral of retorts till the mimetic effect and the mechanism of vendetta make it self-perpetuating. Sadly trust disappears and is lost in communities that once lived together for years and intermarried. Taylor concludes that such forms of categorical nationalist violence are generated by threats surrounding the modern idea of identity. Al Qaeda mobilized this sense of treat to an idealized notion of Islam in the cause of terrorism.

Modernity has sought to recruit even more peoples into such universal identities away from earlier, more local ones dependent on kinship groups, clans or tribes. Earlier identities were usually defined as a network of close, mainly filial type relationships. Modern identities by contrast are based on categories. "They bind people together in virtue of their falling together under a category, such as Serb or American or Hindu, wherein we all relate in a uniform way to a whole" (Taylor 2004, 31). The movement that draws people out of network identities to categorical ones is accelerating because it has been favored by elites, or globalization and migration, or because the economy now undermines traditional ways of making a living. Categorical identity offers people not only a sense of orientation and direction but more importantly a sense of collective agency. People need not be powerless before globalization and can mobilize against its onslaught. However, this also means that the temptations toward scapegoating and holy wars have multiplied exponentially where the universal and globalized institutions of modernity are perceived as a menace.

Taylor concludes his musings with a sober warning: "Violence around categorical identities is one of the most pressing dangers of the coming century. It could literally destroy our world" (Taylor 2004, 32).

Violence, Hatred and Exclusion in Modern Societies.

In general the level of violence in society is today much lower than in former centuries. Many countries have experienced such a prolonged period of internal peace that it began to seem normal. The same nations wage highly destructive wars overseas or become embroiled in civil conflicts. The liberal aspiration for perpetual peace among the nations inspires us but when we contemplate the horrors of modern warfare and ethnic cleansing we are cast into gloom.

How should this paradox be explained? We have built society on the conception of a cooperative order among individuals all enjoying equal rights. Their actions are mutually directed to helping each other to realize their life goals especially through the structures of the economy and the welfare state. This is no vague ideal but is how society's institutions and practices are actually structured. The modern social order has succeeded for the most part in controlling excessive behavior and in curtailing violence.

It can, however, also generate contempt and exclusion, motives for violence in less controlled contexts. There are levels of hatred that have to be constrained and kept below the threshold of violence. A factor that makes this acceptable to society is that of the scientific objective viewpoint of "the disengaged self," as Taylor calls it. It separates us from the numinous powers of violence and sexuality and will not permit any display of holy anger. It shows us coolly and calmly what is to be done so that we may become agents of healing, reform and human betterment.

A peculiarity of Taylor's philosophy is his conviction that the therapeutic movement in psychology and its way of treating people should be properly described under the heading of objectification. Problem cases in modern society are not persons who have suffered or done some evil but have pathologies that have to be healed. This appears to be the very opposite of the revolutionary's moralizing attitude. Problem personalities become patients without guilt or moral failure. Taylor claims that evil has dignity because it is a failure to do good while pathology is sheer incapacity. "Thinking of these people as sick, pathological, needing therapy makes them other, not real interlocutors, not really embodying alternative possibilities that can draw us, tempt us" (Taylor 2004, 34). The patient is typecast as an outsider, a contrast case who cannot assume the responsibilities of a true interlocutor. Examples might extend to the policy of political correctness and its attitude to those classified as "homophobes" or "misogynists." Taylor thinks that the use of shaming and rough treatment as necessary means of imposing conformity to societal norms is but a subtle form of aggression. The question then becomes whether this might not be a throwback or recurrence of holy anger. The tactic of distancing can be a cover for seriously manipulating others. Dostoyevsky's *The Possessed* depicts this mechanism of disengagement in all its complexity as a sham under which the vulnerable can be violated.

These two forms of hatred—identity driven and liberal-moral driven—can combine in a crusade against entrenched evil. The modern conception of morality encourages this distancing, disengaged stance and can generate violence in reaction to violence. The opposition to apartheid in South Africa sometimes suffered from this symptom in spite of supporting a just cause. By taking the numinous out of violence life becomes tame and domesticated, but it also may level out any aspiration to be heroic or saintly. Nietzsche, of course, rebelled against the abolition of a warrior ethic as too high a price to pay for humanizing our condition. His long-reaching influence resonates in fascist ideology and in the outbreaks by skinheads who find uninhibited violence the only means of coming to an identity.

The Mystique of the Victim
Since the fall of Nazism another narrative based on the New Testament values has won wide acceptance. It parallels the story of freedom and democracy and propounds as the goal of human effort the redressing and redeeming of all historical wrongs and inequalities by recognizing and rescuing all victims. It corresponds to the idea of punishing and wreaking vengeance on all perpetrators of evil and on all victimizers.

Like other forms of violence it too is a paradoxical engine of destruction. In Girard's opinion the cult of the victim is the religion of the modern world. It makes absolute claims that have to be understood in terms of the modern moral order that provides the standards of mutual respect and equality against which victims can be identified.

However, it transcends other forms of violence insofar as it drives us toward the ultimate order of reality by unmasking the hidden victimizations that history has covered over or denied as it marched forward triumphantly. It is eschatological and reflects Christian concerns which it has, however, diverted from their original intent. The Gospel too involves a reversal showing the victim to be innocent. It points to the resurrection of the victim, of the despised and rejected. The Reformation and modern humanism set out to reassert and to restore the goodness of ordinary life, of family and to work against a false idea of monasticism as spiritual superiority. In large measure this sensitivity underpins the ethic of our day. It yields a transfigured idea of the modern moral order that often now serves as a substitute for religion. It provides a way to overcome injustice but also draws battle lines between the victim and the perpetrator of evil as an enemy. It dichotomizes good and evil in a way that would horrify Nietzsche and advocates of the heroic. Taylor analyses its workings in these words: "For the greatest disenchanters, evil has to return to their picture, because they have a sense of themselves as actuated by a pure, good will, and have to see somewhere their opponent, pure evil. So there are new myths of evil that are not allowed to be such theoretically. They have to fit the myths of good will" (Taylor 2004, 36). In Rousseau's vision we are in our deepest nature utterly good, and evil comes from mistaken or bad upbringing whereby people become incapacitated and therefore in need of therapy. The source of evil resides in the "system" and those who manage it are identified as the enemy worth of being expelled and destroyed.

Conclusion

In *A Secular Age* (2007) Taylor set out to read the narrative of violence as a subtheme in the great drama of secularization. He observes that the desire for transcendence is not limited to religious people but has its secular practitioners as well. They feel the tension between the wild instincts of sexuality and violence and the claims of the moral order. Violence is something with which believer and secularist alike have to struggle in their search for fulfillment. In our world we are incapable of effecting an eschatological division between the forces of good and evil just as it was impossible to separate the wheat from the weeds in the Gospel (Mt 13: 24-30). This truth is reflected in the fact that the word "sacrifice" has become problematic in contemporary culture (Girard 2006, 79-81). Christ is the only truly and fully innocent victim and he alone can unlock this "mystery of iniquity" and reverse a history of violence. He stands at the turning-point of history as our hope of resurrection and final reconciliation.

References:

Girard, René. 1972. *Violence and the Sacred*. Trans. Patrick Gregory. Baltimore: John Hopkins University Press.

_____. 2006. Non solo interpretazioni. Ci sono anche i fatti. In *Verità o fede debole? Diologo su cristianesimo e relativismo,* ed. Pierpaolo Antonello, 75-98. Pisa: Transeuropa.

Taylor, Charles. 1992. The Politics of Recognition. In *Multiculturalism and "The Politics of Recognition,"* ed. Amy Gutman, 646-660. Princeton: Princeton University Press.

_____. 2004. Notes on the Sources of Violence: Perennial and Modern. In *Beyond Violence. Religious Studies of Social Transformation in Judaism, Christianity and Islam,* ed. James L. Heft, 15-42. New York: Fordham University Press.

_____. 2007. *A Secular Age*. Harvard: Harvard University Press.

Exclusion: A Practical-Theological and Pastoral Challenge

Norbert Mette

Abstract: *The phenomenon of social exclusion names the simple fact that human beings are declared superfluous and disposable. Recent social developments with their dominant systems of regulation favour the advantage of some while the majority of the global population are reduced or destroyed to an unthinkable extent. This is a very threatening "sign of the times" which cannot leave indifferent those who are passionately committed to the belief that future generations can live in human dignity: especially Christians. This essay will first offer some examples of the sociological discourse about exclusion. Then it will discuss how this development critically relates to Christian faith and theology.*

Exclusion: a New Phenomenon

The 5th General Conference of the Roman-Catholic Bishops of Latin America and the Caribbean took place in May 2007 in Aparecida, a shrine of St. Mary in Brazil. The conference's concluding document (cf. Aparecida 2007) presents an analysis of the social, economical, political, cultural and religious realities in that region using liberation theology's methodology of "seeing—judging—acting." Among other things, the document addresses a phenomenon which is explicitly characterized as both new and even worse than oppression and exploitation, namely, social exclusion. "What is affected," states the document, "is the undermining of belonging to the society in which one lives, because one is no longer on the bottom, on the margins, or powerless, but rather one is living outside. The excluded are not simply 'exploited,' but 'surplus' and 'disposable'" (65). Repeatedly the document deals with the fact of exclusion. At the conference in Aparecida the bishops renewed the "option for the poor" as they had done at former conferences, but now augmented it with the new term "the excluded" (cf. 391).

What is the meaning of the term "excluded" or "social exclusion"? It refers to a qualitative change in poverty which has plagued the majority of the population on the South American continent and in the Caribbean for centuries. The German theologian and expert on Latin America, Ulrich Schoenborn, describes this change as follows:

> When "the poor" were referenced in the past, the people under consideration were those not able (or as yet not able) to integrate themselves into modern society. They were marginalized because, for example, there was an imbalance between the extension of the urban infrastructures and the demographic changes in their countries. They were further marginalized because the traditional social structure, the kinds of production, the structures of distribution and the models of

consumption had been modernized or replaced in the course of time. Nevertheless "the poor" had the hope that they could jump on the train of development. Today "the poor" who have participated to a limited extent in the world of labor and consumption experience the fate of "exclusão," exclusion. The process of modernization in industry and state has led to the situation that far fewer workers are admitted to the working place and therefore the aim to satisfy the social needs of human beings has disappeared from society's ethical catalogue. This phenomenon of exclusion refers not only to the classical "sectores populares" or the workers, but also more and more to the middle classes. "Being poor" means today being superfluous and therefore being excluded (Schoenborn 1996, 213).

The US based Spanish sociologist Manuel Castells has succinctly characterized this change as movement "from a situation of social exploitation to a situation of functional ignorance" and commented that "it will be a privilege to be exploited, far worse than exploitation is the fact of being ignored" (Castells 1991, 213). Because of recent changes in poverty a different relationship to the excluded is noticeable. In the past members of society were not totally indifferent to the poor, and in many situations strove to integrate them into the economy and to improve their situation even if that meant subsidizing them with alms. Today those segments of the population which cannot keep up in the face of increasingly accelerated modernization, especially in the economic sector, are simply written off. From the viewpoint of a neoliberal doctrine which exclusively relies on the self-regulatory mechanisms of the market, inequality in society is an unavoidable structural condition. It is even interpreted as an advantage because inequality encourages competition which inevitably implies winners and losers. Therefore, it would be inappropriate to feel pity for the losers. This would be contradictory to the current logic of the market with its decisive criteria of effectiveness, profitability and functionality.

Sociological Approaches

Social exclusion is not a phenomenon which is limited to the countries of the Third World. In the process of neoliberally dictated globalization it increasingly includes more and more people in the so-called affluent societies. The German sociologist Heinz Bude identifies four reasons for this development (Bude 2008, 9-35). A first reason is connected with the functional role of work in which skilled science-based and service-orientated work is considered to be the normal model in an economy of high industrial productivity. For those who do not have the requisite knowledge and skills for this kind of work, the condition of their employment is at best precarious. A second reason for this spreading exclusion in Germany, according to Bude, is the result of Germany becoming a nation with a split in the immigrant population. One part is integrated more or less successfully into society, whereas the other part— whose size is difficult to estimate—loses access to society, isolates itself and seems susceptible to radical ideas because of its excluded status. A third reason Bude offers is rooted in the modern welfare state that has developed a different attitude toward those receiving welfare: from allowing them to be passive recipients to expecting them to be active collaborators. This new perspective expects welfare recipients to take the initiative so that instead of simply being cared for, they are supported so that they can find work and then earn their own living. Those who are not able or willing to do so are left outside. As a fourth reason Bude cites changes which have occurred in the state of the society, especially with regard to the social positioning of the individuals. Niklas Luhmann has characterized this development as a change "from ties of kinship to a career-oriented one". That means that in premodern societies the social status of individuals was determinate by the social background in which they were born (e.g., nobility, farmer, etc.). In modern society, however, everyone creates their own destiny. Those who are competent, mobile and flexible have the chance to be successful; those who are immobile, anxious and narrow-minded fall by the wayside. However, careerists can also fail. Thus a further characteristic of this new exclusion is that it not only extends to people who are socially off balance and discriminated against, but also reaches even into the higher social classes. The point of reference here is the manner of participation in social life, namely, if a person is "inside" or "outside." This does not totally eclipse the conventional differentiation between "above" and "below," but it allows it to be seen from a new perspective.

How can the fact of social exclusion be explained theoretically? For some time in sociology there has been speculation and debate about this question. In this context the term "inclusion"—the opposite of "exclusion"—also becomes relevant. There is also a controversy about how the relation between inclusion and exclusion is to be defined. Two positions exemplify this controversy.

Niklas Luhmann is considered to be a representative of a dichotomist view of the relation between inclusion and exclusion (Luhmann 2008). As will be demonstrated, however, his theory of social system leads to aporia. For Luhmann the difference between inclusion and exclusion is a general one and an integral part of his theory of a social system. This difference refers to the manner in which human beings are thought to be relevant or irrelevant in social communication; this difference has to do with the needs of the social order. A result of this social order is that certain fixed possibilities are allowed and others are excluded. For example, in a religious community a person who acts in accordance with the norm of this community is accepted with a status of full membership; a member who offends against these norms will be excommuni-cated. In principle excluded possibilities still remain because inclusion presupposes that exclusion exists (in this example, the possibility of offense against the norms). The relation between both concepts (inclusion/exclusion) depends on the respective form of social differentiation in a society. In segmentary lineage societies (normally tribal ones) the inclusion in society is determined through the degree of consanguinity of the members, thus the banning of marriage between different groups. In stratified or hierarchical societies (such as the medieval European ones) the inclusion takes place through the assignment of a social status (e.g., nobility, guild or caste) for which the society has already several possibilities—both equal and unequal. According to Luhmann's theory a modern, functionally differentiated society is not able to make such uniform regulations of inclusion because of structural reasons. Modern society delegates its regulation and organization to the separate and differentiated functional subsystems, which in turn make distinctions between persons whose participation is relevant and those whose participation is not.

Regarding the manner of exclusion in the different formations present in contemporary society, Luhmann writes:

> In previous formations present in society the exclusion from one segment could be compensated for when it resulted in the inclusion in a different segment. However, complete exclusion from society in general was a marginal phenomenon. Thus, especially segmented societies know of a great deal of individual mobility between different formations. A comparable regulation of inclusion is not possible in functionally differentiated societies because in general they do not provide for the possibility of individuals who do not participate in one subsystem to do so in another subsystem. An excluding inclusion in a subsystem no longer exists (2008, 241).

Modern society functions in accordance with a kind of inclusion that in principle each person has access to all functional subsystems. Everyone having legal capacity, can start a family, has a right to medical care in case of an emergency, and can participate in business. "The logic of functional differentiation," Luhmann remarks, "excludes social exclusion, but has to allow that it will differentiate within the functional subsystems in accordance with system-specific criteria" (Luhmann 1998, 227).

Irrespective of the conclusion that there is a theory-immanent contradiction if the talk about inclusion presupposes that exclusion exists, Luhmann himself had to recognize how deeply moved and surprised he was on his visits to *favellas* in mega cities in Latin America and to dilapidated settlements which are the legacies of the closing-down of the coalmines in Wales. He writes:

> [T]here are after all exclusions, namely on a massive scale and with a kind of misery which defies description... We know there is talk about exploitation or social oppression or *marginalidad*, about an intensification of the contrast between the center and the peripheries... But if you look exactly you will find nothing that could be exploited or oppressed. You will find an existence which is reduced to the physical body in the self-perception of oneself as well as in the

perception of others—a body which tries to survive until the next day. In order to survive people need, on the one hand, the ability to perceive dangers and to procure the most necessary things and, on the other hand, resignation and indifference towards civic standards—including rules, cleanliness and self-perception. Furthermore, if you project what you see, you could easily realize that this could become the leading difference of the next century: inclusion and exclusion (1998, 228).

How this experience has caused Luhmann to change his architecture of system-theory cannot be explained in detail. His argumentation shows that he endeavors to switch from the perspective of consternation again to the distanced perspective of observation.

The conclusion that for him personally there is evidence "that where there is exclusion human beings are no longer regarded as people but as bodies" demonstrates that he cannot have had any personal contact with the excluded and their perception of themselves. Instead he seems to make their situation fit his own sociological ideas in a way that borders on cynicism without ever having checked their situation empirically. At least in his admission that in view of the described situation "society could not expect advice or assistance from sociology" (1998, 230), he realizes an aporia in his theoretical system which does not have contact with empirical reality and thus is closed logically

Some years ago the French sociologist Pierre Bourdieu and his staff took a totally different approach towards the "world of the excluded," documented in a book pointedly titled *The Misery of the World* (1997). As the subtitle indicates, it contains "testimonies and diagnoses of everyday suffering in society". The intention of this study is understanding, i.e., the understanding of the diversity of the suffering caused by contemporary society, and to discover something of the reasons behind this development. The blurb for the German edition of this book notes:

> Human beings, who otherwise have no chance to have their say and to be heard, give an account of their real lives, their hopes and frustrations, their injuries and suffering. Together these images of life and society "from below" amount to a merciless investigation of the present French society—and not only the French one, characterized by increased competition, structural mass unemployment, the dismantling of the welfare state, social marginalization or exclusion of more and more groups in the population, intensified through the stealthy retreat of the state from its responsibility for the welfare state and the increasing deregulation of the economy and society. The great and small miseries and sufferings of these people in everyday life appear in the Janus-faced form of the economic situation or material social forces, on the one hand, and painful experiences with social hierar-

chies which are linked to their respective personal status in the social community, on the other hand.

With his hermeneutic approach to the "misery of the world," Bourdieu wishes to effect two changes. On the one hand, he wishes that all who are suffering can find a way to trace their suffering back to social reasons and so emancipate themselves from feelings of personal guilt. On the other hand, he wishes to show the privileged (in this case in France), as tangibly as possible, the downside of an affluent society. He summarizes this latter concern by saying, "Nothing is less innocent, than to let things run their course" (1997, 826).

A Theological Approach

After this brief review of the sociological debate the question arises, why does the phenomenon of social exclusion concern theology and the church? My thesis is that the phenomenon of social exclusion—through which human beings are declared to be superfluous and the prerequisites and funds for participation in social life are subsequently withdrawn—and the way this reduction and destruction of human life for the selfish advantage of a few is deemed acceptable is an obvious and very threatening "sign of the times" which cannot leave indifferent those who are passionately committed to the present and future generations living with dignity. This matters to Christians especially.

In order to show how this matters to Christians, we will reference ten points which characterize a broad theological debate in Latin America and the Caribbean which has resulted in official announcements by the Roman Catholic Church. Of course, this debate cannot simply be transferred to other regions of the world, as it needs to be contextualized within any other specific regional reality. At the same time, the theological debate in Latin American and the Caribbean in all of its strengths and weaknesses may be informative to all religious thinkers and leaders who oppose the phenomenon of social exclusion.

1. As self-critically admitted in Aparecida's text (cf. 397) and in the discourse of the theology of liberation as well, the talk of the "option of the poor" is currently degenerating from a doctrinal formula to an empty one. Any serious theological discussion of poverty and exclusion must by necessity engage recent socio-scientific analyses. In addition, theologians need to encounter personally those who are forced to live in poverty and misery as well as with those who, because of their direct work with the poor, can give them information about the current developments in this field. Poverty and exclusion are hard facts and affect real people. It is necessary to be in contact with them instead of only talking about them.

2. The received ideas on the "world of misery" have to be considered more seriously by critically viewing the economic, political and cultural factors behind this devel-

opment. Critical analyses can demonstrate that many of the decisions taken, especially in the economic sector, are not as rational as they may first seem to be.

3. This ideology-critical contribution is a central task of theology because the dominant economic and political system endeavors to represent itself as a form of transcendence, thus giving itself a quasi-religious legitimacy. Its claim to absoluteness is expressed in the motto "outside of the market there is no salvation".

4. Theology cannot backpedal on the "option for the poor," as the Magisterium of the Roman Catholic Church has confirmed repeatedly in the last years. On the contrary, this concept has to be developed further in the light of "the increasingly outrageous social injustices" (Jürgen Habermas) manifested in the scandal of social exclusion in which human beings are declared to be superfluous. As Leonardo Boff postulates in this context, one's view has to be widened beyond the suffering of individual human victims to the suffering of the whole of creation (Boff 2002).

5. Theology in the so-called affluent societies has the deficit that it is not largely embedded in its own context as the (liberation) theologies in the Third World understand themselves to be. An actual example is how theology in our context is reacting to recent precarious social developments or to the world's financial crisis. Often our theology is content to make moral appeals to the well off that they should abandon their insatiable greed which has occupied them and should share their money with the poor. But such appeals do not suffice to find an effective way out of the recent crisis which has come about not only because of the actions of individuals but also structural reasons.

6. The German theologian Hadwig Müller, emphasizing her understanding of the theological view of the "option for the poor," concludes that this is not an additional element in the gospel but the essential and constitutional dimension of the project of God and Jesus. That would mean that "The option for the poor is not a part of a theology of caritas or moral theology, but it is part of fundamental theology" (Müller 2001, 184). The pivotal point to emphasize is God's justice and love and—along with the other side of the coin, as it were—each individual in their God given dignity.

7. It is this point which makes the phenomenon of exclusion so explosive. In God's eyes no human being is superfluous. The workbook of the campaign for fraternity in Brazil's Christian churches in the year 2000, which had the motto "A new millennium without excluding the excluded," took the story of Mk 3.1-6 as foundational for showing what has to be done in theological reflection and Christian practice: Jesus calls an unnamed person who suffers from a paralyzed hand into the middle of the synagogue, where the Torah has its place in services on the Sabbath, and heals him. This is the reason why the law-abiding people are indignant. The gospels were written at a time in which there were many kinds of exclusion of human beings from society, e.g., because of illness, for collaborating with the Roman oppressors, for

behavior which was morally reprehensible, etc. Such exclusion was legitimatized religiously. Jesus breaks down these barriers and communicates with the excluded. He explicitly connects his message of the coming of the kingdom of God with this practice. For him true and full salvation takes place in this kingdom which includes all human beings and excludes nobody.

> By joining the sinners and custom officers the historical Jesus counters the social exclusion of human beings through religion. By praising the poor he gives hope to those who from an economic point of view are regarded as irrelevant for participation in the economy. By healing the sick and suffering whose punishment was regarded as God given, he contradicts the religiously legitimatized stigmatization of such people. By exorcizing demons he counters the traumatic consequences of Rome's rule in Israel. Jesus by searching for an inclusive physical community tries to redress the dynamics of the political, economical and religious processes of exclusion (Etschmüller 2008, 5).

8. By caring for the poor, the sick and sinners, Jesus calls into question the prevailing standards of self-assertion and the winning of power through exclusion. Thus, he provoked the political and religious leaders of his time. In their eyes Jesus' preaching and deeds were an extraordinary danger to their privileged status quo. Consequently, they did everything possible to eliminate this danger, using the mechanism of exclusion against Jesus. They executed him in the hope that his ideas would definitely be eliminated, too. But Christians believe that God, with whom Jesus lived and ministered in an intimate way, did not forsake Jesus on the cross. Through the resurrection God rehabilitated him and his way of living as the way God lives: in justice and love.

9. In history this resurrected and living Jesus meets us personally in the poor, the thirsty, the naked, the sick and in strangers and prisoners (cf. Mt 25.31-46). How people treat them is decisive for their own life. Without communion with the poor and excluded we will be unworthy of the Eucharist (cf. 1 Cor 11). To put it succinctly, whosoever instigates social exclusion or tolerates it, instigates the exclusion of God.

10. To the extent that the church acts like the good Samaritan, it bears witness to this good news and makes its contribution to the building of the kingdom of God. In a 1995 document of the Roman Catholic Church of Brazil the following characteristics are mentioned which serve as criteria for evaluating the practice of the Church:

- it is present and sensitive to the needs of the "weak";
- it neither hides suffering nor tries to justify it, for it cannot be exculpated;
- it does not oppress and exclude;

- it identifies itself with the values and sufferings of the "weak";
- it denounces the mechanism of exclusion and fights against it;
- it embraces the sufferings of the excluded;
- it gains its own identity as the church of the poor;
- it restores the dignity of the poor, the excluded and those who cannot speak for themselves;
- it transforms the "weak" as objects of charity to subjects in their life and history for the benefit of all human beings and their salvation (CNBB 1994, 98).

In spite of the noble values expressed in these characteristics, the 1995 document that contains them is nevertheless characterized by a negative undertone suggesting that help for the excluded is expected from others. The ecclesial status of the poor and excluded, however, is much more radical. They reflect a specific dimension of the biblical revelation that is not seen and cannot be seen without them: the option of God which is specifically for them. The Concluding Document of the 3rd General Conference of the Roman-Catholic Bishops of Latin America and the Caribbean justifiably notes: "The commitment to the poor and oppressed and the emergence of the Christian base communities have helped the church to discover the evangelical potential of the poor. They continually confront the church with questions by calling for a return to the values of the gospel which are solidarity, service, convenience and receptiveness for the gift of God which many of them live in their daily lives" (1147). Truly, the poor and the excluded are evangelizing the church.

US missiologist Philip L. Wickeri has characterized the contrast between neoliberal globalization and the Christian faith as follows: Globalization involves the transformation of social relationships and interactions embodying four types of change, "the stretching of social, political and economic activities across all kinds of borders; the intensification of the flow of trade, investment, culture and migration; the acceleration of global interactions and processes; and their deepening impact on local conditions everywhere" (Wickeri 2008, 466). The result would be a splitting of the world into those who profit from globalization and those who are left behind. The Christian faith, however, embodies the promise of life in abundance for everyone (cf. John 10.10). Christian hope is the expression of a faith and a love to which there are no added conditions and in which everyone is included (even those who are not Christians). This is diametrically opposed to the maxims of the dominant system; participation instead of exclusion, sharing instead of accumulation, gratuity instead of speculation. In complete contrast to neoliberal globalization, the way these promises are to be realized has to be in accordance with the gospels.

The neoliberal way to success consists of brutal competition without any consideration for the victims. In contrast, the Christian way—even if one must contritely admit that often enough hegemonic means were and are used in the church's name—consists of the sensible perception of exactly these victims, of compassion with them and of a tenacious commitment to more justice and love in the world, above all in an "economy of sufficiency" which excludes no one. While the neoliberal way means to strive without compromise to achieve one's aims, the Christian way means that one is continually obliged to help those in need and to support all those who wish to preserve the earth as a habitable place for all.

Concluding Remarks

Exclusion does not only refer to the erasure of Christians but also to the marginalization of members of other religions and philosophies of life, sometimes even more harshly. All of Christianity's resources must be mobilized and brought together if exclusion is not to have the final word. Furthermore, there must be a mutually beneficial, and possibly controversial exchange between religions about which resources they can collectively draw upon when resisting every attempt to advance the idea that human beings are to be excluded and unnecessary. Such resources must also support a shared insistence on the fundamental dignity of every human being.

The subject "exclusion" makes us aware of the fact that the cultural-hermeneutic approach of practical theology has to be broadened with more intense economic analyses. Without such analyses, practical theology is in danger of reducing its ability to perceive reality. A consequence could be that the structurally caused social suffering and distress of peoples might be addressed without real comprehension in pastoral practice. Therefore each religion, and even theological discipline, must be critically self-reflective about the extent to which they have made and are making a contribution to the eradication of exclusion.

References:

Aparecida. 2007. http://www.celam.org/MisionContinental/Documentos/Ingles.pdf (accessed 7 December 2009).

Boff, Leonardo. 2002. *Schrei der Erde, Schrei der Armen.* Düsseldorf: Patmos.

Bourdieu, Pierre. 1997. *Das Elend der Welt.* Konstanz: UVK. 1993. *La misére du monde.* Paris: Seuil.

Bude, Heinz. 2008. *Die Ausgeschlossenen. Das Ende vom Traum einer gerechten Gesellschaft.* München: Hanser.

CNBB, Conferência Nacional dos Bispos do Brasil. 1994. *Eras Tu, Senhor? Campanha da Fraternidade–1995: A Fraternidade e os Excluidos, Manual.* São Paulo: Paulinas.

Etschmüller, Gregor. 2008. *„für uns gestorben nach der Schrift." Bausteine zu einer realistischen Kreuzestheologie.* manuscript.

Luhmann, Niklas. 1996. Jenseits von Barbarei. In *Modernität und Barbarei,* ed. Max Miller and Hans-Georg Soeffner, 219-230. Frankfurt am Main: Suhrkamp.

Luhmann, Niklas. 2008. Inklusion und Exklusion. In *Soziologische Aufklärung 6* (3rd ed.), 226-251. Wiesbaden: Verlag für Sozialwissenschaften.

Müller, Hadwig. 2001. Option für die Armen. *Jahrbuch für kontextuelle Theologie* 9:173-192.

Schoenborn, Ulrich, 1996. Ausgeschlossen vom Markt–ausgeschlossen vom Heil? Anmerkungen zur „teologia dos excluídos." *Una Sancta* 51:209-218.

Wickeri, Philip L. 2008. Globalization and Transnational Christianity. In *Negotiating Borders. Theological Explorations in the Global Era*, ed. Patrick Gnanapragasam and Elisabeth Schüssler-Fiorenza, 465-483. Delhi: ISPCK.

Pastoral Ministry in a context of Ethnic Diversity: Reflections from Nairobi

Gerard Whelan SJ

Abstract: *This article describes six years (2000-2006) the author spent as pastor of a Catholic parish in Nairobi, Kenya, where he employed a pastoral decision-making strategy based on a critical realist methodology grounded in the thought of Bernard Lonergan. A year after the departure of the author from Kenya violence broke out across the country that killed hundreds of people. Thankfully, the area of the city where the author worked was relatively untouched by the violence; he believes that one contributing reason for this is that the critical realist method employed helped to underscore the importance of addressing issues of ethnic tension and took some steps to do this. Furthermore, the author inherited a pastoral situation influence by an approach to pastoral planning based on liberation theology. He proposes that this approach was so focused on issues of economic and class inequality that it neglected issues of ethnic tension, as well as issues of religious and moral formation of parishioners. He concludes on a theoretical point of how a liberation approach to pastoral decision-making can be deepened and improved upon by one based upon critical realism.*

Introduction

From 2000 to 2006 I was pastor of the Catholic parish St Joseph the Worker Parish in Kangemi (Nairobi), Kenya. This engagement included a commitment to help build up the social fabric in one poor part of the capital city—a contribution to national development especially suited to religious institutions. I had a particular interest in employing an approach to pastoral decision-making that I had been teaching for some years in courses in practical theology at the Jesuit School of Theology in Nairobi—an approach based on the "critical realism" of the philosopher and theologian Bernard Lonergan (d. 1984).

Subsequent events in Kenya make me aware that the historical narrative in which we think we are playing a part is not always the narrative that is in fact going forward. In the early months of 2008 ethnic clashes broke out in many parts of Kenya after a controversial national election; hundreds of people were killed, thousands of people displaced and forced to live in makeshift camps, and the social fabric of the country is severely damaged yet today. That such conflict should occur came as a surprise to me as to many others. In retrospect, I recognize that a key pastoral question of my efforts in Kangemi becomes: to what extent did the parish leadership recognize the kind of political and ethnic tensions that were brewing and to what extent did we do anything to address these issues?

In fact, the pastoral team can look back with a certain confidence on the years 2000-2006 and conclude that we were not completely found wanting in this matter. During the months of insecurity in early 2008, Kangemi remained relatively untouched by the violence when it hit other slum areas of Nairobi. This relative peace could be explained in numerous ways, but there is reason to think that one explanation is that pastoral actions we undertook during our six years helped make Kangemi a less ethnically divided place. The following narrative attempts to show how a pastoral strategy based a critical realist methodology had some success in recognizing the "signs of the times" in years leading up to this conflict and responding to them.

A point that will emerge in the course of this narrative is that the parish whose leadership I inherited had been founded by fellow Jesuits who employed a related but not identical methodology, i.e., liberation theology as it emerged in Latin America in the 1970s and 1980s. My experiences in this parish confirm my opinion that liberation theology can benefit from a methodological deepening offered by critical realism and that this deepening is especially relevant in relating to issues of culture such as ethnocentrism—issues that were to play a pivotal role in the conflict of 2008.

Kenya's "original sin": an unjust distribution of land

Our first point with respect to the roots of conflict in Kenyan society relates to land ownership; some have called this issue the "original sin" of the state of Kenya. This problem brings a particularly ethnocentric edge to issues of economic injustice in the country. The borders of Kenya took shape about 1890. As in most other African colonial territories of this time, little attention was given to the fact that the borders of this colony cut across the territories of various ethnic communities. The various ethnic communities that subsequently found themselves within these new borders often had little in common with each other. Two further factors would make nation-building particularly difficult in Kenya: the exceptional diversity among the peoples found within its borders, and the fact that the state came to be perceived as associated with land-grabbing. Kenya exhibits diversity in different ways that is a delight for tourists and a challenge to any national government. The state enjoys greater ethnic diversity than almost any other African country. It is a zone of convergence for some of the largest ethnic (often called racial) groupings on the continent. These include the Bantu-speaking peoples, the most numerous in Africa, as well as Nilotic, Hamitic and Semitic communities. It also includes strikingly different climatic zones, a fact related to geographic phenomena such as the East African Plateau and the Great Rift Valley. Related to climatic difference are the different economic sets of activities in which pastoralist agriculturalist peoples engage, accompanied by consequent cultural differences. Finally, further regional diversity is exemplified by the influence of Arab and Muslim culture on the Bantu-speaking and Somali communities of the coastal region, while the other regions of the country were the focus of intense Christian missionary activity.

In this challenging context for building a culture of unity one must also recognize that the Kenyan state has, from its inception until today, been perceived as consistently unjust in its treatment of land ownership. This perception unfolded in three stages: 1) colonial times, 2) under the Presidency of Jomo Kenyatta (1957-1979), and 3) under the presidency of Daniel Arap Moi (1978-2002).

Regarding stage one, it is notable that the British government found parts of Kenya (the "White Highlands") to be attractive for its own citizens so it encouraged the migration of European settlers. With this in mind the government created legal structures to permit extensive expropriation of land. In steps beginning with the "Foreign Jurisdiction Act" in 1890, the colonial administration divided the land of Kenya into two major categories: "government land" and "trust land." Government land was any area that was likely to be valuable for creating public utilities or settling white farmers. Huge swathes of the best agricultural land were designated as government land. Land of less value was called trust land and assigned formally to different ethnic groups.

It would take decades for the destructive effect of these legal decisions (elaborated in legislation in 1939) to become evident. At first, local ethnic communities continued to live on a large proportion of the newly designated government land; during succeeding decades, however, they would find themselves increasingly displaced. During the era of British rule, as a response to a campaign for independence by indigenous Kenyans in the "Mau Mau rebellion," the British government during the 1950s began allocating government land not only to White immigrants but also to selected Africans who they trusted to be loyal to them and not to support independence-seeking rebels. In the words of historian M.P.R. Sorrenson, this "Land consolidation would create a class of land-owners that would refuse to have any truck with the nationalist politicians" (1967, 250-1).

The second stage in the history of unjust policies concerning land ownership occurred during the long presidency of Jomo Kenyatta. As president of the newly independent Republic of Kenya in 1963, he chose to imitate the British practice allocating land to his own loyalists so as to assure political loyalty. Kenyata felt that he could most rely upon those of his own ethnic community and so those receiving gifts of land under his government were predominantly Kikuyu.

A third phase in the process of dislocation from land began in 1979 when President Kenyatta died and a successor was chosen from one of the minority pastoralist communities. President Daniel Arap Moi was a compromise candidate from within the single ruling party in which ethnic tensions were already evident between the larger, non-pastoralist, ethnic communities. An attempted coup in 1982 made President Moi feel insecure in his hold on power and so he accelerated the practice of bestowing gifts of government land upon political supporters—this time mostly to his own community. One problem Moi encountered was that his community had been a victim of expropriations of land during the previous regime. What resulted were ethnic clashes that amounted to ethnic cleansing from these pastoralist lands. The worst incident occurred in the Rift Valley in 1992 when 1,500 people were killed. It is not surprising that with such injustice prevailing in rural areas the rate of migration to the cities was high. Furthermore, the practice of allocating land to political loyalists was applied also to cities. In centers such as Nairobi, there emerged some of the worst slums in the world but, unlike most other slums in the developing world, residents were compelled to pay a considerable proportion of their income to landlords who were given rights to rent collection by the government. Kenya climbed high in world rankings for unequal distribution of wealth as well as for corruption. The tension emerging from the slums combined both the resentment of people who felt economically marginalized as well as ethnic discrimination.[1]

An imbalanced Pastoral Strategy
The area of Kangemi, 12 kilometers from the centre of Nairobi, is a typical example of Kenyan urban poverty, characterized both by economic and ethnic injustice. Within this context Jesuits performed admirable work since the founding of St. Joseph the Worker Parish in 1985. However, the methodology they employed led them to stress issues of class discrimination and to neglect issues of ethnic discrimination; they also tended to neglect issues of role of moral and spiritual formation in pastoral work. By 2000 these decisions contributed to division and a reduced effectiveness in fulfilling the parish mission.

When the Jesuits helped found the parish in 1985 the area population was about 35,000. During my ministry there (2000-2006) the population was closer to 100,000. Kangemi suffers from a lack of basic infrastructural services such as sanitation, clean water, education and healthcare; unemployment is high and the proportion of the population under the age of 15 is 50%.

In terms of ethnicity, two main groups each comprise about 40% of the population. The first is the Kikuyu, not surprisingly as this was originally an area inhabited by the Kikuyu. The second is the Luhya, one of the other large ethnic groups of Western Kenya. Such a demographic mix is a recipe for polarization and this tension has pointedly played itself out politically. The Luhya community is the poorer community in the area but is able to muster its numbers to elect the local Member of Parliament; he in turn promoted policies that favored his own ethnic community. During my first week in the parish riots broke out throughout the area; the reason was that the member of parliament had allocated an area of government land to

---

[1] Satellite photos of Nairobi highlight its remarkable inequality. Within the city limits, there is an equal area occupied by the slums, where up to 3 million people live, and a series of about six golf courses. http://maps.grida.no/go/graphic/nairobi-interesting-neighbours-golfcourses-and-slums {accessed 1.viii.10].

Luhya slum dwellers so that they could build shacks there; local Kikuyu burnt down the first of these houses.

The founding team of St. Joseph the Worker Parish in 1985 had a two-prong strategy for the parish. The first was building pastoral life around small Christian communities (SCCs); the idea for SCCs was borrowed from the "basic Christian communities" in Latin America associated with theologies of liberation. In fact, some of the Jesuits working in the parish in its early years came from Latin America. This option for SCCs echoed the position of the Catholic Episcopal Conferences of Eastern Africa and Madagascar who proposed making small Christian communities a fundamental component of evangelization within their region at their 1973 meeting in Malawi. The second strategy involved initiating a range of development projects in areas of health, education and income-generating activities.

Throughout the 1990s the Kangemi Catholic parish became well known in Kenya and beyond as a model parish for implementing the bishop's priority for the SCC pastoral strategy. One result of this strategy was the stimulation of a wide level of general community activism in Kangemi. The area was known for opposing the illegal brewing of alcohol and for identifying and ousting corrupt government officials. Similarly the development projects run by the parish made a significant contribution to the area. Furthermore, much civic education was conducted helping to make Kangemi a politically literate place during years of political turbulence towards the end of the Moi's presidency.

While successes were evident, the passing years also revealed problems. In the late 1990s a kind of management crisis befell the parish. A number of development projects experienced financial problems and tension became apparent between parish priests and certain members of the pastoral council. It also became clear that all was not well in the SCCs, e.g., they had not been expanding to keep pace with the expansion of the population of the area, and some leaders were using their position to gain financial advantages for themselves.

When appointed pastor in 2000, I was asked by my Jesuit Superior to place the parish on an improved financial footing and to concentrate on improving the formation of lay leaders. In examining the kind of formation offered to members of SCCs, there seemed to be a stress on social justice activism that outweighed other dimensions living the Christian life. Some of the theoretical concerns I had about liberation theology (cf. CDF 1984 and 1986) were supported by weaknesses that I witnessed in the parish of St. Joseph the Worker. It seemed clear to me that opting for a kind of political activism had not sufficiently taken into consideration the moral and spiritual formation of the members both individually and as members of their communities. This kind of activism tended to be based on a form of social analysis that stressed class inequality but seemed to leave issues of culture and ethnicity unaddressed. Similarly, there was so much stress on trying to change social structures that there was little stress on the extent to which relations within the parish might be reflecting larger social injustices..

A Pastoral Strategy based on Critical Realism

From 2000 to 2006 we tried to correct and complement the pastoral strategy employed in Kangemi parish in previous years with one that had roots in critical realism (Lonergan 1992 and 1985; Doran 1990; Ormerod 2000). I say "we" because while pastor I was a member of a group of priests and religious women who formed a pastoral team for the parish. Over time, we felt that we witnessed positive results from our somewhat different pastoral strategy. With hindsight, one particularly important characteristic of our newer method was that it recognized the significance of cultural issues and so made efforts at addressing problems of ethnocentrism that existed both within our own Christian community and more broadly in Kangemi. In the long run this may have contributed to reduced violence in our area when conflict broke out across the country in early 2008.

Space does not permit an elaboration of how a critical realist set of categories for pastoral decision-making are generated. Rather, I simply employ these categories in what follows and hope this gives the reader a sense of what is distinctive about this approach. Above all, this approach employs a distinction of the mission of the Church *ad intra* and *ad extra* and Lonergan's understanding of ministry as mediating "development from above" (Lonergan 1985) and a scale of values (Lonergan 1990, 31-32).

Planning for Holiness

Regarding formation of members of our SCCs, in a certain sense our policy was simple: we would begin by placing a priority on the formation of religious and personal values *ad intra* to the parish and hope for results that would enable us to proceed towards other goals that form part of an integral approach to evangelization. In this matter we had to withstand criticisms from certain quarters that our approach was "spiritualizing" and "conservative."

This stress on promoting religious and personal values continued for about two years. It was perhaps inevitable that this shift of policies would produce a backlash in certain quarters and for a time my relations with certain members of the parish leadership was difficult. After two years in the parish the ordinary time arrived to elect or re-elect leaders in the SCCs, in the Parish Pastoral Council, and to a five-person executive committee for this council. Unbeknownst to me and to members of our pastoral team, parishioners who had attended the retreats and other formation activities began to organize themselves into what they called the "spiritual party," so as to oppose what they called the "projects party" within these elected bodies of the parish. During the elections, a clear victory was attained for the "spiritual party" and those of us on the pastoral team only began to catch on to what had happened when we saw a large number of new faces appearing in the leadership of these different groups. I recognized a number of the individuals who had been evidently most graced on our retreats appearing in these ranks. It was also evident that a greater diversity of economic and ethnic background was appearing in our leadership.

Evangelizing Culture *ad intra* to the parish

Next the process of moving to prioritize cultural values *ad intra* to the parish could be initiated. We attempted this in a consultative manner. The underlying ideas here were: 1) personal religious conversion should always bear fruit in moral conversion; 2) morality relates to how we live together in community, and 3) if we cannot model moral relations within our Christian community we will have little to offer in an effort to promote Christian values beyond the boundaries of our community.

When asked what might be the ideas and values in which our parishioners most needed formation, members of SCCs pointed to two areas: family life and ethnic inclusivity. During the two years that followed, the stress was less on retreats and scripture courses and more on formation activities related to these two themes. We devoted considerable attention to promoting family life but here I will report primarily the work we did on the issue of ethnicity.

One example of an almost unconscious ethnic injustice was that parish leaders virtually always came from the Kikuyu community and not from the Luhya; this remained mostly the case even after the elections of our new "spiritual party" to membership on the pastoral council. However, a difference between the new pastoral council and the previous one was that the new group acknowledged that ethnic imbalance was a problem that needed to be addressed. We initiated an association of Catholics that came from the Western Province of Kenya which is the heartland of the Luhya community. This was, in effect, an exercise in positive discrimination as only the Luhya community were invited to create such a group. This group undertook a variety of activities such as the formation of a savings and welfare cooperative which extended structures of Luhya solidarity from home villages to urban life. While benefiting from this particular association, members of this new group understood perfectly how regrettable it would be if it were to become a mono-ethnic "church within a church" cut off from the rest of the parish and so accepted an obligation to remain as active members of their (multi-ethnic) SCCs.

After a year or so into our efforts to promote ethnic inclusivity we began to notice a marked increase of individuals attending Sunday liturgies and SCCs. This created for us a new challenge: we had too few SCCs, members were not able to fit into the small houses of the area to conduct meetings, and new members who experienced this problem tended to fall away again. Ideas began to emerge about the need to increase the number of our SCCs and ultimately to build a second church within the area. Increasing the number of SCCs seemed to answer an obvious need but it quickly came up against obstacles which reminded us how difficult it can be to change culture even *ad intra* to a Christian community. SCC members had developed strong bonds of loyalty and friendship and did not take kindly to the thought that some of their best friends might soon be praying in a different SCC from their own. To be frank, in some cases an element of this resistance clearly related to issues of class and ethnicity. There was little doubt that the changes of structure that we were proposing would bring advantages, above all, to recent migrants to the area who tended to be poorer and from the Luhya ethnic community.

Recognizing that changing ideas and values takes time, the pastoral council and I decided to delay any forced implementation of an increase of our SCCs. Instead we spent about six months offering formation meetings to SCCs where we explicitly addressed this issue. Finally, most opposition turned to active cooperation and we succeeded in creating these new small communities.

Evangelizing social structures *ad intra* to the parish
In the final two years of my time in the parish we had a feeling of operating in a pastoral environment of a "virtuous circle." We felt that our promoting of religious, personal and cultural values were leading to a mutual reinforcement of all of these levels with progress being made in each of them. Now that we were confident that the integrity of the scale of values *ad intra* to the parish was being addressed reasonably well, it seemed time to address ourselves to ministry *ad extra* to the parish. A related issue here is that during our earlier prioritizing of spiritual formation we had initiated prayerful contacts with other Christian communities in the Kangemi area and even with a local Mosque. The respectful friendships we had built up by these explicitly religious means served us well as we began to undertake activities that appertained to issues of social justice.

Evangelization *ad extra*
We then began a parish-wide consultation process about what were the greatest cultural and social problems in the Kangemi area. At a certain stage we expanded this consultation process to some of the other religious communities in the area with whom we had good relations. We noted that most of the other religious communities were predominantly populated by members of just one ethnic community—given the ethnic make-up of Kangemi this meant that they were either predominantly Kikuyu or predominantly Luhya. We were recognized as being a more ethnically mixed religious community and so could play a catalytic role between different faith-based organizations in the area. In our process of consultations, Kangemi residents identified three main problems in the area: 1) crime, 2) addiction to alcohol and drugs, and 3) HIV/AIDS. In our pastoral planning for 2004-2006, we organized ourselves around the need both to act and to be seen to act on each of these three issues.

The story of how we took action on each of these issues is a complex one and I will only highlight a few points. First, we proceeded on these issues in a manner that was collaborative with other institutions beyond our Catholic parish. I have already mentioned how this included other Christian ecclesial communities as well as

Muslims in Kangemi, but we also sought to collaborate with the local government and police. Second, our efforts met with some success. We found that we could mobilize large numbers of Kangemi residents (Catholic and non-Catholic) around our three priority issues. One example was a march against the selling of illegally brewed alcohol which attracted many thousands of participants and which gained national media attention. A final point refers to a previous comment concerning how some friends and colleagues had felt uneasy about our pastoral emphasis on spiritual and moral formation during 2000-2002. Such commentators were often influenced by what I would call a more classical liberation theology methodology. Some of these commentators expressed surprise to find us apparently returning to a more liberationist approach by 2004-2006. Our hope was that such commentators would recognize that our critical realist approach was integrating issues of "the promotion of faith and the struggle for justice"; this expression, taken from the General Congregation 32 of the Society of Jesus (1975), became a kind of summary of the Jesuit approach to mission in the years after Vatican II. We believe this approach contributed to assuring effectiveness in the struggle for justice.

Conclusion

From January to March of 2008 Kenya was wracked by ethnic violence. The causes of this were complex but related to the matters explained in the first section above. The immediate cause was irregularities in a national election. A clear perception by many was that the Kikuyu-centered coalition government engaged in electoral misbehavior (a perception shared by international observers) and old resentments were ignited amongst other ethnic communities.

As previously noted, these resentments had been fuelled over the years by what was perceived to be land-grabbing across the country and consequent economic inequality. In the course of this violence, deep and long-term damage was inflicted both on the cultural superstructure and the economic infrastructure of the country. The healing of historic hurts will be made far more difficult by these recent ruptures. Healing of this rupture will have to begin with a just political agreement where a truly democratic government is elected, and grievances—not least on issues of land-ownership—that have fuelled ethnic tension will have to be addressed. It is far from clear that the political settlement that put an end to immediate violence in 2008 has the characteristic of such a real sharing of power.

Happily, Kangemi remained relatively untouched by the violence that erupted in certain other locations. Reasons for the relative peace of Kangemi are multiple; one of these is that tension between Kikuyus and Luhyas was not the worst of the faultlines that appeared nation-wide. However, we have reason to believe that our efforts at addressing issues of ethnic diversity within our Catholic parish, as well as our ecumenical efforts to address social problems in the area, made some contribution to the less violent atmosphere in Kangemi. With all due respect to our predecessors in

St. Joseph the Worker Parish, it appears that the kind of methodology they employed was in need of modification. In the early years of the existence of the parish there seemed to have been a neglect of various aspects of formation *ad intra* in a haste to engage with issues of economic injustice *ad extra*. In fact, what followed at times was a somewhat superficial engagement with issues *ad extra* because the kind of social analysis that was informing this praxis seemed to pay little attention to issues of ethnicity.

I have briefly outlined how a critical realist approach to pastoral planning stresses the importance of forming community *ad intra* to a Christian institution before, or at least in tandem with, efforts to promote an integral evangelization *ad extra*. This community-building *ad intra* needs to attend first to issues of religious and moral conversion of individuals and then needs to guide a process where deepened religious motivation helps members of the Christian community recognize limitations to the set of ideas, values and symbols that influence them. This amounts to an evangelization of culture *ad intra* to a parish that will not succeed unless it occurs within just social structures, such as SSCs, which facilitate participation of all members of a community and that serve as safe locations for the formation and change of attitudes and values. It is in the context of this kind of growth *ad intra* that a ministry *ad extra* can begin where religion can contribute to a strengthening of social fabric that is essential to national development. We are confident that our employing of such methods met with some success during 2000-2006 in Kangemi. At the time, we tended to focus on success in addressing problems such as crime, addiction and HIV/AIDS; in retrospect, perhaps what was most significant is that we developed means to address these issues in a multi-ethnic manner.

References:

CDF (Congregation of the Doctrine of the Faith). 1984. "Instruction on Certain Aspects of the 'Theology of Liberation.'"

CDF. 1986. "Instruction on Christian Freedom and Liberation."

Lonergan, Bernard. 1992 (1957). *Insight: A Study in Human Understanding*. Collected Works of Bernard Lonergan, Vol. 3. Toronto, University of Toronto Press.

_____. 1990 (1971). *Method in Theology*. Toronto, University of Toronto Press.

_____. 1985. Healing and Creating in History. In A *Third Collection*, 100-112. Toronto: University of Toronto Press.

Sorrenson, M.P.R. 1967. *Land Reform in the Kikuyu Community*. Oxford: Oxford University Press.

Doran, Robert M. 1990. *Theology and the Dialectics of History*. Toronto: University of Toronto Press.

Ormerod, Neil. 2000. System, History and a Theology of Ministry. *Theological Studies* 61:432-446.

Whelan, Gerard. 2008. Robert Doran and Pastoral Theology: Reflections from Nairobi, Kenya. In *Lonergan Workshop, Volume 20,* ed. Frederick Laurence, 357-90. Chestnut Hill MA: Boston College.

_____. 2009. Method in Practical Theology. *The Lonergan Review* 1, no. 1:221-38.

Contributing Authors

Esther Acolatse is Assistant Professor of Pastoral Theology and World Christianity at Duke University Divinity School in Durham, North Carolina, the United States.

Riet Bons-Storm is retired Professor of Women Studies and Pastoral Theology and Care of the University of Groningen, the Netherlands.

Lynn Bridgers is the Associate Director of the Master of Theological Studies Program for St. Norbert College in Albuquerque and teaches Religious Studies at the University of New Mexico, the United States.

Rein Brouwer is Assistant Professor of Practical and Empirical Theology at the Protestant Theological University in Utrecht, the Netherlands.

Leah Dawn Bueckert is Spiritual Care Coordinator with North Eastman Health Association in Manitoba, Canada.

Taylor Christl is a Research Associate and Doctoral Candidate in the Faculty of Rehabilitation Sciences at Technische Universität in Dortmund, Germany.

Johan Cilliers is Professor in Practical Theology (Homiletics and Liturgy) at the Faculty of Theology at the University of Stellenbosch, South Africa.

Jack Curran is a Vice President for development and Assistant Professor at Bethlehem University in Palestine.

Joyce S. Dubensky is the Executive Vice President and CEO of the Tanenbaum Center for Interreligious Understanding in New York City, the United States.

Barbara Flunger is Junior Researcher in the department of Practical Theology and Pedagogy at the University of Würzburg, Germany.

Edward Foley is Duns Scotus Professor of Spirituality and Ordinary Professor of Liturgy and Music at Catholic Theological Union in Chicago, the United States.

Wilhelm Graeb is Ordinary Professor of Practical Theology at Humboldt-University in Berlin, Germany.

Christoph Käppler is Professor for Social and Emotional Development in Rehabilitation and Education at Technische Universität in Dortmund, Germany.

Terence Kennedy C.Ss.R. is Professor of Fundamental Moral Theology in the Alphonsiana Academy and Visiting Professor at the Gregorian University in Rome, Italy.

Norbert Mette is Professor of Religious Education and Practical Theology at Technische Universität in Dortmund, Germany.

Peter Meyer is Lecturer and Researcher in the field of Practical Theology in the Department of Protestant Theology at Goethe-University in Frankfurt am Main, Germany.

Christoph Morgenthaler is Professor for Pastoral Care and Counseling and Pastoral Psychology in the Faculty of Protestant Theology at the University of Berne, Switzerland.

Aristide Peng is a Research Associate and Doctoral Candidate in Psychology of Religion at the University of Berne, Switzerland.

Uta Pohl-Patalong is Professor of Practical Theology at Christian-Albrechts-Universität of Kiel, Germany.

Esther D. Reed is Associate Professor of Theological Ethics at the University of Exeter, England.

Daniel Schipani is Professor of Pastoral Care and Counseling at Associated Mennonite Biblical Seminary in Elkhart, Indiana in the United States.

Robert Schreiter is Vatican Council II Professor of Theology at Catholic Theological Union in Chicago, the United States.

Friedrich Schweitzer is Professor of Practical Theology and Religious Education in the Protestant Faculty of Theology at the University of Tübingen, Germany.

Valburga Schmiedt Streck is Professor of Practical Theology and Pastoral Counseling at the Escola Superior de Teologia in São Leopoldo, RS, Brazil

Constanze Thierfelder is Lecturer in Practical Theology at the Philipps-University in Marburg and executive pastor of the parish of Wetter in Hessen, Germany.

David Tracy is the Andrew Thomas Greeley and Grace McNichols Greeley Distinguished Service Professor Emeritus of Catholic Studies and Professor of Theology and the Philosophy of Religions in the Divinity School at the University of Chicago, the United States.

Raymond J. Webb is Professor of Pastoral Theology at the University of Saint Mary of the Lake in Mundelein, Illinois in the United States.

Gerard Whelan lectures in Practical Theology and Fundamental Theology at the Pontifical Gregorian University in Rome, Italy.

Claire Wolfteich is Associate Professor and Co-Director of the Center for Practical Theology at Boston University School of Theology in Boston, the United States.

Sabine Zehnder is a Research Associate and Doctoral Candidate in Psychology of Religion at the University of Berne, Switzerland.

Hans-Georg Ziebertz is Professor of Practical Theology and Religious Education in the Faculty of Theology at the University of Würzburg, Germany.

International Practical Theology

edited by Prof. Dr. Chris Hermans (Nijmegen), Prof. Dr. Maureen Junker-Kenny (Dublin),
Prof. Dr. Richard Osmer (Princeton), Prof. Dr. Friedrich Schweitzer (Tübingen),
Prof. Dr. Hans-Georg Ziebertz (Würzburg) in cooperation with the International Academy of
Practical Theology (IAPT), represented by Bonnie Miller-McLemore (President) and
Jean-Guy Nadeau (Vice President)

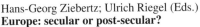

Hans-Georg Ziebertz; Ulrich Riegel (Eds.)
Europe: secular or post-secular?
Religion is back on the agenda. Western societies
are searching for an adequate understanding of religion. Media move religion into focus as a resource
of significance in modern societies, but also as a
source of tension and conflict. Politics is testing
how to manage religious pluralism. Education is developing concepts of interreligious dialogue in order to promote a better intercultural understanding.
The book discusses if the concept post-secularity
allows a suitable understanding of the public presence of religion.
Bd. 9, 2008, 216 S., 19,90 €, br., ISBN 978-3-8258-1578-3

Hans-Georg Ziebertz; William K Kay;
Ulrich Riegel (Eds.)
Youth in Europe III
An international Empirical Study about the
Impact of Religion on Life Orientation. With
a preface by Silviu E. Rogobete
This book draws upon empirical data collected
from 10,000 adolescent young people in 10 European countries. The first volume of this project
was about young people's lifeperspectives and the
second about their religious attitudes and practices.
The current and final volume of this cross-cultural
study connects both research dimensions. The analyses make clear that the influence of religion on
values, life-orientation and politics differs strongly
between different groups within Christianity and
between Christians, Jews and Muslims. Many findings contain obvious surprises because they refute
mainstream opinion on many topics.
Bd. 10, 2009, 272 S., 19,90 €, br.,
ISBN 978-3-8258-1579-0

LIT Verlag Berlin – Münster – Wien – Zürich – London
Auslieferung Deutschland / Österreich / Schweiz: siehe Impressumsseite

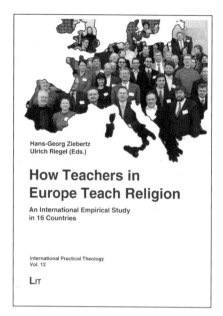

Hans-Georg Ziebertz; Ulrich Riegel (Eds.)
How Teachers in Europe Teach Religion
An International Empirical Study
In 2007 about 3500 teachers in 16 European countries participated at a cross-cultural study "Teaching
Religion in a multicultural Europe". The empirical
survey researches existing teaching procedures in
religion and theology. The book presents the results
which are different approaches, strategies and ways
of thinking when it comes to teaching religion in
a multicultural context. This research was stimulated by the TRES Network (Teaching Religion in
a multicultural European Society) which has been
selected and approved by the EU Commission for a
Socrates thematic network.
Bd. 12, 2009, 408 S., 34,90 €, br.,
ISBN 978-3-643-10043-6

Annemie Dillen; Anne Vandenhoeck (Eds.)
Prophetic Witness in World Christianities
Rethinking Pastoral Care and Counseling
Prophets have a reputation of changing the relation
between people and God for the better. Christianity
has a long history of prophets who direct the faithful towards more justice and righteousness. What
can Christians learn from prophets for daily life,
for contemporary theology and pastoral care? This
book undertakes the endeavor to look at prophetic
acting from a biblical, pastoral and ethical perspective. The contributions of both, pastoral theologians
and pastors from around the globe, make this study
a unique exercise to keep the prophetic perspective
in theological reflection and pastoral practice.
Bd. 13, 2011, 248 S., 24,90 €, br.,
ISBN 978-3-643-90041-8

LIT Verlag Berlin – Münster – Wien – Zürich – London
Auslieferung Deutschland / Österreich / Schweiz: siehe Impressumsseite